The History of GANGSTER RAP

From Schoolly D to Kendrick Lamar

The Rise of a Great American Art Form

SCHOOLLY D / ICE-T / BDP
EAZY-E / NWA

1987

SOREN BAKER

ABRAMS IMAGE, NEW YORK

D1295822

// Contents

V Introduction

VIII Foreword

1 Native Son

13 "Squeeze the Trigger"

29 Niggaz Wit Attitude

45 The Revolution Gets Televised

59 Ice Cube: "A Gangsta's Fairytale"

75 "Say Hello to My Little Friends": Gangster Rap Meets Scarface and the Geto Boys

89 Gangster Rap Is the Name

107 California Dreamin': The Aftermath

123 A Doggy Dogg World

137 Bangin on Wax: There Goes the Neighborhood

151 G-Funk Meets Mob Music

167 Death Around the Corner: The So-Called East Coast/West Coast Beef

183 It Ain't My Fault: Master P and the No Limit Revolution

201 Dr. Dre and Snoop Dogg Reignite, Sending Detractors "Up in Smoke"

213 Your Life's on the Line

225 Money Turned Boys into Men

239 Gangster Rap at Thirty

252 Acknowledgments

255 Works Cited

258 Photo Credits

258 Index

MC Eiht and Mack 10 on the set of *Thicker Than Water* in Los Angeles in June 1998.

IN THE MID-1980s, GANGSTER RAP DIDN'T HAVE A NAME. BUT VIRTUALLY EVERYONE WHO HEARD IT REALIZED ITS POTENCY.

At the time, I was a pre-teen growing up in suburban Maryland, and gangster rap made the stories I read about in the newspaper and saw on the evening news come to life in a way I didn't know was possible. Instead of watching or listening to some stuffy, detached (usually white male) reporter recount the violence ravaging black, urban America, I suddenly found myself listening to Schoolly D, Ice-T, Boogie Down Productions, Just-Ice, Eazy-E, and N.W.A. They had created a new style of rap, one that contained graphic, X-rated stories of gangs, guns, violence, drugs, sex, and mayhem told in a brash, unapologetic manner.

Gangster rap, as it came to be known in the late 1980s, started as first-person street reporting from those living in, and surrounded by, America's urban warzones, and exploded in popularity once the focus became the lives of gangbangers and the people around them. These typically profane, often insightful, and sometimes horrifying stories from this group of disenfranchised young, black men opened my eyes to the depth and complexity of America's atrocious racial legacy, and also introduced me to a new generation of storytellers backed by mesmerizing music that resonated with me even more than the other rap I loved. Gangster rap was the telling of a reality seldom seen and rarely discussed in popular culture.

Dana Dane, the groundbreaking Brooklyn, New York, rapper whose 1985 song "Nightmares" and 1987 song "Cinderfella Dana Dane" are widely regarded as two of the best story raps of all time, said that gangster rap swept through New York and the music industry in the late 1980s with magnum force. "We had hardcore rap, but now it was getting even deeper in regards to bringing the inner city and the hood lifestyle to the forefront," Dana Dane told me. "It made cats like myself and Salt-N-Pepa, who were doing radio-friendly music, try to figure out if we were still going to fit in. It raised the stakes."

Given that this wave of gangster rap emerged from Southern California, New York rappers, who to this point in the late 1980s had been the only driving force of rap, were unprepared to be unseated as the culture's leaders. They were also unaware of the significance of this new type of rap, one that exponentially ratcheted up the intensity, violence, profanity, and sexuality of the music, reflecting the gang-related lifestyle of the Los Angeles metropolitan area.

Growing up on the East Coast in the mideighties, I soon noticed the cultural bias that New York artists and (a few years later) New York–based journalists typically had against rap that didn't come from New York's five boroughs. I also noticed that once the labeling of this segment of rap evolved from street rap, hardcore rap, and reality rap into gangster rap, there was a separation among rap artists.

"We didn't understand the culture at the time," Dana Dane told me, "and where it was coming from."

This unfamiliarity bred contempt. Yes, early artists from Philadelphia, Los Angeles, Miami, and Houston often mimicked the sound, style, and flair New York rappers employed in their music, but when gangster rap took off commercially, thanks to Ice-T, Eazy-E, and N.W.A, there was a division. These so-called gangster rappers were viewed as lesser artists by other rappers because they focused not on lyrical agility, per se, but on tales from the hood. Thus, gangster rappers became, in effect, the disenfranchised among the disenfranchised.

That's also why the perception of hardcore rappers in Los Angeles, who were labeled as gangster rappers, differed from their New York counterparts. Kool G Rap, Fat Joe, The Beatnuts, and Mobb Deep adopted the same style and subject matter as gangster rappers, but were not viewed by many artists, journalists, and fans as gangster rappers, because they did not rap about Los Angeles gang culture. This group of New York rappers also didn't fancy themselves as gang members, nor were they perceived that way by the outside world.

Indeed, the "gangster," "street," "reality," or "thug" rappers not from Los Angeles typically rapped about the blanket persona and habits of a traditional gangster and the criminal lifestyle rather than gangbanging itself. Thus, I have focused this book on West Coast artists, while also including extensive coverage of The Geto Boys (based in Houston, they emerged before the West Coast began its musical dominance, referred to themselves as gangsters, and operated under the direction of gangster label head James Prince), Master P and his No Limit Records (whose artists operated as a gang-like unit, carrying themselves as "soldiers" while billing themselves as gangsters, included the gangster rap superstar Snoop Dogg, and were based in Richmond, California), as well as 50 Cent (who, despite being from the New-York area aligned himself with Dr. Dre and the Game, had his own G-Unit crew, and name-drops and raps about Los Angeles gangs in several of his songs, most notably "What Up Gangsta").

It was also important for me to include almost an entire chapter on Schoolly D, whose music has been sampled scores of times, and whose lyrics and flows have been incorporated by everyone from the Notorious B.I.G to Nicki Minaj. Although many people think the genre started with either N.W.A or Dr. Dre, Schoolly D is known by rap cognoscenti as the creator of gangster rap,. Most of all, I wanted to write about the major players who pushed the music forward, from lesser-known acts such as Schoolly D and Above the Law to more recognized trailblazers such as Ice-T and Master P.

As I was working on this book, my friend Big Tray Deee, one half of the platinum gangster rap group Tha Eastsidaz, provided an explanation of gangster rap that served as my barometer: "We didn't start gangster shit and we didn't start gangster rap. But the lifestyle that we push and espouse, and what LA means to the gangster world overall, our voice has helped shape the lives of many youngsters right now [who] call themselves Gs, gangsters, or what have you."

So, New York rappers such as Kool G Rap, Fat Joe, The Beatnuts, Mobb Deep, Wu-Tang Clan, and JAY-Z, as well as Cleveland's Bone Thugs-N-Harmony, Miami's Trick Daddy, and Memphis's 8Ball & MJG and Project Pat, among many others, could be, and are, considered gangster rappers by some. For my purposes, though, they are all immensely talented and successful artists, but they didn't shape or redirect gangster rap itself. The artists I focus on in this book did. They are the ones who are the heart of this book, the acts whose words, music, style, and business shaped the genre.

I also wanted to hone in on the story of the music itself. Who made the important singles, albums, and projects? Why were the artists and the art they made noteworthy? How did their music lead to the next generation of artists and the evolution of the genre?

That's why I dedicate much of this book to focusing on the music and the business that influenced the music. These are essential and untold stories, ones not previously presented in a detailed context, that show how they intersect creatively and commercially.

As a fan, music has always been the thing for me. That's why *The History of Gangster Rap* does not delve extensively into beefs, or diss records, other than particular ones that changed the trajectory of gangster rap. That's why the rivalry between 2Pac and the Notorious B.I.G. is covered, as is Ice Cube's beef with N.W.A, but I don't explore the Westside Connection's feud with Cypress Hill, for instance. The first two resulted in dramatic changes in the music being made and how the rap music business evolved. By contrast, the latter resulted in a few clever and searing songs, but not much else.

Enough time has passed since gangster rap's inception in the mid-1980s for me to get a broader view of how gangster rap has influenced everything from music to fashion to film to American culture overall. I was fortunate enough to be a listener and a fan during gangster rap's infancy, and, as a journalist who has written about rap (and gangster rap) for more than twenty-four years in such publications as the *Los Angeles Times*, *The Source* and the *Chicago Tribune*, I've seen its growing pains, its raw emotion, and its flashes of brilliance. Over the years, I saw it develop its balance of intellect and chaos, something that continues today through the material of popular Compton artists such as Kendrick Lamar and YG, as well as the work of Bronx, New York, rapper Cardi B, whose "Bodak Yellow" song title and lyrics pay homage to the Bloods. Gangster rap remains vital because the societal circumstances that inspired it still exist.

It is within these pages that I'll explore those societal circumstances and how a great American art form rose, and continues to rise, out of them. Thank you for reading.

SOREN BAKER
April 2018

Foreword

But I identified with gangster rap because it spoke to my soul. The hard times, the things I was witnessing, the things I was curious about, it seemed as though the music that I was gravitating to had the answers.

As I look back on it now, gangster rap was the soundtrack to my life because things were really rough for me as a kid. My parents were very religious. They hated rap music, so they wouldn't let me consume it the way I wanted to. I couldn't have it blaring in my room. My listening was very hush-hush. The music was an outlet for my aggression and my anger, and discovering new music began to be something my friends and I did together. That was dope to me.

I was really into Ice Cube when he broke away from N.W.A. I was drawn to his writing and how he expressed himself. That was something that was mind-boggling to me. When his first album, *AmeriKKKa's Most Wanted*, came out in 1990, there was no Internet and I didn't have access to MTV, so I didn't know the ins and outs, or the reasons why Ice Cube had split from N.W.A. I just thought that he had a solo record. But then when you actually heard the record, that was the *Nigganet*. That's where you got the information that you were looking for. I thought the album was crazy. I thought it was fanfuckintastic. I wore it out because the production was so dope—my favorite production team, the Bomb Squad, was involved; they'd broken through with Public Enemy. I was like, "Wow." Cube's expressions, his voice inflection. I was in awe of all of it.

Cube was a storyteller. He killed it on that album. Other people told stories, but not like Cube's. You could visualize them. You didn't have to see a video to see what he was talking about—he was painting pictures you could see in your mind. It was relatable content, and for the people that couldn't relate, who were curious about South Central, this was about as close as they were going to get to it. They'd stay way the fuck away from there.

As I was listening to gangster rap as a kid, I had no idea I wanted to be an artist. In fact, at the time, I wanted to be an architect, to tell you the truth. I did architectural drafting, computer-aided drafting. That was my shit. That's what I wanted to do, build bridges and boats and shit. But then, I went to jail, and there goes that.

So when I actually got out to California (I was about seventeen or eighteen) and met up with James Broadway, there were groups around him that he was producing for: Mad Kap, King Tee, Tha Alkaholiks. It was an exciting time and those were the first artists that I was around. I would just rap for however long the rap turned out to be. There was no structure. There were no bars. It was just rapping.

Eventually, I saw how the process happened. I saw what made a good idea into a good song, and then what made a good song into a great record. Understanding the process lit a spark in me. I started to be like, "I can actually do this." I haven't ever looked back.

Now that gangster rap has been around, we've seen it transform. We've seen it be the scapegoat for a lot of shit that's really not its fault. We've seen it launch careers. We've seen it kill careers. We've seen it kill people. I say it's killed people because the one thing about gangster rap is either you're authentic or you're not, there is no in-between. A lot of people try to live up to that authenticity when they're really not that type of gangster, and it gets them killed.

Then there are people that *are* authentic, and it gets them killed, too, so the music can't be the only factor you consider. What I'm saying is that gangster rap – the music itself – is overshadowed by the people in its environment, and that's where the problems come into play. That's with anything, but the stigma that comes along with gangster rap doesn't exist in country, doesn't exist in pop, doesn't exist in polka music, folk dancing, Riverdancing. You don't hear about motherfucking rival river dancing bands shooting each other. There's a danger that comes along with telling these stories.

Gangster rap has fed a lot of people. It's changed a lot of lives. It's changed my life. It's given me something to really reflect on as a fan and as a man. And that's why Soren Baker's *The History Of Gangster Rap* is important—to document the things that some of us may have forgotten, and to relive the moments that have been seared into our souls.

XZIBIT
Chatsworth, California
April 2018

MELODY MAKER

SCHOOLLY·D

GANGS GUNS & THE HIGH LIFE: BLOWING AWAY
THE YO·BOY MYTH + JUST ICE MURDER RAP

Native Son

OPPOSITE:

Schoolly D (right) and his DJ Code Money appeared on the cover of the November 15, 1986, edition of British publication *Melody Maker*.

IN 1982, RAP GOT A GLIMPSE OF ITS FUTURE.

President Reagan gutted school programs and Martin Luther King Jr. did not yet have a holiday. The Los Angeles Lakers defeated the Philadelphia 76ers to win the NBA finals, and the Crips and Bloods gangs ruled South Central. The first CD player was sold; disco was dying and gangster rap was about to be born. Snoop Dogg was eleven years old and Ice Cube was thirteen, and they lived in Long Beach and South Central, respectively. A seventeen-year-old Dr. Dre got his first set of turntables after listening to Grandmaster Flash's "The Adventures of Grandmaster Flash on the Wheels of Steel." A twenty-four-year-old Ice-T was transitioning from a life of crime to being a rapper at Radio Club, aka Radiotron, the only rap club in L.A.

At this point, rap records were mostly party songs brimming with braggadocio and good-natured rhymes. In 1979, rap took its first major commercial step forward with the release of the Sugarhill Gang's "Rapper's Delight," the genre's first mainstream hit. The song's music was blatantly appropriated from Chic's disco record "Good Times" and its rhymes, in part, were lifted from Grandmaster Caz.

TIMELINE OF RAP

1985
Key Rap Releases

1. LL Cool J's *Radio* album

2. Doug E. Fresh & The Get Fresh Crew's "The Show" b/w Doug E. Fresh & M.C. Ricky D's "La Di Da Di" singles

3. Schoolly D's "P.S.K. What Does It Mean" and "Gucci Time" single

US President

Ronald Reagan

Something Else

The first Internet domain name, symbolics.com, was registered.

Rappers Wonder Mike, Master Gee, and Big Bank Hank delivered simple, playful lyrics about their affinity for fashion, the desire to get with women, and the awkwardness of eating substandard food at a friend's house. Even at a time when rapping was in and of itself revolutionary, the Sugarhill Gang's lyrics, and those of such contemporaries as Kurtis Blow and the Funky 4 + 1, were little more than conversational, simplistic, and occasionally witty barbs that rhymed. Since the overall genre was in the infancy of its artistic evolution, most rappers of this era were still developing their styles and songwriting skills. Still, their delivery, concepts, and rhyme patterns, which were relatively straightforward, were nonetheless groundbreaking.

When 1982 came along, pioneering Bronx hip-hop DJ Grandmaster Flash and his rap crew, the Furious Five, came with it. With "The Message," the group's revolutionary recording, rapper Melle Mel described the desolate neighborhoods that many members of the rap community called home. "Broken glass everywhere," Melle Mel rapped at the start of the first verse. "People pissin' on the stairs, you know they just don't care."

"The Message" was a dark, somber song that spoke profoundly of the reality that many black people in America were experiencing and which stood in stark contrast to the festive music most rappers were releasing at the time.

For many rap fans, it was the first time they'd heard any sort of profanity on a record. A young Jayo Felony, a future gangster rapper who would be signed to Def Jam Recordings, was floored when, at the chaotic end of "The Message," Melle Mel and his crew are seemingly apprehended by police and an officer (or someone impersonating an officer) blurts out, "Get in the goddamn car." Those lyrics are remarkably tame compared to those uttered by rappers today, but in 1982, they were shocking.

The lyrics resonated with Jayo Felony and the rap-buying audience in a new, piercing way because they signaled a key change in rap. For the first time, the rage, chaos, and feelings of helplessness of blacks in America had been presented in a rap song. Moreover, Melle Mel presented himself as someone caught in systematic degradation and oppression. Although political messaging had been present in other rap songs, by Kurtis Blow for instance, it had never been presented in such a stark, serious, and striking manner.

Then, in 1984, gangster rap forefather Schoolly D flipped the script. Inspired by "The Message," the pioneering Philadelphia rapper made a record called "Gangster Boogie," in which he played the role of someone who menacingly instilled fear in and perpetuated crimes against the people living in the abhorrent conditions of the ghetto that Melle Mel had described. Schoolly D pressed it up on vinyl and took it to radio DJ Lady B, whose "Street Beat" show on Power 99 in Philadelphia was one of the most influential rap radio shows in the country at the time.

Lady B gave it to Schoolly D straight: No record company was going to sign him or distribute his records. The reason? He was rapping about weed and guns. Schoolly D, though, did not think his music was abrasive.

"I was being an artist," Schoolly D said. "I grew up listening to [comedic legend] Richard Pryor on the radio on Saturday night. Late Saturday nights, the DJ would put on [his album] *That Nigger's Crazy*. We didn't think nothing of it. It was art. To us, it was art. To you [outsiders], it was just like, 'We've got to stop these voices.' Motherfuckers were listening. Then when they started listening, it was like they didn't understand. I tell people now, 'I don't give a fuck what y'all thought. You have to understand that. I was making records for my peers, to uplift my situation, and it was workin'. I wanted to tell my stories the way I wanted to tell my stories. That's why I never wanted to change my art."

Faced with the sobering reality that he might never get radio play or a record deal, Schoolly D started saving up to press his own records. He connected with the buyers at influential mom-and-pop Philly record shops such as Funk-O-Mart and Sound of Market. Philadelphia was a bit player in rap at the time, but the city was on the cusp of an explosion thanks to Pop Art Records, which released early singles from burgeoning rap artists Roxanne Shanté, Steady B, and MC Craig G. For the mom-and-pop shops, independently released rap records were particularly attractive because corporate record stores typically didn't carry

MIX MASTER SPADE

This pioneering rapper-singer-mixtape maestro helped popularize early Compton rappers. As Los Angeles–area rap evolved in the mideighties from the electro sounds of Egyptian Lover, World Class Wreckin' Cru, and others, Mix Master Spade made mixtapes and singles with a singsong style that featured collaborations with such protégés as Toddy Tee ("Just Say No") and King Tee ("Ya Better Bring a Gun"). The Compton Posse leader helped his city develop a buzz on the local market prior to N.W.A putting it on the global map a few years later.

STREET LIT
AS A PRECURSOR
TO GANGSTER RAP

THE WORKS OF generations of rappers were inspired by the pulp street novels of such revered writers as Iceberg Slim and Donald Goines. Their gritty stories featured graphic tales of pimping, prostitution, and murder, and the narratives were often inspired by the authors' real-life experiences. Ice-T took his name in order to pay homage to Iceberg Slim, while Goines's *Crime Partners* was adapted into a 2001 film that featured Ice-T and Snoop Dogg. Goines's *Never Die Alone* was made into a 2004 film starring DMX.

AUTHOR	FIRST PUBLISHED	SEMINAL BOOK
Iceberg Slim	1967	*Pimp*
Donald Goines	1971	*Dopefiend*
Charlie Avery Harris	1976	*Macking Gangster*
Odie Hawkins	1979	*Sweet Peter Deeter*

much rap. Schoolly D was encouraged by the feedback he got from Philly's independent record retailers.

"All the record stores said that if I pressed the record up, they'd sell them," Schoolly D said. "So I did it."

Launched in 1983, his Schoolly-D Records was the first artist-owned rap label. It was also the first to release what would be considered a gangster rap song, 1985's "P.S.K. What Does It Mean?" The booming, self-produced song featured Schoolly D rapping about smoking weed, driving a Mercedes, buying cocaine, pulling a gun on another rapper, hijacking said rapper's show, and taking a girl (who he later determines is a prostitute) home, where he "fucked her from my toes to the top of my head."

The way Schoolly D rapped—with an ominous, off-kilter flow—stood in stark contrast to the other rappers of the era. Ice-T, for instance, remembers being drawn to the song the first time he heard it. He was at a club in Santa Monica, California, and was initially hooked by the beat, but he was also taken aback by how Schoolly D flowed.

"At that time, everybody was yelling on records," Ice-T said. "The cadence was so different."

As an artist, Schoolly D had taken several significant steps with "P.S.K. What Does It Mean?" For one thing, he stood apart from most of his rap contemporaries because he was a solo artist. In 1984 and 1985, many of the biggest rap acts, including Run-DMC, Whodini, and the Fat Boys, were groups. Another distinction was that he rapped in first-person narrative, and in a brash, violent, sexual, and menacing way, about the street lifestyle.

"Our first inkling of gangster rap was Schoolly D, 'P.S.K.,'" platinum rapper-producer and Compton, California, gangster rap act DJ Quik said. "I don't know how I got that record. But I know that once I got it, I couldn't let it go. I played that shit wherever I could play it. The music kind of low-key scared you into liking it, like a bully."

As the song gained popularity, Schoolly D noticed that his artistic stance made some listeners uncomfortable, especially coming from a black man who was willing to exact violence on others.

"Richard Pryor would say this all the time: 'If the shit I was saying had music behind it, it wouldn't get played, not anywhere, because the message with music and a black man who didn't give a fuck—or gave a fuck—was dangerous in America,' and is still dangerous to this day," Schoolly D said. "You see it. How the fuck are police officers—and twenty of 'em—with guns afraid of one little black boy? What do they say? 'I was in fear of my life.' But they don't give a fuck about going in the hoods and rounding up gangs, but they swear to God it's always that one motherfuckin' black dude that's getting shot."

Violence notwithstanding, in the "P.S.K. What Does It Mean?" narrative, the protagonist decided he "ain't doing no time" and showcased his so-called "educated mind" in deciding not to shoot the "sucker-ass nigga trying to sound like me." Philadelphia was emerging from a neighborhood gang era when Schoolly D was crafting the song, and he said it was this short-lived period of peace and civility that inspired him to look at his city's culture of violence from a mindful perspective.

"I felt in '85, when I was writing that, I was feeling like, 'Wow. We can actually go into other neighborhoods and don't have to worry about getting shot. We can date other girls from other black neighborhoods,'" Schoolly D said. "It was kind of like I felt like we were educating ourselves. I was like, 'I'm not going to do no time just for some sucker-ass shit. If I do time, it's going to mean something.' That's what I was trying to stress, but the more I said that, the more it got drowned out. People were like, 'Yeah. But you said this in the beginning. . . .' I'm like, 'Did you read the whole fuckin' book?' It made me very angry and it made me close up. So it was just like, 'People don't really want to know the real truth. They just wanna know I could shoot and stab, or rape and murder.' It's a shame that it has to be that way, but it's not all that way."

"P.S.K. What Does It Mean?" also sent shock waves throughout the music world thanks to its thunderous self-produced beat. Unlike most other rappers, Schoolly D produced and composed his own music. He grew up listening to jazz and funk, and he gravitated to songs with lengthy guitar solos and robust horn sections.

Material from Ohio Players, James Brown, Chicago, and the Beatles were among his favorites. While listening to these musically disparate groups, he appreciated the instrumental portions of songs. Thus, "P.S.K. What Does It Mean?" contains several extended instrumental sections during its six-plus minutes.

"The song was about not just rapping," Schoolly D said. "It was also about the music. Since I was going to write the music and the music was going to represent me, I spent a lot of time writing that music."

It "sounded like a church cathedral eight city blocks big," Questlove said of "P.S.K. What Does It Mean?" "That much echo. I was more hypnotized at the way the drums kept coming in offbeat at the top of each phrase ending."

"It was groundbreaking, the drums that they used," independent rap juggernaut and Kansas City rap pioneer Tech N9ne said. "You never heard anything like that before."

The influence of "P.S.K. What Does It Mean?" resonated for years. It is one of the most sampled and referenced songs in rap history. The sonically sparse song is a genre-shifting piece of art that influenced generations of artists, even though it never went gold or platinum, and even though it is not often referenced by the artists who appropriated it. In fact, many of the artists who used "P.S.K." were far more commercially successful than Schoolly D.

For instance, in 1991, the popular UK rock group Siouxsie and the Banshees co-opted the beat on their biggest hit single, "Kiss Them for Me." In 1997, the Notorious B.I.G. covered it on "B.I.G. (Interlude)," a cut from his ten-times platinum *Life After Death* album. More recently, Nicki Minaj emulated Schoolly D's flow on "Beez in the Trap," her 2012 single featuring 2 Chainz.

Part of the allure of "P.S.K. What Does It Mean?" can also be traced to *P.S.K.*, an acronym for the Park Side Killers gang with which Schoolly D was affiliated. Although Schoolly D never rapped about being in the gang on the song, word spread through rap circles that Schoolly D was representing and flaunting his gang membership, adding another layer of mystery, intrigue, and menace to the selection.

"I was like, 'Okay, so this is like a little anthem for a gang,'" Ice-T said.

Also included on the "P.S.K. What Does It Mean?" single was another one of Schoolly D's most significant songs, "Gucci Time." On this cut, the Pennsylvania artist opens the track by saying he wants to beat people up for biting his material. For many young rap listeners, it reminded them of what they'd hear on the streets.

"C'mon, man, that's gangster shit," Tech N9ne said. "That's like real people talking to you on a dope-ass hip-hop beat. His tone was like nobody's. He's the pioneer of gangster rap."

In fact, the way Schoolly D rapped about his wealth, his material possessions, and his unflinching attitude and willingness to beat people down separated Schoolly D from other rappers.

"'Lookin' at *my* [sic] Gucci, it's about that time,'" Tech N9ne said. "*He* had a Gucci, not looking at some other nigga's Gucci wishing [he] could have one. It reminded me of the dope dealers in the hood. I was like, 'He must be a dope dealer.' That was my first stereotype of Schoolly D. He struck me as somebody who didn't have to talk about nobody else or what they seen. It's what *he's* doing."

The third "Gucci Time" verse features Schoolly D rapping about pulling a gun on a pimp whose girl he was enjoying himself.

Reached in my pocket / Pulled out my gun / Shot the pimp in the head / Mother-fucker fell dead / But now she in jail on a ten-year bid

Like "P.S.K. What Does It Mean?," "Gucci Time" quickly became one of the most sampled songs in rap history. The first major usage came on Beastie Boys' "Time to Get Ill," a selection from *Licensed to Ill*, their breakthrough 1986 album that sold more than ten million copies. Other rap artists either just recited the chorus—"Lookin' at my Gucci it's about that time"—or modified it for their own personal fashion sensibilities, from Common—then going as Common Sense on 1994's "Chapter 13 (Rich Man vs. Poor Man)"—to the Big Tymers—on their 2002 hit single "Still Fly." JAY-Z rapped over the instrumental, referenced the lyrics, and was inspired by the title for his "Looking at My S Dots," which celebrated his 2003 Reebok deal.

Buoyed by the success of "P.S.K. What Does It Mean?" and "Gucci Time," Schoolly D released his eponymous debut album in 1985. The six-track project also included "I Don't Like Rock 'N' Roll," "Put Your Filas On," "Free Style Rapping," and "Free Style Cutting." The latter was an instrumental selection that featured the turntable work of Schoolly D's DJ, DJ Code Money.

SAMPLERS vs. INSTRUMENTS

IN THE MIDEIGHTIES, most rappers moved away from using live instruments to make their music. Instead, they worked with drum machines, samplers, and turntables. This evolution largely eliminated musicians and instruments from the actual music-making of rap. Now, producers and production crews were self-contained units who could program, sample, and scratch

KEY EQUIPMENT

DRUM MACHINES
Roland TR-808
Linn LM-1

TURNTABLE
Technics 1200

SAMPLERS
E-mu SP-1200
Akai MPC60

On "I Don't Like Rock 'N' Roll," Schoolly D marked a line in the sand, distancing rap—and himself—from rock music. He also dissed Prince (who, in the eighties, had said that people who made rap weren't musicians, among other slights), boasted of carrying a .38 automatic pistol, and scored himself and his girl of the moment some marijuana.

Like "Gucci Time," "Put Your Filas On" is a celebration of the type of ghetto fabulousness that would become synonymous with rap within a few years. It was also a nod to the line of athletic gear particularly popular with drug dealers in the mid-Atlantic region of the United States at the time.

> *"The fuckin' label was handwritten. There was nothing pretty about this shit."*
>
> **BIG BOY**

Released in 1985 on Schoolly-D Records, *Schoolly D* marked several turning points for rap: It was released by a rapper not from New York and by his own record company. It was also self-funded and self-produced, Schoolly D hand-drawing his own art for his early singles and albums and printing the song information on his releases.

"The fuckin' label was handwritten," Los Angeles's Real 92.3 radio personality Big Boy said. "There was nothing pretty about this shit."

Schoolly D also provided rap with its first look into the life and mind of an artist who was part of the street culture and boasted about his criminal activity—instead of just describing the deplorable conditions surrounding him.

"When you heard it, it was some of the most gulliest, gutter—to this day—gangster shit that you heard," Big Boy said. "That's the way we were talking. If we were on some, 'Fuck this motherfucker,' then to hear someone on record say, 'Fuck this motherfucker,' you were like, 'Oh, shit.'"

Unlike other rappers who wanted to distance themselves from urban squalor, Schoolly D placed himself in the middle of it, making it clear that he was representing the streets because he was of—and from—the streets he was rapping about. He made himself the prototype for gangster rappers.

"Being from Philly and being from the Northeast, I had to make sure [to put] more heart and soul into it," Schoolly D said. "When you put more heart and soul into something like that, people are more afraid. . . . I was representing a person, a one-minded person, Schoolly D, and that's more dangerous than a gang. It is because you beat down the leader of a gang, the gang disbands. You beat down a man, he becomes a martyr."

TODDY TEE

Released in 1985, Toddy Tee's "Batterram" documented the vehicle—a modified ex-military tank outfitted with a battering ram affixed to the front—the Los Angeles Police Department used to break down the doors of suspected L.A. drug and crime houses in the eighties. The song's upbeat, keyboard-driven sonics belied the horror described in the lyrics, including the batterram, which shoved a person's living room into his den. The following year, Toddy Tee, who was from Compton, and Mix Master Spade detailed the drug epidemic ravaging South Los Angeles on "Just Say No," a song whose music was decidedly upbeat for such bleak subject matter. "Batterram" and "Just Say No" hinted at what gangster rap would become.

In 1986, Schoolly D released the first version of *Saturday Night! – The Album*. Originally consisting of seven songs, the project's cover art was again drawn by Schoolly D, but, unlike his previous work, Schoolly D's name was written without a dash between the *y* and the *D*. Being essentially a one-man shop (record company owner, rapper, producer, drum programmer, keyboardist) afforded Schoolly D little time for quality control over the artwork he created for his material. He also provided another explanation for the discrepancies between how he wrote his name, which also included writing it with one *L*—"Schooly D."

> ## *"When you put more heart and soul into something like that, people are more afraid."*
> **SCHOOLLY D**

"In the beginning, it depended on how much weed I was smoking," Schoolly D said. "Sometimes you'd be seeing double and you think you put those two *Ls* down, but you know you didn't. Then I was like, 'Whoa. It must mean something.'"

Interested in seeking out the possible significance of using Schoolly D versus either Schoolly-D or Schooly D, he spoke to a mystic.

"She was like, 'I'm going to tell you something about numerology,'" Schoolly D said. "She said, 'I was thinking about you. I was hoping I'd meet you and sit down with you. When you spell it with the one *L*, you're going to do great things at home with your family. When you spell it with the two *Ls*, great things will come to you with your business, your money. You should think about when you did this and when you did that.' It was some numerology, but most of it was how high I was."

Saturday Night! – The Album's selection "Saturday Night" contained what was becoming Schoolly D's signature storytelling style: violent, profane tales about his drug-induced, sex-chasing life on the streets of Philadelphia. Like "P.S.K. What Does It Mean?" and "Gucci Time" before it, "Saturday Night" became a popular sample source. The Roots used its music on their 1999 song "Without a Doubt," and Diddy protégé Loon used the "Saturday Night" instrumental as the music for his 2003 single "How You Want That." Method Man also paid homage to "Saturday Night" on his hit 1995 single "I'll Be There for You/You're All I Need to Get By" with Mary J. Blige by saying Schoolly D's "cheeba cheeba, y'all" chant.

With *Saturday Night! – The Album* continuing the success Schoolly D had enjoyed with his self-titled debut album, he embarked on several tours throughout the United States and Europe. When he returned after an extended stay promoting his material in Miami, his mother told him he needed to sit down and call an emerging rapper who had tried to reach him several times. The resulting phone call inspired gangster rap's first West Coast superstar to make music unabashedly on his own terms.

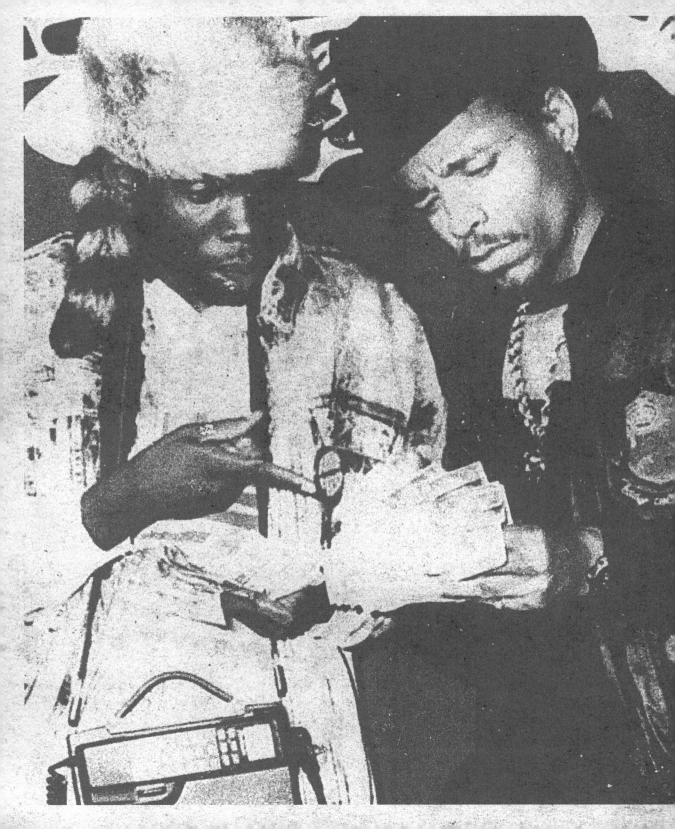

"Squeeze the Trigger"

IN 1986, LOS ANGELES WAS A CITY UNDER SIEGE.

OPPOSITE:

King Tee (left) and Ice-T are proof that rhyme pays.

Tens of thousands of reported members of various sets of gangs populated the streets of the Southern California epicenter, notably the Crips and the Bloods. As these notorious factions warred over territory, money, drugs, and women, nearly two hundred gang-related deaths were taking place annually as crack, cocaine, marijuana, alcohol, and firearms flooded the streets.

Against this backdrop, New Jersey transplant Ice-T was emerging as one of Los Angeles's hottest rappers. As other East Coast rappers were bringing a street persona to their own material, Ice-T had enjoyed international exposure with small roles in the 1984 b-boy movies *Breakin'* and *Breakin' 2: Electric Boogaloo*. He was also rising through the ranks of Los Angeles's nascent rap scene, one that was leaning more on disco and electronic influences than the boom bap style of Queens, New York, rap trailblazers Run-DMC.

Early singles such as "Cold Wind-Madness" (produced by Jimmy Jam and Terry Lewis, later famous for their work with Janet Jackson, among others) and "Ya Don't Quit" showed Ice-T's promise as a clever writer, but his friends

1986
Key Rap Releases

1. Run-D.M.C.'s
Raising Hell album

2. Beastie Boys'
Licensed to Ill album

3. Salt-N-Pepa's *Hot,
Cool + Vicious* album

US President

Ronald Reagan

Something Else

*The Oprah Winfrey
Show* broadcast
nationally for the first
time.

urged him to write some of the street-based rhymes that he would say to them in private. He decided to humor these requests on the B side of his 1986 single "Dog'n the Wax (Ya Don't Quit Part II)."

But before he released the song, he and his manager, Jorge Hinojosa, put in a series of calls to gangster rap pioneer Schoolly D. They talked to his mother, who served as Schoolly D's de facto messenger service. Just back from hanging out with the 2 Live Crew in Miami, Schoolly D placed a three A.M. call to Ice-T, who wasn't available.

"They called me back and were like, 'Before you say anything, I want to play the song,'" Schoolly D said. "[Ice-T] played me '6 'N the Mornin'' over the phone, and I was like, 'Hell yeah.' He was like, 'Respect, because I wouldn't do this [without your blessing], because if I did it, it would seem like I was biting you, but I'm not biting you. You just inspired me.' We talked about it, and that was that. That was love. To me, to push the art form forward, I felt like we all had to work together."

In an August 2015 Twitter exchange, Ice-T reciprocated the respect when he responded to a question wondering why some say Schoolly D is the first gangster rapper.

"I even say that," Ice-T tweeted. "PSK inspired 6 n the morning. Schoolly was hinting at it. I just said it."

Schoolly D indeed lit the gangster rap fuse with "P.S.K. What Does It Mean?," and the genre exploded with the release of Ice-T's "6 'N the Mornin'." Ice-T was inspired by the lyrics and rhyme style of Schoolly D's work, and he and producer the Unknown DJ drew a portion of their sonic inspiration from the Beastie Boys' 1986 song "Hold It Now, Hit It."

An elaborate story rhyme, "6 'N the Mornin'" ratcheted up the intensity and brazenness of Schoolly D's material exponentially and took gangster rap from the East Coast streets of Philadelphia to the West Coast streets of Los Angeles.

"It was play-by-play an L.A. day," Ice-T said.

"It's like a short film with music, with a score and soundtrack all in one," adds KK, one half of the Compton rap duo, and DJ Quik protégés, 2nd II None.

Throughout the song's ten verses, Ice-T unfolds a narrative in which he escapes the police raiding his house, beats a woman with the help of his crew, gets arrested for possession of an Uzi and a hand grenade, stabs a fellow inmate in the eye, gets out after serving a seven-year sentence, starts pimping, is involved in a shoot-out where six people are shot and two die, steals a car, has wild sex, and catches a flight to New York City.

Ice-T called the song "faction."

"They're factual situations put into a fictional story," Ice-T said. "[My friend] Sean E Sean did have a Blazer with a Louis [Vuitton] interior. We did get busted with a hand grenade. All these different things happened at different times, but I made it all happen [in] '6 'N the Mornin'.' Then I go to jail for seven years. No, I couldn't possibly have actually gone to jail for seven years. So there's a lot of fiction and faction put in."

Listeners were drawn to the song's realistic elements. "'6 'N the Mornin',' the shock value on that was so consistent of what we was going through," says Gangsta D, the other half of 2nd II None. "Before, it was like you keep that under the hush, 'cause you're trying to get away with something. But, that's what he gave to the game."

"They're factual situations put into a fictional story."
ICE-T

Ice-T's lyrically visual style and his genuine street credibility—he was a known hustler—helped propel the genre from the underground rap world to mainstream recognition. His semi-autobiographical storytelling also earned the rapper comparisons to musical and literary legends.

"[T]his reformed criminal is the rap equivalent of pimp-turned-paperback-writer Iceberg Slim," the *Village Voice*'s Robert Christgau wrote of Ice-T in 1988.

Born Tracy Marrow, Ice-T came up with his stage name in order to pay homage to Iceberg Slim, the pimp turned author whose 1967 book, *Pimp: The Story of My Life*, was a poetic and bleak depiction of the world of black pimps that resonated with Ice-T, Ice Cube, and others. There was a vicious, brutal current that ran through *Pimp* and Slim's other works, a stark mixture of rawness and reality told in a hypnotic way that captivated readers. Ice-T brought a similarly vivid realism and personal perspective into his presentation of the criminal underworld on "6 'N the Mornin'," from pimping and drug dealing to robbery and murder.

But where Iceberg Slim's cautionary tales resonated largely and most prominently within the black community, Ice-T's work was appreciated, consumed, and enjoyed by some of music's most respected white voices as well as droves of young white followers.

Bob Dylan, one of the most celebrated singer-songwriters in music history and a 1988 inductee into the Rock and Roll Hall of Fame, for instance, said, in *Chronicles, Volume One*, his 2004 memoir, that he became a fan of Ice-T's music after being introduced to it by U2 front man, Bono. During the sixties, Dylan's work on such songs as "The Times They Are A-Changin'," "Chimes of Freedom," and "Blowin' in the Wind" examined the social unrest consuming America marked by the civil rights and antiwar movements.

Just as Bob Dylan served as the soundtrack to his era, Ice-T emerged at the forefront of the burgeoning gangster rap movement with "6 'N the Mornin'." Like Dylan, Ice-T was providing a voice to the voiceless and serving as an unofficial spokesman for people pushed to the limits of survival and sanity by America's government.

Dylan's material was in line with the progressive thoughts of his era, while Ice-T's music depicted the aftermath of the civil rights movement. It told the story of the fallout of a generation of kids whose parents marched in the streets of America for equality but whose families and communities were undone by the ravages of the drug epidemic of the early eighties, crack cocaine in particular.

Ice-T was surprised that people wanted to hear music about life on the streets of Los Angeles.

"It was fascinating to me that people liked that," Ice-T said. "I was like, 'Yo, people want to hear this gangster shit.' That's when my music started to change. I started to go in that direction. It was funny for me. I was like, 'Oh. That's what they want? Well, I've got tons of that shit.' It would have been difficult for me to make dance records, or to try to deny who I was, but I just didn't know that that lifestyle could become a genre of music."

Gone was the political correctness of yesteryear. "6 'N the Mornin'" was full of profanity and was presented in an explicit, gritty way, but it wasn't mindless rage. Yes, the song depicts a life of crime, but in the third verse, Ice-T's character gets arrested and sent to jail for seven years. In the sixth verse, he explains why he and his crew ran from the police: "Cops [would have] shot us on sight / They wouldn't [have] took time to ask."

In "6 'N the Mornin'," Ice-T presented a moral overtone, showing that despite some of the glamour and excitement that came with living a life of crime, there were also serious, life-altering—and sometimes life-ending—consequences to being in this world. For the protagonist in Ice-T's song, it was a seven-year stretch behind bars.

Even with the visual quality of Ice-T's raps, during this era, outlets for rap videos were virtually nonexistent because MTV (Music Television) had yet to embrace the genre, essentially relegating rap videos to community access programs. Boogie Down Productions, though, brought a visual portrayal of

PMRC

FORMED IN 1985, the Parents Music Resource Center (PMRC) was cofounded by Tipper Gore and aims to limit children's access to music it considers inappropriate. Material deemed too violent or too sexual, or which contains drug references, is the target of the PMRC. The group, whose influence and significance has waned over the years, originally wanted to initiate a ratings system for albums similar to the one used by the Motion Picture Association of America (MPAA) for films.

More than a dozen record companies agreed to put an advisory sticker on the packaging of their albums, though the initial warning sticker was generic and did not specify the type of content deemed explicit.

Rappers did not take kindly to Gore's group. Ice-T, for one, blasted the PMRC and Gore on "Freedom of Speech," a song from his 1989 album, *The Iceberg/Freedom of Speech . . . Just Watch What You Say!*:

> *Think I give a fuck about some silly bitch named Gore? / Yo, PMRC, here we go, war / Yo Tip, what's the matter? You ain't gettin' no dick? / You're bitchin' about rock 'n' roll, that's censorship, dumb bitch / The Constitution says we all got a right to speak / Say what we want, Tip, your argument is weak / Censor records, TV, school books, too / And who decides what's right to hear, you? / Hey PMRC, you stupid fuckin' assholes / The sticker on the record is what makes it sell gold*

Paris, a San Francisco rapper whose music advocated a Black Panther Party agenda but who was often

mislabeled a gangster rapper because of his all-black attire and the violent content of some of his lyrics, agrees with Ice-T that the PMRC actually spurred the sales of raucous rap.

"Anything that was provocative just sold more back in the day," Paris said. "The idea of censorship and Tipper Gore and the PMRC, all they did was fuel sales because they would censor us or talk about it, but it didn't bar us from stores. The big difference is that now if people want to censor you, they just ignore you altogether. But back then, if they censored you, there was this kind of fake political type of outrage that occurred that only made each side more emboldened. If you were against what we were talking about, those voices were very loud and very vocal. But to the people who bought our records, that gave us an increased sense of a voice with them. It didn't hurt anybody, as far as I can tell, who was doing the kind of stuff I was doing, or gangster rap. Our sales just went through the roof."

More than a decade after Ice-T's "Freedom of Speech," Eminem examined the potential societal ramifications of the PMRC's actions on the outro of his 2002 song "White America," a cut from his *The Eminem Show*, which sold more than ten million copies.

> *To burn the [flag] and replace it with a Parental Advisory sticker / To spit liquor in the faces of this democracy of hypocrisy / Fuck you Ms. Cheney, fuck you Tipper Gore / Fuck you with the freest of speech this Divided States of Embarrassment will allow me to have*

gangsterism to their music. On the cover of their debut album, 1987's *Criminal Minded*, Bronx-based group members KRS-One and DJ Scott La Rock posed with pistols, a hand grenade, and a clip of bullets. The cover image matched the gangster raps of *Criminal Minded* songs "My 9mm Goes Bang" and "Criminal Minded," which were also released as singles, in 1986 and 1987, respectively.

The *Village Voice*'s Robert Christgau bristled at the overt explicitness of *Criminal Minded*. In his 1988 review of the album he wrote, "KRS-One's talk of fucking virgins and blowing brains out will never make him my B-boy of the first resort. I could do without the turf war, too." Yet Christgau also found merit in KRS-One's work on Boogie Down Productions' debut album, saying, "[H]is mind is complex and exemplary—he's sharp and articulate, his idealism more than a gang-code and his confusion profound."

Given its status as one of the first gangster rap albums, *Criminal Minded* garnered scant mainstream media coverage. In 2004, though, it earned a perfect five-star rating in Rolling Stone LLC's *The New Rolling Stone Album Guide*.

However, in the mideighties, the profanity-laced, violent, and confrontational music of such East Coast street rappers as Schoolly D (Philadelphia, Pennsylvania), Boogie Down Productions (Bronx, New York), and Just-Ice (Bronx, New York), who had a 1987 song called "The Original Gangster of Hip Hop," was largely discounted or ignored by the mainstream media. It was, however, being listened to, studied, and appreciated by a growing number of fans, including future gangster rappers and producers.

"We were inspired by their music," platinum rapper-producer DJ Quik said. "Our ear was to that shit. When those guys started talking that street shit out there, it was like you had to be from the streets to be able to relate. In a sense, you had to be all-seeing. You had to be hip, in the know. It was just a wave we had where it was like nonverbal communication, like 'I can relate to that.' And that's inspirational, like 'I want to do a song like that.' As a young writer, who wishes they didn't write the last hit song? It was like someone whistled over the gate. You whistle back."

Gangster rap's siren song was not limited to the music, though. Schoolly D and Ice-T knew the power of the provocateur and added notes to their early singles calling out that they contained explicit language.

Schoolly D's and Boogie Down Productions' popularity as independent acts led them to record deals with Jive Records, distributed through RCA Records, home to multiplatinum R&B singer Billy Ocean and platinum rap act Whodini,

BOOGIE DOWN PRODUCTIONS

SCOTT STERLING WAS working at a homeless shelter in the Bronx in the mideighties when he met Lawrence "Kris" Parker, a homeless teen and aspiring rapper. The two bonded over their love of rap and formed Boogie Down Productions (BDP), with Sterling rechristened as DJ Scott La Rock and Parker going as rapper KRS-One, an acronym for Knowledge Reigns Supreme Over Nearly Everyone. The duo's 1986 single "My 9mm Goes Bang" featured KRS-One rapping about shooting and killing a drug dealer named Peter and, later, his crew, who came to avenge his death. BDP's debut album, 1987's *Criminal Minded*, featured landmark rap singles "South Bronx" and "The Bridge Is Over," songs that thrust the group into the rap limelight because of KRS-One's disses leveled at MC Shan, a popular Queens, New York, rapper whose "The Bridge" single trumpeted the Queensbridge housing projects he called home. BDP's brazen gangster rhymes endeared them to fans, but the course of the group was forever changed in August 1987 when Sterling was shot and killed after coming to the aid of BDP affiliate D-Nice, who had gotten into an altercation over a woman. Upon Sterling's death, Parker changed the direction of BDP's music from gangster to conscious. He wrote, produced, directed, and mixed the group's second LP, 1988's *By All Means Necessary*. The album is one of the first conscious rap releases.

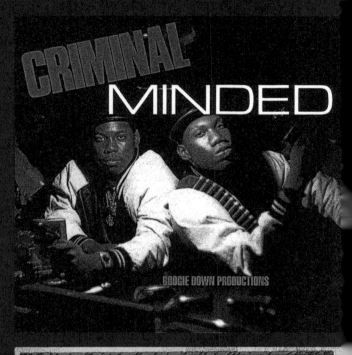

while Ice-T's deal with Sire Records, distributed through Warner Bros. Records, placed him on one of music's most respected labels.

At the time, Sire Records was enjoying staggering commercial crossover success with Madonna and critical accolades thanks to cutting-edge British rock band Echo & the Bunnymen, Canadian country-pop singer-songwriter k.d. lang, new-wave English musicians Depeche Mode, New York punk rockers the Ramones, and art rock band Talking Heads, among others.

Prior to signing Ice-T, the imprint had never counted a black artist among its roster, let alone a rapper. But the label's cofounder and Artists and Repertoire (A&R) man, Seymour Stein, a 2005 inductee into the Rock and Roll Hall of Fame, saw something special in Ice-T. Stein admitted that he didn't understand Ice-T's work, but he recognized him being of the same ilk as the other artists he signed. Stein knew from hearing Ice-T talk that he was a musical visionary, so he signed him. Throughout his debut studio album, *Rhyme Pays*, Ice-T built upon the creative canvas he started with "6 'N the Mornin'." With the frantic, mesmerizing "Squeeze the Trigger," for instance, Ice-T rapped about having an alarming arsenal of firearms, including an Uzi and a twelve-gauge shotgun. But it was his other observations that made the record remarkable and poignant.

Cops hate kids, kids hate cops / Cops kill kids with warning shots / What is crime and what is not? / What is justice? I think I forgot / We buy weapons to keep us

WEST vs. EAST

Jheri curls	Shaved heads
Red or blue bandanas	Gazelles
Lowriders	Train/subway
Rick Ross	Larry Davis
Small houses/apartments	Projects
24/7 rap programming	Mix shows
KDAY	Kool DJ Red Alert/Mr. Magic

strong / Reagan sends guns where they don't belong / The controversy is thick and the drag is strong / But no matter the lies, we all know who's wrong

Ice-T's masterful insight connects the police brutality of the eighties with the Iran-Contra affair that rocked the second term of Ronald Reagan's presidency. In a scandal that led to the indictment of several government officials, a number of the president's senior officials secretly facilitated the sale of weapons to Iran, which, at the time, was under an arms embargo. The Reagan administration members wanted to use the arms to secure the release of hostages. At the same time, they wanted funds from the sale of the weapons to Iran to be used to fund the anticommunist Contras movement in Nicaragua, which had been prohibited by Congress.

With his "Squeeze the Trigger" lyrics, Ice-T showed that rappers were paying attention to more than just their blocks. Although locked in their local worlds, they were vitally concerned with global events. Ice-T's perspective became all the more prescient once it was discovered that at least some of the money sent to Nicaragua was used to fund the explosion of the drug trade in South Los Angeles, of which the CIA was, if nothing else, aware.

The influx of drugs, money, and guns turned mideighties Los Angeles into a war zone. The city's streets were in such tumult that the police department used modified ex-military tanks armed with battering rams to enter hostile environments, making the juxtaposition of a crack house and a hostage situation all the more powerful. Toddy Tee's 1985 single "Batterram" bemoaned the use of the vehicle, which destroyed the houses of several families not involved in the drug trade.

On "Squeeze the Trigger," Ice-T gave America one of its first looks into the specific neighborhoods where both the cops and the gangs inflicted terror on residents. Ice-T took a bold step by naming several of the city's gangs and a handful of its most dangerous neighborhoods.

From the Rollin' '60s to the Nickerson "G" / Pueblos, Grape Street, this is what I see / The Jungle, the '30s, the VNG / Life in L.A. ain't no cup of tea

"'Squeeze the Trigger' was just a record about me saying that the world's fucked up and this is what I see," Ice-T said. "This is what I'm dealing with. I'm not coming from the same place you're coming from. It was basically my life. These different sets are what I'm dealing with. When I said those on 'Squeeze the Trigger,' people had *no idea* what I was talking about. L.A. people did. Just speaking in L.A. dialect unapologetically was putting gangster rap in motion, just saying things that you knew no one would really understand, but it was so hood."

That type of street specificity endeared Ice-T to large swaths of Southern California rap fans, allowing him to make inroads that other rappers had not.

"The difference is that Ice was out here with West Coast gangster rap—gangbanging, Crips, Bloods, Eses," said Hen Gee, a member of Ice-T's Rhyme Syndicate posse. "They didn't have that in any other region. Ice was the spokesman that introduced it to the world."

"Los Angeles artists gravitated more to the reality rap side, and what was going on and the conditions people were living in," said CJ Mac, who worked extensively with WC and released his 1999 album, *Platinum Game*, through Mack 10's Hoo-Bangin' Records. "That's what Los Angeles gravitated toward more so than the party, hip-hop rap. So, the streets were more influential in the music because that's what we thrived on, just trying to make it out. Any story of anybody relating to how you were living is what we wanted to hear."

> *"The world's fucked up and this is what I see. This is what I'm dealing with. I'm not coming from the same place you're coming from."*
>
> **ICE-T**

Ice-T put some specific gangs on the national map, but it was clear that his work didn't glamorize gangbanging. His most damning indictment of the lifestyle on *Rhyme Pays* arrived on "Pain." Here, Ice-T opens the song by rapping about a robber who gets incarcerated and laments building his own personal hell.

No matter how cold you roll / You simply cannot win / It's always fun in the beginning / But it's pain in the end

In the second verse, Ice-T tells the story of a lifelong criminal who joins a gang and scoffs at the thought of working a nine-to-five but is consumed by thoughts of being incarcerated. These trepidations are eventually overcome, but before the protagonist can move on, he is shot at close range by one of his friends.

The third verse tells the tale of a self-proclaimed "neighborhood terror" who scares his mother as he builds his street empire. But it all comes crashing down when the FBI raids his house, leading to ten criminal charges and an eighteen-year prison sentence.

Although Ice-T was rapping about the criminal lifestyle, he was not endorsing it. Instead, he was presenting the stark consequences associated with that life choice as cautionary tales, like his mentor and namesake Iceberg Slim had.

"My whole angle always was, I'll be street, but I will always tell you the horrors that go along with this life," Ice-T said. "That was what I set out to be, unique. I wasn't just going to document the streets. I'm going to say, 'Yeah. This looks very glamorous, but you could end up dead.' Most of my characters I did in my stories would end up dead or shot."

"That's part of Ice," Hen Gee said. "He always wanted to teach. He had more of the vision, the vocabulary."

As he had done on "6 'N the Mornin'," Ice-T also wove explicit sexual adventures into *Rhyme Pays*. Much like Schoolly D and Too $hort before him, Ice-T boasted of his sexual prowess and the throngs of women at his disposal on such songs as "Somebody Gotta Do It (Pimpin' Ain't Easy!!!)," "I Love Ladies," and "Sex."

When Stein first heard the early version of *Rhyme Pays*, he called Ice-T and his manager, Jorge Hinojosa, into a meeting. Stein wanted to voice his concerns. Prior to *Rhyme Pays*, Stein's only concerns when releasing an artist's album were whether or not it was creatively rich and musically vibrant, and whether or not it had commercial potential.

But Ice-T's album gave him a third concern. Stein was an older, white, Jewish man who was about to position himself as the outlet for black rage. He didn't question the validity of the record's content. He did, however, wonder what he was doing. He understood his other artists. Their music had melodies and choruses that he enjoyed and appreciated. They even had instruments. Ice-T's *Rhyme Pays* was the antithesis of virtually everything he knew.

As they sat in the A&R department in Warner Bros. Records, Stein explained to Ice-T

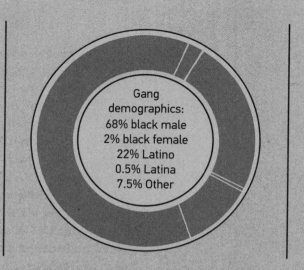

Gang demographics:
68% black male
2% black female
22% Latino
0.5% Latina
7.5% Other

LOS ANGELES GANGS IN 1986

Gang members:
150,000 Crips / 25,000 Bloods

Average age:
16

Square miles of gang territory:
28

Colors:
2 (blue and red)

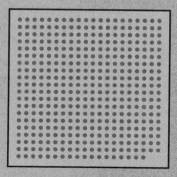

Gang deaths: 398

RIGHT:
"What Ya Wanna Do?"
DJ Evil E (left) and Ice-T
weigh their options.

and Hinojosa that he was surprised by the project's lyrical content. "Ice went through the record and explained specific lyrics to him that he didn't understand," Hinojosa said. "Seymour was very quiet and then Ice said, 'Maybe that feeling you're having is money.' Seymour nodded his head and agreed to release the album." *Rhyme Pays* was put on Sire Records' schedule and Ice-T soon proved that Stein's move was a prescient one.

Ice-T's *Rhyme Pays* was released in 1987. It benefitted from Ice-T's popularity in the streets, his creative reach, and Sire Records' major label push. Despite earning scant support from radio and video outlets, the album hit No. 26 on the Top R&B/Hip Hop Albums and No. 93 on the Billboard 200 charts and was certified gold with sales in excess of a half million units. With the album selling more than five hundred thousand copies, it was clear that gangster rap was appealing to a wider audience than just the black kids in the hood. It was taking hold in the suburbs with young white fans, too.

The mix of sex and criminality indeed made for an alluring musical concoction, even to some white, mainstream music critics. "[H]is sexploitations and true crime tales are detailed and harrowing enough to convince anybody he was there," the *Village Voice*'s Robert Christgau wrote of *Rhyme Pays*. "Wish I was sure he'll never go back." In 1987, rap had shown its sustainability, and more rappers began releasing albums, not just singles. That year, Ice-T's *Rhyme Pays* and Just-Ice's *Kool & Deadly (Justisizms)* became the first to have warning stickers about explicit content plastered on the covers of the albums themselves.

On the one hand, this tactic was indeed a warning for parents who may have been purchasing the product for their children. On the other hand, it was a sly marketing tool that gave the albums a certain cachet among consumers, especially ones seeking edgy material. These artists were rapping about doing the very things that helped lead to the conditions Melle Mel detailed on "The Message," and they were proud of it.

What Schoolly D, Ice-T, Boogie Down Productions, Just-Ice, and other artists had started as an independent, underground musical force was growing with an ever-increasing fan base eager to consume this new brand of rap—and with the labels, both big and small, ready to give them a platform.

Yes, the Sugarhill Gang, Kurtis Blow, Whodini, Run-DMC, LL Cool J, Dana Dane, and Beastie Boys had all gone either gold or platinum by 1987, but the rap landscape was changing. The first-person presentation of gangster rap made it more urgent, more sensational, and more vital than any other music in the marketplace, rap or otherwise. Gangster rap wasn't just artists rapping about what they saw, but also what they did. They were products of the streets whose art reflected their life experiences—gangs, violence, drugs, and sex.

This is masterfully illustrated by Ice-T's landmark 1988 single "Colors," the first rap song that was the title track of a major motion picture. The film from Academy Award nominee Dennis Hopper showcases an experienced cop (Academy Award winner Robert Duvall) and a rookie (eventual two-time Academy Award winner Sean Penn) as partners who patrol the streets of Los Angeles as gangs begin taking over the city.

Using Ice-T's "Colors" in such a high-profile film marked a significant development for gangster rap because, up to this point, rap songs were typically used in small-scale independent films about hip-hop culture (1983's *Wild Style* and 1985's *Krush Groove*) and films about breakdancing (1984's *Breakin'*, *Beat Street*, and *Breakin' 2: Electric Boogaloo*). By contrast, *Colors* was a Hollywood studio film starring two of the industry's biggest names—Duvall and Penn—as well as such future stalwarts as award-winning actors Don Cheadle and Damon Wayans.

In unflinching terms, "Colors" mirrors the film's subject matter and details the kill-or-be-killed gangbanging lifestyle that was ravaging Los Angeles. The video version of the song features Ice-T providing two distinct perspectives. One came from the vantage point of an active gang member detailing his status as a "nightmare walking, psychopath talking" gangster. The other commentary arrives in spoken-word passages after each rapped verse. This viewpoint is from the eyes of a kid who wishes he was not a part of the madness. Strikingly, Ice-T articulates the pain, disappointment, and struggle from both characters' perspectives, even though they put up dramatically different facades.

NIGHTMARE WALKING, PSYCHOPATH TALKING GANGSTER:

Tell me what have you left me / What have I got? / Last night in cold blood my young brother got shot / My homeboy got jacked / My mother's on crack / My sister can't work 'cause her arm show tracks / Madness, insanity / Live in profanity / Then some punk claimin' they're understandin' me / Give me a break / What world do you live in? /

VOICE OF REASON:

My brother was a gangbanger / And all my homeboys bang / I don't know why I do it, man, I just do it / I never had much of nothin', man / Look at you, man / You've got everything going for yourself / And I ain't got nothing, man / I've got nothing / I'm just living in the ghetto, man / Just look at me, man / Look at me

The song continues in kind, alternating between the chilling commentary of the two characters:

NIGHTMARE WALKING, PSYCHOPATH TALKING GANGSTER:

My game ain't knowledge, my game's fear / I've no remorse, so squares beware

VOICE OF REASON:

No matter whatcha do, don't ever join a gang / You don't wanna be in it, man / You're just gonna end up in a mix of dead friends and time in jail

Ice-T says that showing the pros and the cons of street life is essential in order to accurately depict the lifestyle and to remain credible with the music's target audience.

"If you've actually been out there with gangsters and drug dealers, they're going to keep a close eye on you," Ice-T said in an August 2000 interview. "There's no true way to deal with gangsterism without showing both sides of it and being honest.

"My music was an attempt for me to show [life on the streets], but be truthful," Ice-T added. "And the truth of the matter is that when you're winning, it's the most exciting thing in the world. But the downside is a motherfucker."

With "6 'N the Mornin'," *Rhyme Pays*, and then "Colors," Ice-T brilliantly showed both sides of the lifestyle, putting his stamp on the emerging gangster rap movement in the process. He became known as the genre's truth teller, a high-profile poet and provocateur whose aim was not merely to agitate, but to educate the world about the crises transpiring in black urban America.

As Ice-T was riding high thanks to the success of "Colors" (which was named the nineteenth greatest hip-hop song of all time by VH1 a decade after its release), another 1988 release would change the course of rap history forever. It also put a previously anonymous Los Angeles suburb on the national radar, thanks in large part to a song then-emerging rapper-producer Dr. Dre didn't want to release because he thought no one would care about it.

EAZY-E

EAZY-DUZ-IT

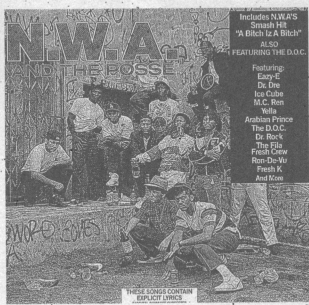

Includes N.W.A'S
Smash Hit
"A Bitch Iz A Bitch"
ALSO
FEATURING THE D.O.C.

Featuring:
Eazy-E
Dr. Dre
Ice Cube
M.C. Ren
Yella
Arabian Prince
The D.O.C.
Dr. Rock
The Fila
Fresh Crew
Ron-De-Vu
Fresh K
And More

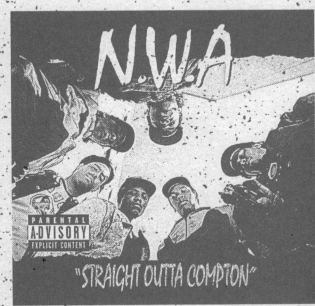

N.W.A

"STRAIGHT OUTTA COMPTON"

Niggaz Wit Attitude

IN 1988, RAP FOUND ITS VOICE. AND IT WAS FUCKIN' PISSED.

OPPOSITE:
Eazy-E & N.W.A went
from popular singles to
multi-platinum albums.

As Dr. Dre was entering his mid-twenties and producing an increasingly diverse group of artists in his native Compton, California, twenty-three-year-old Eazy-E was looking for a way to invest his proceeds from drug dealing into a legal venture. DJ Yella, Dr. Dre's twenty-year-old production partner, was experiencing the clash between the R&B and rap worlds, while seventeen-year-old Compton resident MC Ren was becoming more and more enraged with the reality of being a poor, young, black male in suburban Los Angeles. At the same time, nineteen-year-old Ice Cube was shuttling between school in Arizona and his parents' house in South Central Los Angeles.

While the members of N.W.A (Niggaz Wit Attitude) navigated their respective travails, the exploding crack epidemic was having an especially devastating impact in black urban neighborhoods, as were the draconian drug policies of President Reagan's second term, which seemed to target the poor. The enforcement of the Rockefeller Drug Laws, with the help of a militarized police force, filled new private prisons with tens of thousands of petty drug users and sellers—many of

1988
Key Rap Releases

1. N.W.A's *Straight Outta Compton* album

2. Public Enemy's *It Takes a Nation of Millions to Hold Us Back* album

3. Slick Rick's *The Great Adventures of Slick Rick* album

US President

Ronald Reagan

Something Else

Al-Qaeda formed in Pakistan.

whom were black—for fifteen-year to life sentences. As a result, a generation of poor and disenfranchised children often had to look outside their own households for male role models.

"These kids growing up in the eighties, they never had a father figure," Kendrick Lamar said. "I was the only one out of my homeboys in my neighborhood that had a pops in my life. He wasn't perfect. He was still in the streets, but he was always there to pull me back in whenever I bumped my head. Other kids didn't have that, so they go out into the streets and their father figures are the big homies down the block."

These "fatherless" children turned to the streets to find a family unit, often through sports, gangs, crime, or, thanks to the emerging hip-hop culture, rap music.

At this point, rap was in the midst of what would be considered by much of the genre's cognoscenti as its golden era. In 1988, the genre graduated from a curiosity into a full-blown national musical movement thanks to an explosion of trailblazing albums from artists who would become key figures in its development.

Public Enemy's *It Takes a Nation of Millions to Hold Us Back*, for instance, is viewed as the best rap album of all time by many rap scholars because of the unique pro-black lyrical fury of Chuck D and its revolutionary aural tactics. Producers the Bomb Squad cut and pasted musical samples, speeches from black leaders, and wild sound effects into a mesmerizing mix that entered new sonic territory, all of whose heft was balanced out by Chuck D's comedic rhyme foil, Flavor Flav.

In the aftermath of DJ Scott La Rock's murder, Boogie Down Productions shifted from being a gangster rap group to one delivering edutainment with their *By All Means Necessary* album. Eric B. & Rakim followed up their landmark 1987 album, *Paid in Full*, with *Follow the Leader*, whose "Microphone Fiend" and "Follow the Leader" singles showcased Rakim's steely, poised, and precise delivery, as well as his poetic prowess. Slick Rick's *The Great Adventures of Slick Rick* featured his comedic tales, while Big Daddy Kane's *Long Live the Kane* established him as one of the most versatile rappers in the genre, one equally adept at delivering social commentary, braggadocio, and material catering to women.

As gangster rap gained traction in the music industry thanks to the success of Schoolly D, Ice-T, Boogie Down Productions, and Just-Ice, rap remained a largely New York movement, with Empire State artists releasing the majority of the material and selling the most units, as well as the most concert tickets, often in major metropolitan hubs like Los Angeles, Chicago, and Houston. Bucking this trend, Ice-T released his second gold album, *Power*, in 1988.

SETTING THE SCENE

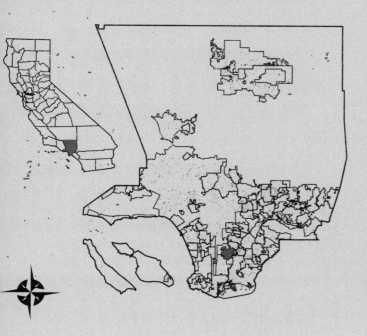

PHYSICAL LOCATION: Compton

DATE OF INCORPORATION: May 1888

SIZE: 10.2 square miles

POPULATION: 81,286 (as of 1980), 90,454 (as of 1990)

BLACK PEOPLE LIVING IN COMPTON: 48,570 (as of 1990)

HISPANIC PEOPLE LIVING IN COMPTON: 38,316 (as of 1990)

WHITE PEOPLE LIVING IN COMPTON: 1,613 (as of 1990)

FAMOUS PEOPLE BORN OR RAISED IN COMPTON: former NFL commissioner Pete Rozelle; National Baseball Hall of Fame member Duke Snider; Nirvana bassist Krist Novoselic; and actors James Coburn and Kevin Costner

YEARS BETWEEN INCORPORATION AND BECOMING GROUND ZERO FOR GANGSTER RAP: 100

In the same year, Oakland, California, rapper Too $hort offered a sexually explicit look at the world of street-level pimps and prostitutes on the platinum *Life Is... Too $hort*; Compton, California, rapper King Tee blended a b-boy sensibility with a gangster ethos on *Act a Fool*; and Philadelphia duo D.J. Jazzy Jeff & The Fresh Prince became crossover kings with the lighthearted *He's the DJ, I'm the Rapper*. Yet it was an album from a previously anonymous Los Angeles suburb that was the tipping point for changing the geographical and contextual premise of rap—and, arguably, music history.

Released in its initial version on August 8, 1988, N.W.A's *Straight Outta Compton* set in motion a tidal wave that still resonates throughout music today. Yet, despite its monumental importance, *Straight Outta Compton* had a hard time finding a home, and its most famous song almost didn't get recorded, let alone released.

The individual members of N.W.A took varied routes to stardom. Dr. Dre and DJ Yella were members of the Prince-inspired electro/R&B/rap group World Class Wreckin' Cru, which enjoyed local success in the mideighties with the independent single "Surgery." The group's regional success earned them a short-lived major recording contract with Epic Records (home to Michael Jackson at the time). The Cru quickly returned to the independent world, though, and scored another hit in 1987 with "Turn Off the Lights," a steamy R&B collaboration with Dr. Dre's then-girlfriend Michel'le.

As World Class Wreckin' Cru released light fare, Ice Cube was in the group C.I.A. (Cru' in Action!) with rapper Kid Disaster (K-Dee) and DJ/producer Sir Jinx, who happened to be Dr. Dre's cousin. At the same time, Eazy-E's friend MC Ren was a talented rapper from Compton whose rage was starting to boil.

With fewer than ninety thousand people living in Compton in the mideighties and a tiny music scene, Dr. Dre and Eazy-E befriended each other just as World Class Wreckin' Cru was having creative differences. Group leader Alonzo Williams wanted to remain true to the electro dance scene the Cru and such acts as Egyptian Lover and Arabian Prince had helped popularize. Williams also had become tired of bailing Dr. Dre out of jail for a series of minor offenses, so the next time Dr. Dre needed someone to get him from behind bars, he rang Eazy-E. Always the businessman, Eazy-E wanted Dre to reciprocate his generosity by helping him produce some songs for the rap crews he was working with at the time.

Williams's pushing Dr. Dre away professionally and personally coincided with rap's surging popularity in the streets. As the members of N.W.A and the

MASTERED AT: Bernie Grundman Mastering
MASTERED BY: Brian "Big Bass" Gardner

BRIAN "BIG BASS" GARDNER

THE MUSIC RELEASED on Ruthless Records benefitted from Dr. Dre and DJ Yella's brilliant production, but it also had some other key contributors. One of them was Brian "Big Bass" Gardner, who began working at Bernie Grundman Mastering in Hollywood in the mideighties and who worked on early Eazy-E and N.W.A releases, including *Straight Outta Compton*. He earned the "Big Bass" moniker because of the bottom he put into records in the postproduction process, a significant factor in the appeal of rap records. "He put bass in your shit," platinum Compton, California, rapper-producer and audiophile DJ Quik said. "He put bass in your records. He just made it sound big and bassy, like 'Ooooh.' He'd give you a bass bump. It was like getting a double cheeseburger for the price of a single cheeseburger. It was an extra patty and cheese. Ask anyone. Ask Michael Jackson if he was still here, rest in peace. Ask the Jacksons. They'll tell you."

acts surrounding them began collaborating, Eazy-E started pestering Williams to meet with veteran music industry manager and promoter Jerry Heller, who had worked with Elton John, Marvin Gaye, and others in the sixties and seventies. Eazy-E paid Williams $750 to meet Heller, a man who provided Eazy-E with something he lacked: knowledge of the music business.

Eazy-E and Heller, twenty-four years his senior, met at Macola Records, a local pressing plant and indie record distributor, where Eazy-E played him "The Boyz-N-The Hood." Like Schoolly D's "P.S.K. What Does It Mean?" and Ice-T's "6 'N the Mornin'" before it, "The Boyz-N-The Hood" provided a look at a world most of mainstream America knew nothing about. In the version of Compton Eazy-E rapped about (with lyrics written by South Central Los Angeles resident Ice Cube), he positioned himself as the ultimate gangster, operating without remorse as he stopped by the local park and shot and killed a friend who stole his radio (coverage of the song's fictitious murder appeared on the front of the *Los Angeles Times*). From there, Eazy-E picked up his girl and got in an altercation with her before he "reached back like a pimp and slapped the hoe" and also knocked out her father, who was trying to defend her.

The song concludes with Eazy-E heading to court to bail his friends out, only to witness a courtroom shoot-out initiated by his friend's Uzi-toting girlfriend.

He yelled out "Fire," then came Suzy / The bitch came in with a sub-machine Uzi / Police shot the girl but didn't hurt her / Both upstate for attempted murder

GANGSTER RAP

THE TERM *GANGSTER RAP* was coined by the media. *Los Angeles Times* writer Robert Hilburn's 1989 article in which he referred to Ice-T popularizing "the L.A. gangster rap image" is cited as the first time the term was used in print. Prior to the term's usage, most acts considered themselves reality rappers and street reporters. Here, artists opine about the term.

MC Ren: "The gangster rap title, it's like a division. I see a lot of cats embrace it, like 'We do gangster rap.' But you probably can't find nothing with me saying I do gangster rap, or I did gangster rap. It's just hip-hop to me."

DJ Quik: "That's like a label put on you by somebody that's trying to keep the law on you. Put this light on it."

Paris (known as the Black Panther of Hip-Hop): "I think people just assigned young, black men who were doing music and looked a particular way, they just painted us all with the same brush. The violence in the lyrics and the imagery is what got us on people's radar, although the violence I was talking about was completely different than the violence other people were talking about."

Cormega: "I hate the term gangster rap. The media created that word. I've been around hip-hop most of my life, and I've never heard a rapper say, 'I'm about to go make some gangster rap.' It was something the media used to stigmatize us because they didn't respect hip-hop as a culture, period. I'd rather call it reality rap."

CJ Mac: "I think this genre has been named gangster rap by the media. We're just talking about how we lived and the things that we saw around here, and that's what we reported and made music to."

KING TEE

THA TRIFLIN'
ALBUM

PARENTAL
ADVISORY
EXPLICIT LYRICS

KING TEE

THE FIRST PROMINENT rapper from Compton, King Tee released singles "Payback's a Mutha," "The Coolest," and "Ya Better Bring a Gun" in 1987 on Techno Hop Records/ Macola Records. Tila, as he's also known, then signed to Ice-T's Rhyme Syndicate management company and released three acclaimed albums—1988's *Act a Fool*, 1990's *At Your Own Risk*, and 1993's *Tha Triflin' Album*—on Capitol Records (home of the Beatles). The music from the Marley Marl remix of "At Your Own Risk" was used as the theme music for BET's hit *Rap City* program. King Tee is also the leader of the Likwit Crew, a collective of artists including Tha Alkaholiks and Xzibit. He later changed his name to King T and recorded the *Thy Kingdom Come* album for Dr. Dre's Aftermath Entertainment, though it was not released as planned in 1998. Dr. Dre did feature King T on "Some L.A. Niggaz," a song from his *2001* album.

But where Schoolly D rapped with a tinge of menace and Ice-T rhymed with alternating caution and excitement about the criminal world he was describing, Eazy-E's nonchalance in detailing the chaos he created and witnessed made him the ultimate gangster: an ambivalent participant in a world where the line between life and death, incarceration and freedom is often razor thin.

Even though he was essentially new to rap, Heller was sold on Eazy-E's potential and on "The Boyz-N-The Hood," later calling it "the most important rap music I had ever heard. This was the Rolling Stones, the Black Panthers, Gil Scott-Heron; this was music that would change everything."

With no musical industry connections, Eazy-E used Macola Records, the same pay-for-pressing Los Angeles–based label that also handled some of World Class Wreckin' Cru's material, to release three Ice Cube–written songs in 1987 on his upstart Ruthless Records: "The Boyz-N-The Hood," "Fat Girl," and "L.A. Is the Place." "Fat Girl" features sophomoric humor and "L.A. Is the Place" highlights Los Angeles's glamorous side, as well as its violent underbelly. To be sure, though, it was "The Boyz-N-The Hood" that struck a chord with listeners.

"I knew it was special because of the reaction it would get from people," Ice Cube said. "They loved it. Niggas was beating down our doors for the next song. We had a few singles out there, and we knew the reaction. It was just going in there and doing an album."

Eazy-E and the loose collection of artists he had assembled recorded several songs that ended up on various versions of the *N.W.A and the Posse* compilation, Eazy-E's "The Boyz-N-The Hood" and N.W.A's "8 Ball," "A Bitch Iz A Bitch," and "Dope Man" chief among them. In addition to the artists who would eventually make up N.W.A, *N.W.A and the Posse* (originally released in 1987) also featured the Fila Fresh Crew, a group fronted by the D.O.C., a Dallas transplant whose way with words and keen phraseology made him an invaluable asset to the burgeoning musical juggernaut. The D.O.C. became a trusted Dr. Dre confidant and writer for N.W.A's material. He was, effectively, an auxiliary member of the group.

As "The Boyz-N-The Hood" began gaining traction in the streets, Eazy-E, Dr. Dre, Ice Cube, MC Ren, and DJ Yella started recording what would become *Straight Outta Compton* and Eazy-E's *Eazy-Duz-It*. For his part, Heller had meetings with several major record companies, shopping N.W.A's material to his circle of music industry friends. Executives at Capitol Records, Columbia Records, Elektra Records, and other major imprints all balked at releasing the racy subject matter.

But Eazy-E had a backup plan in J.J. Fad, the female rap trio of MC J.B., Baby D, and Sassy C. The group had a hit with the Arabian Prince–produced pop/rap song "Supersonic." Heller thought that he could land the clean-cut outfit a major record deal thanks to Dr. Dre's even more commercially viable remix. He did, with Atco Records, a subsidiary of Atlantic Records.

Released in April 1988, the Dr. Dre version of J.J. Fad's "Supersonic" was a radio hit and went gold in nine months. The trio's *Supersonic* album was released in June 1988 and sold more than five hundred thousand copies in three months, earning Ruthless Records its first breakout hit and its first major cash infusion. It was also a sign of things to come. For Eazy-E, it marked the beginning of his meteoric rise as a businessman. For Dr. Dre, it signaled his production prowess and earned him his first gold record.

But where J.J. Fad was pop-heavy and friendly, N.W.A wanted to live up to their name. "That's what we felt we were," Ice Cube said. "We were tired of shit. We weren't going to hold it in. We were going to just rap about it. It was the perfect name because it was taking control of yourself, in a way, and defining yourself."

"The Boyz-N-The Hood" helped define N.W.A by showcasing an almost detached Eazy-E, but one who

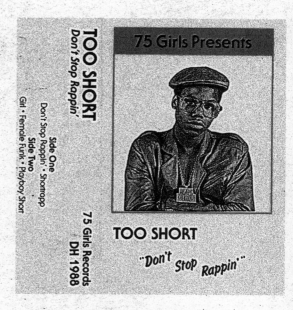

TOO $HORT

IN THE MIDEIGHTIES, Too $hort became a local celebrity in Oakland, California, by selling custom-made cassette tapes on the bus with partner in rhyme Freddy B. After releasing a string of popular independent singles and albums that contained cuts featuring him boasting about his rap prowess ("Don't Stop Rappin'"), bemoaning drug use ("Girl [Cocaine]"), and detailing his wild sexual adventures with women ("Freaky Tales"), Too $hort broke through nationally once he signed to Jive Records (who also counted Whodini and Boogie Down Productions among their roster). He zeroed in on the same world as gangster rappers, but his social commentary on the world of pimps, players, and prostitutes made him distinctive.

was likely a by-product of the fact that he was not originally supposed to be rapping on the song. Ice Cube had written it for New York rap group H.B.O. (Home Boys Only), but the group didn't appreciate the decidedly West Coast lyrics and left the studio without doing the song. Ice Cube was in the group C.I.A., and MC Ren hadn't yet become an official member of the crew. The lack of rappers in the studio opened a lane for Eazy-E to transform from just the brains behind N.W.A to one of its voices.

As Eazy-E's time on the mic grew, so did his comfort level and his panache. Ice Cube, on the other hand, rapped with attitude to spare from the jump. Even though it is labeled as an N.W.A song, "A Bitch Iz A Bitch" is an explicit treatise where Ice Cube rhymes solo and slams gold-digging and attitudinal women, relegating that segment of the female population to bitch status.

But Ice Cube's rancor wasn't limited to women. On the opening verse of "Dope Man," he provides a chilling third-person look into the world of the drug dealer, a heartless character who looks down on his customers, even as they supply him with the capital to make his material dreams possible.

His Uzi up yo' ass if he don't get paid / Nigga begging for credit, he's knocking out teeth

As for the dope man's girlfriend:

THE ROADIUM OPEN AIR MARKET
AKA THE ROADIUM SWAP MEET

A FIFTEEN-ACRE OUTDOOR swap meet in Torrance, California, the Roadium Open Air Market is located about six miles west of downtown Compton and was a place where independent rap artists gained traction in the area by selling their music. Several gangster rappers became local celebrities in the mideighties by selling their material at the flea market. "I don't think I'd be in the music business had I not heard these mixtapes at the Roadium Swap Meet," DJ Quik said. "Some of them, I still have now. Eazy-E and Dr. Dre were putting out these mixtapes. The way they were recording it, Dr. Dre was an animal at tape recording and editing. Motherfuckas don't know. He's not to be fucked with. They're some of the best-sounding cassettes you've ever heard in your life. When I heard them and saw Compton on the address, I'd never seen that before. Whoa. That means this place matters."

Sit and cry / If the dope man strikes you / He don't give a fuck / He got two just like you

Ice Cube's commentary about a woman labeled "Strawberry" was anything but sweet.

Strawberry is the neighborhood ho / Do anything for a hit or two / Give the bitch a rock, she fuck the whole damn crew

Even though the emerging gangster rap subgenre was accused of trumpeting negativity, "Dope Man" certainly isn't a celebration of the culture. "If you smoke 'caine, you a stupid motherfucker" is how Ice Cube starts the third verse. Then, in a remarkable tag-team move, Ice Cube figuratively passes the mic to Eazy-E, the self-proclaimed "dope man," who proceeds to relay that he's got "money up to here but unemployed."

"It was easy to write 'Dope Man,'" Ice Cube said. "The shit was all around us. The eighties were the worst, what cocaine did to people. It was going like a disease from house to house to house to house. The man you respected in 1979 and '81 was washing cars for five dollars in 1985. He'd lost his house, his kids. Everybody left him. Motherfuckers were pulling furniture out his house. He'd be in the house sleeping on the floor. No carpet. He'd pulled the carpet up and sold it. This is a man you used to respect as an elder. Now, he's a crackhead. We had to say something and do something about it, which was just to tell the world what the fuck was going on."

What the world heard was striking. "I remember first hearing N.W.A with *Straight Outta Compton*," the Fat Boys' Kool Rock Ski said. "I'm like, 'Damn. You know, this is crazy.' Look at the stuff we're doing. It's like walking into frickin' Disneyland."

But the words and the feel of N.W.A's material transported listeners to a lifestyle nothing like the Happiest Place on Earth. Ice Cube and Eazy-E's words on "Dope Man" are made all the more powerful by Dr. Dre's searing production, which took its funk and edge from the Ohio Players' "Funky Worm," which is sampled throughout. Unlike the skeletal sounds of gangster rap precursors Schoolly D, Ice-T, and Boogie Down Productions, Dr. Dre's production was layered and vibrant. It had a driving musical pulse thanks to well-placed funk and soul samples from James Brown and the Staple Singers, as well as at least ten other sources, all of which blended into a virtually combustible aural assault.

Then there was "Fuck tha Police" (written as "_ _ _ _ Tha Police" on the album copy). It stands as N.W.A's signature song, but it almost didn't get past the idea stage.

Even though the group's music had gotten some local acclaim, the group members were still struggling. Close to completely giving up on his dream of becoming a rap star, Ice Cube left for school in Arizona. He wrote a verse for a song called "Fuck tha Police." There was a problem, though.

"Dr. Dre didn't want to use it," Ice Cube said. "He didn't want no songs talking about the police. He said that nobody gave a fuck about that, about hearing about the police."

Viewing the song as a lost cause, Ice Cube threw his lyrics in the trash. "One of my homeboys named Phil was like, 'Hell nah,' and pulled it out the trash can," Ice Cube said. "He was like, 'Hell nah. That shit is dope. You can't throw that one away.' Back then, if Dre didn't want to do some shit, it didn't get done."

Discouraged but not defeated, Ice Cube held on to his antipolice rap. N.W.A wrapped work on Eazy-E's *Eazy-Duz-It* album before they finished *Straight Outta Compton*, and Dr. Dre told Ice Cube he needed some more material for N.W.A's project.

"So I waited until everybody was in the room and I brought up 'Fuck tha Police' again," Ice Cube said. "It just caught fire. Ren was like, 'Hell yeah. That's dope.'"

"We always wanted to say that, but nobody was talking like that," DJ Yella said. "The song was true to the ghetto. Everybody hated the police. I guess we just had the balls to say it—and got lucky with it."

The way N.W.A presented the song was almost as noteworthy as the song itself. The group took the groundbreaking step of setting up "Fuck tha Police" as a faux court case, complete with the D.O.C. portraying the bailiff, Dr. Dre handling judicial duties, and Ice Cube, MC Ren, and Eazy-E serving as prosecuting attorneys against the police department.

On the first verse of "Fuck tha Police," Ice Cube took "the stand" and proceeded to lay out his reason for his disdain for law enforcement.

Fuck the police! Comin' straight from the underground / A young nigga got it bad 'cause I'm brown / And not the other color, so police think / They have the authority to kill a minority

Prior to his verse, MC Ren and a police officer acted out a scenario where the rapper gets pulled over. According to the officer, the reasoning was "'Cause I feel like it."

The intro to Eazy-E's verse featured police knocking on his door, executing a warrant, and refusing to announce the alleged transgressions the Ruthless Records owner had committed. Eazy-E questioned the toughness of police officers.

Without a gun and a badge, what do ya got? / A sucker in a uniform waiting to get shot / By me or another nigga / And with a gat it don't matter if he's smaller or bigger

The song concluded with the jury finding the police officer "guilty of being a redneck, white-bred, chickenshit motherfucker" and judge Dr. Dre ordering his staff to get the officer "the fuck out my face."

"Fuck tha Police" marked the first time skits were used as a driving portion of the narrative of a song, giving N.W.A's words a cinematic feel. Listeners were exposed to more than just lyrics and music. The lines were fully executed events, commercials of a sort.

"When we were making records, the records were a whole thing," the D.O.C. said. "The songs were individual, but as a piece of art, everything went together. We made the record so that you could put it on and play the thing all the way through, so the commercials were just something that took you from one place to the next place with something that made you laugh, made you have fun, and [made you enjoy] the listening experience."

"We wanted to make it three-dimensional," Ice Cube said. "Not just a record, but a whole experience."

Eazy-E, though, didn't want controversy to be N.W.A's only calling card. He had just tasted success with J.J. Fad and wanted to hedge his bets on N.W.A's commercial prospects. Hence the profanity-free "Express Yourself" and the album-closing "Something 2 Dance 2," a song featuring Arabian Prince that sounds more like a World Class Wreckin' Cru cut than N.W.A material.

"I hated it," said Ice Cube, who does not appear on "Something 2 Dance 2." "I was like, 'This shit don't even match.'"

ODD MAN OUT: ARABIAN PRINCE

The son of prolific Holloway House writer Joseph "Skippy" Nazel Jr., Arabian Prince produced the original version of Ruthless Records' first hit: J.J. Fad's "Supersonic." The Compton electro rapper-producer was also a member of N.W.A and appeared on the group's "Panic Zone" single in 1987, as well as on the cover of N.W.A's *Straight Outta Compton* album and the collection's "Something 2 Dance 2." By the time *Straight Outta Compton* was released, Arabian Prince had left N.W.A over creative differences and returned to his dance-electro roots. A party record in the midst of ultragangster material, "Something 2 Dance 2" was removed from later pressings of *Straight Outta Compton*.

Arabian Prince, who appears on the cover of *Straight Outta Compton* yet only raps on "Something 2 Dance 2," left the group over creative differences before the album was released. Like Dr. Dre's World Class Wreckin' Cru bandmate Alonzo Williams, Arabian Prince neither agreed with nor approved of N.W.A's ultraviolent and ribald material.

"It's like we opened up one door and closed the other one," DJ Yella said. "We were going from one era to another one."

Indeed, the music N.W.A was making was more primal than Little Richard's squeal, more provocative than Elvis's suggestive hips, more violent than Johnny Cash's shooting a man just to watch him die, and more timely than the overtly sexualized and fantasy-based R&B and electro music of the eighties. N.W.A's entrance came with profanity-laced assaults; sex in the roughest, most descriptive manner possible; and violence executed with rage and without remorse. Eazy-E, Ice Cube, MC Ren, Dr. Dre, and DJ Yella presented themselves as a gang on the record and gave listeners little reason to believe they weren't one off the record.

But being gangster rappers wasn't something N.W.A sought out. "It was called reality rap before gangster rap," Ice Cube said. "That's what N.W.A is, reality rap."

> *"It's like we opened up one door and closed the other one. We were going from one era to another one."*
>
> **DJ YELLA**

Regardless of how they were labeled, one of N.W.A's objectives was to show that their Los Angeles experience was far different from the one presented by the glamour of Hollywood, Randy Newman's 1983 song "I Love L.A.," and the successful run the city had with the 1984 Summer Olympics. Eazy-E, in particular, was focused on putting his city on the map. "Nobody knew nothing about Compton, really—not unless you lived here," Ice Cube said. "We heard everybody putting their cities on the map—South Bronx, Brooklyn—so he [Eazy-E] felt compelled to put Compton down the same way."

Eazy-E's plan worked. "Eazy-E taught us we mattered," platinum rapper-producer and Compton, California, native DJ Quik said. "Dr. Dre nailed it home. Ice Cube wrote the soundtrack to our life. It was like we really didn't have to talk. We could just play an N.W.A record. It said every mood you were in."

After defecting from music compilation label K-Tel, white Canadian music executives Bryan Turner and Mark Cerami launched Priority Records, which was distributed by industry juggernaut EMI. The company was flush with cash after the success of the California Raisins, a fictional R&B group presented as raisins that had sold more than one million copies thanks to their cover of Marvin Gaye's "I Heard It Through the Grapevine." Turner and Cerami also knew the power of rap through their background at K-Tel, which had released several successful rap compilations. Priority Records agreed to distribute N.W.A's and Eazy-E's releases. In a move that would later prove problematic for Eazy-E, he did not initially have the members of N.W.A sign as solo artists to Ruthless Records.

In a revolutionary agreement, Ruthless Records' contract with Priority Records did not make Ruthless and their acts exclusive to Priority, as was typically the case whenever a smaller label signed a deal with a larger company. Indeed, the way the contract was set up, the other acts on Ruthless Records (Michel'le, the D.O.C., Above the Law) were free to sign with other labels. Thus, once N.W.A's and Eazy-E's material took off, the freedom afforded to Ruthless by Priority was a key component to the development of Ruthless's success as a business. Ruthless Records was not tied to one company and could use its leverage to get better deals from labels competing for its acts.

In 1988, the fledgling Priority Records was about the lowest-tier label Heller could go to. But Priority had a much larger reach than Macola thanks to its national distribution deal with industry powerhouse EMI. That muscle helped get Ruthless Records releases in record stores throughout the country and its artists' names

A GANGSTER'S STORY

ALTHOUGH N.W.A'S *STRAIGHT OUTTA COMPTON* garners most of the attention, Eazy-E's *Eazy-Duz-It* was also a landmark gangster rap release. The 1988 album includes the sensational remix of the seminal "Boyz-N-The Hood," as well as "We Want Eazy," and "Eazy-Er Said Than Dunn," both of which were mainstays on *Yo! MTV Raps* and helped establish Eazy-E as both the face of N.W.A and of gangster rap.

"Eazy was the first person on a whole record who talked the way people I looked up to talked," says gangster rapper Glasses Malone, who grew up in Watts, California. "It was all of the private intel he was making public. He was the first person to me using the word bitch so freely, so openly. I was hearing that every day. It was like he became a reflection of everything I saw every day at the time, and that was the first time I ever saw it from somebody. It was from somebody who you could see around the city, like a guy that's really from around there."

Yet the firestorm that *Straight Outta Compton* cut "Fuck Tha Police" generated moved the attention, if not sales (*Eazy-Duz-It* sold more than 1 million copies its first seven months in stores), away from *Eazy-Duz-It*. Nonetheless, Glasses Malone believes that Eazy-E was the embodiment of what people loved about N.W.A and its music.

"*Straight Outta Compton* is Eazy-E," Glasses Malone said. "It's more Eazy-E than anybody else. Everybody else was more rapping and stuff, and Dr. Dre as a producer. Eazy-E actually is *Straight Outta Compton*. *Eazy-Duz-It* is like the raw, pure version of *Straight Outta Compton* straight out of Eazy-E's mouth. I don't really think it got its just due."

MACOLA RECORDS

MACOLA RECORDS GAVE West Coast gangster rap its launching pad in the mideighties. The Hollywood-based independent label, manufacturer, and distributor released early recordings from Ice-T, King Tee, World Class Wreckin' Cru, C.I.A., Eazy-E, N.W.A, J.J. Fad, Arabian Prince, the Unknown DJ, Laylaw, Cli-N-Tel, and the D.O.C.'s the Fila Fresh Crew, among others.

in the rap media. What really generated N.W.A's firestorm, though, was an unintended ally: the United States government, specifically the FBI.

In August 1989, Milt Ahlerich, assistant director of the FBI Office of Public Affairs, sent Priority Records a letter voicing the orgnanization's displeasure with "Fuck tha Police," though the letter does not mention it by name. "Advocating violence and assault is wrong, and we in the law enforcement community take exceptions to such action," the letter says, per the *Los Angeles Times*. "Recordings such as the one from N.W.A are both discouraging and degrading to these brave, dedicated officers."

Pat Charbonnet, N.W.A's publicist at the time, told the *Los Angeles Times* that the letter "makes valid everything [the rap group] said on the record. Their life is a lifetime of hassle and it never stopped being that way."

Danny Goldberg, then chairman of the Southern California affiliate of the American Civil Liberties Union (ACLU), argued in October 1989 that the letter would, in fact, further the belief that the government remained at odds with America's lower-class citizens.

"It reinforces the notion among minorities that the government is against them," Goldberg said. "[N.W.A] is a positive role model about how you can get out of poverty, and then the FBI writes them a letter. The result is to add to the feelings of alienation and separation from society, and those are the things that give rise to violence. . . . Rap is one of the most positive role models, a positive way for poor people using their energies, making art and poetry out of their social dilemma. They should be applauded by the police."

On the contrary, police in several cities throughout the United States tried to prevent N.W.A from performing, fearing that the group would encourage their fan base to be violent toward police officers.

"I think Eazy took the attitude of somebody like Donald Trump," the D.O.C. said. "I mean that guy's said some of the most ridiculous shit in the world, right, some of the most inflammatory shit in the world. He doesn't give a fuck about anybody and talks shit to you to your face: 'Suck my dick. You can't get in my country. Kiss my ass.' He said all of this shit and he got [elected] fuckin' president. The [Republican strategist] Roger Stone school says, 'If you're mad with me, you're upset with me, you're talking shit, arguing with me, I've already won the game.' I think Eazy was sort of in that school."

Up to this point, N.W.A was an independent rap group that was getting little radio play outside of Los Angeles AM rap station KDAY and scant coverage in the mainstream media. Then the FBI wrote them a letter. It generated national publicity for them. It also gave the group an identity as being infamous.

"That song right there separates us because that's something everybody wanted to say, much more than *bitch*, *hoe*, *pussy*, and all the other nasty words on there," Ice Cube said. "That phrase right there is something the whole world had been wanting to say."

Having the excitement drummed up in the press was one thing. More than that, N.W.A needed a vehicle to help spread their message. They found an unlikely partner in a music channel that had heretofore essentially ignored black music.

The Revolution Gets Televised

ALTHOUGH RAP WAS KNOCKING ON MAINSTREAM AMERICA'S DOOR IN 1988, IT WAS GANGSTER RAP THAT KICKED THE DOOR OFF ITS HINGES.

OPPOSITE:
Fab 5 Freddy (left) and Ice-T attend a fifteenth anniversary screening of the movie *Wild Style* in Los Angeles on June 18, 1998.

Gangster rap was enjoying increasing success as N.W.A's *Straight Outta Compton* and Eazy-E's *Eazy-Duz-It* surged in popularity. Ice-T, now thirty years old, was riding high on the success of two gold albums and was preparing to embark in earnest on his acting career, while eighteen-year-old Scarface was joining the Ghetto Boys (later changed to Geto Boys), Houston's premier rap outfit. Several other future gangster rap figures, including DJ Quik (eighteen) and Compton's Most Wanted's MC Eiht (twenty-one), were releasing music independently in Compton. At the same time, DJ Muggs (twenty) was one-third of the 7A3, his group before Cypress Hill.

In 1988, America's inner cities were still reeling from Reagan's devastating

1989
Key Rap Releases

1. De La Soul's *3 Feet High and Rising* album

2. The 2 Live Crew's *As Nasty As They Wanna Be* album

3. Big Daddy Kane's *It's a Big Daddy Thing* album

US President

George H.W. Bush

Something Else

The Tiananmen Square Massacre rocked China.

policies and the severe drug laws that helped to fill a burgeoning number of private prisons that profited from government and corporate contracts. This was seen by many as a new and diabolical twist to crush and enslave black people. The irony that Reagan's "War on Drugs" initiative was at odds with his role in the Iran-Contra affair, which was a catalyst for drug distribution and use in America's inner cities, especially South Los Angeles, was lost on no one.

This reality was articulated eloquently by rappers who were experiencing the aftermath of this scourge firsthand. The authenticity and artistry of their words fueled the sale of millions of records and made them the de facto spokesmen for the hood. But the outlets that usually supported popular music at the time—namely radio and MTV—typically shunned rap in general, and gangster rap in particular. The reality of—and the art inspired by—what was happening in the streets of major cities throughout the country was essentially being overlooked by the local and national media.

Thus, consumers were forced to turn to alternative outlets to hear, discover, and enjoy the rap and gangster rap records from artists such as Schoolly D, Ice-T, N.W.A, and others who were selling hundreds of thousands of copies. Word of mouth, college radio play, and a smattering of mix shows on commercial radio became key resources for rap fans. The popularity of rap at college radio, in particular, was an important step to opening the minds of a generation of young, white, privileged kids to the plight of being black. The cultural impact of this was a tremendous catalyst in bringing young whites and blacks together and would later be seen as an important step in electing a black man to the highest office in the world.

Where rap (and especially gangster rap) got next to no backing was where most would have assumed it would get the most support: commercial black radio. At the time, black radio was playing highly stylized and sanitized artists who sang about love, money, and parties, and whose music was largely devoid of any social commentary or reality. Rappers and their music were the polar opposite of what black radio and BET (Black Entertainment Television) were promoting as black music. Whereas R&B artists wore suits or custom-designed outfits, rappers wore white T-shirts, khaki jeans, baseball hats, and sneakers. Even worse, rappers cursed on records and used the words *nigger* and *nigga* with increasing regularity.

"When we were young, all the old R&B heads thought that rap was a piece of shit," the D.O.C. said. "They didn't give a fuck about it. It wasn't going to be shit."

Even though most rappers made "clean" versions of their songs, black radio program directors were reportedly repulsed by the images, graphic language, and subject matter of rap.

"Those lyrics were something that the parent police just didn't want broadcast on the airwaves," DJ Quik said. "The PTA, they wasn't happy about some of the shit we were doing. That's the total opposite of what they're teaching in school. I don't mean to make fun of it, but that shit was belligerent, audacious, explicit. . . . This shit was wild. It was just debauchery at its finest."

The way rap—especially gangster rap—was virtually ignored at radio stations did not match the music's surging popularity with the radio stations' listening audiences.

"Rap was still like stepkids, but they were selling shitloads [of records]," said Chris LaSalle, who worked in promotion and marketing at Profile Records (Run-DMC, Dana Dane, Rob Base, and DJ E-Z Rock) from 1985 until 1989.

There was such a disconnect between black radio stations and the rap world that artists openly began taking shots at the radio establishment that had largely shunned them. On their "Rebel Without a Pause" single, for instance, Public Enemy's Chuck D rapped, "Radio, suckers never play me." Also in 1988, pioneering Seattle rapper Sir Mix-a-Lot buttressed the video for his "Posse on Broadway" with skits featuring real-life local radio DJ Nasty Nes. In the video's open, Nes is approached by the rapper and his crew, who ask him to play their new song on his radio show. Nes balks, saying that his radio station plays real music, not rap. By the end of the video, Nasty Nes is playing the record on the station repeatedly and is shown wearing a gold chain and hat à la Sir Mix-a-Lot's posse.

Just as rap struggled to get on the radio,

MTV AT A GLANCE

PHYSICAL LOCATION: New York, New York

YEAR FOUNDED: 1981

INITIAL CONCEPT: MTV was built as an album-oriented rock music channel

FIRST VIDEO PLAYED: "Video Killed the Radio Star" by The Buggles

FIRST VIDEO MUSIC AWARDS: 1984

TOP FIVE VIDEOS OF 1988:

"Sweet Child o' Mine" by Guns N' Roses

"Pour Some Sugar on Me" by Def Leppard

"Need You Tonight/Mediate" by INXS

"Rag Doll" by Aerosmith

"Man in the Mirror" by Michael Jackson

SONGS ON URBAN RADIO

Billboard's Hot R&B/Hip-Hop Songs

Michael Jackson, "The Way You Make Me Feel"

Keith Sweat, "I Want Her"

Billy Ocean, "Get Outta My Dreams, Get Into My Car"

Pebbles, "Mercedes Boy"

Johnny Kemp, "Just Got Paid"

Bobby Brown, "Don't Be Cruel"

NOTE: The lone song featuring a rapper to top Billboard's Hot R&B/Hip-Hop Songs chart in 1988 was Rick James's "Loosey's Rap," which featured female rapper Roxanne Shanté and was included on his 1988 album, *Wonderful*.

rap videos had limited exposure, enjoying play almost exclusively on regional public television shows such as New York's *Video Music Box*, which was launched in 1983 by Brooklyn entrepreneur Ralph McDaniels. Even BET provided minimal support of videos for early rap hits, including Run-DMC's "Rock Box" and "King of Rock."

"They turned down those two videos off the bat," LaSalle said in a 1986 interview with *Billboard*, "because they were too hard."

In 1988, even though rap was selling records in numbers rivaling its rock and R&B counterparts, it did not have the mainstream media penetration other musical genres enjoyed. That all changed almost instantly with one television program.

Yo! MTV Raps debuted on MTV on August 6, 1988, bringing rap—and later gangster rap—to America's living rooms. The premiere episode was hosted by Run-DMC and featured D.J. Jazzy Jeff & The Fresh Prince.

In addition to being the third-highest-rated show after MTV's Video Music Awards and Live Aid, *Yo! MTV Raps* was groundbreaking on several other levels. For one, MTV had long shunned videos by black acts. Founded in 1981, the network had developed such a reputation for not supporting music by black musicians that rock icon David Bowie called out VJ (video jockey) Mark Goodman during a 1983 interview.

"The only few black artists that one does see are on about 2:30 in the morning until about 6:00," Bowie said. "Very few are featured prominently during the day."

Future rap power brokers noticed the same problem. "When I was a kid, you waited for Michael Jackson or Prince or Lionel Richie to come on," said the Roots' Questlove. "You'd have to sit through four hours of Thomas Dolby and Genesis and Duran Duran."

Even Michael Jackson, whose blockbuster *Thriller* album was released in 1982, had a hard time getting videos aired on MTV. In 1983, though, the video for

Jackson's "Billie Jean" became a staple on the channel, making it the first video from a black act to get major rotation on the network.

Although *Thriller* would quickly become the bestselling album in music history, few videos from black musicians—and, by default, even fewer rap videos—earned a spot on MTV. Those that did typically had some sort of rock crossover appeal, such as Run-DMC's "Walk This Way" collaboration with rock band Aerosmith and clips from white rap group Beastie Boys' album *Licensed to Ill*, both released in 1986.

"Basically, these rappers had to emulate rock and roll, in order to get on MTV," said author and producer Dan Charnas.

Yet, the unofficial and unstated barrier between rap and white America vanished once *Yo! MTV Raps* hit the airwaves. The program, which arrived at a time when MTV had approximately two hundred and forty thousand viewers at any given minute, featured interviews with artists and music videos, eventually expanding to include weekly performances from artists as well.

Yo! MTV Raps was created by one-time MTV production assistant and future major motion picture director Ted Demme and fellow music documentarian Peter Dougherty. A serious rap fan and proponent of the genre, Demme essentially willed the show into existence. "I was always a hip-hop fan growing up in New York and just thought there was a lack of hip-hop music on the channel, and back then, obviously a lack of black music on the channel," Demme said.

Despite Demme's perseverance with the MTV brass, a lack of interest by the network's power players meant Demme and Dougherty were given just a few thousand dollars to shoot a pilot. But once the Run-DMC–hosted episode got great ratings, MTV quickly ordered the show into production. For the host of

MTV VIDEO MUSIC AWARDS

AUSTRALIAN ROCK GROUP INXS was nominated nine times and won five awards at the 1988 MTV Video Music Awards. George Harrison and U2 were each nominated eight times, while no rap videos were nominated in any category. Rap was represented at the ceremony by the Fat Boys, who performed their "Louie Louie" and "The Twist" singles with Chubby Checker, and by D.J. Jazzy Jeff & The Fresh Prince, who, with Justine Bateman, presented the Best Stage Performance in a Video award to Prince (featuring Sheena Easton for "U Got the Look").

YO! MTV RAPS VS. RAP CITY VS. PUMP IT UP!

LESLIE "BIG LEZ" SEGAR was one of the hosts of BET's *Rap City* from 1993 to 2000. She looks at the three major rap video shows.

YO! MTV RAPS (MTV, 1988–95, BASED IN NEW YORK): "*Yo! MTV Raps* was groundbreaking, without question. They got people to really sit down and show you who they were, that they were artistic, creative, prolific, human, and that they liked to have fun and it wasn't all about the music. It showed [the artists] weren't as volatile as their rhymes made them seem."

RAP CITY (BET, 1989–2008, BASED IN WASHINGTON, DC): "We wanted to do not just what was on the Top 10 Billboard and take hip-hop out of the studio and into the backyards of all these people. We would go everywhere. We went to Chicago and would be at [prominent independent urban music retailer] George's Music Room, where Common would get love. Then we'd go down to Houston, where [Rap-A-Lot Records owner] Lil' J [J. Prince] was shooting horses. Nobody thought hip-hop would be at a farm or a ranch. Then we had the whole dancehall era, [when we] would go hang out in Jamaica with [reggae artists] Buju Banton and Patra, and [we'd] really show people what the fuck is up with all this music."

PUMP IT UP! (FOX TV, 1989–1992, BASED IN LOS ANGELES): "Dee Barnes was one of the first female hosts that I'd seen in a male-dominated thing do her hip-hop thing. She rolled out the welcome mat for me as a female, making it be like, 'Okay. Go ahead and do your thing and show these boys you represent hip-hop to the fullest.' She didn't try to sell T&A. She wasn't flirtatious. She didn't ask ridiculous questions. She asked real, poignant, hardcore things about the lyrics, about politics, the labels."

the show—which aired on the weekends—MTV tapped Fab 5 Freddy, a visual artist who is credited with bridging the gap between New York's uptown hip-hop scene and the city's downtown art world. His status in the Manhattan scene led him to be name-dropped on Blondie's 1981 single "Rapture." Blondie singer Debbie Harry rapped that "Fab 5 Freddy told me everybody's fly" on the song, which would later be a full circle moment for the man born Fred Brathwaite. The video for "Rapture" is considered the first video featuring rap played on MTV. Seven years later, Fab 5 Freddy was hosting *Yo! MTV Raps* and giving much of the world its first look at rap videos, interviews with rappers, and rappers performing on television.

To this point, popular rap videos such as Run-DMC's "Walk This Way" and Beastie Boys' "(You Gotta) Fight for Your Right (to Party!)" and "No Sleep Till Brooklyn" were relatively straightforward performance pieces. Even the clip for Grandmaster Flash and the Furious Five's "The Message" featured Melle Mel rapping on a stoop and on a city street for much of the video before he and his crew are apprehended and hauled away in a police car. Yes, Melle Mel and the rest of the Furious Five were in deplorable surroundings, but they were rapping about them, not helping create them. They were reporters, not perpetrators.

Similarly, the video for Ice-T's "Colors" featured scenes from the 1988 film after which it is named. As Ice-T raps in a graffiti- and debris-adorned alley, images of actor Sean Penn's character are shown chasing and abusing the blue- and red-clad actors portraying gang members in the movie. As striking as the video for "Colors" was, Ice-T acted as a narrator in the clip, much as Melle Mel had done in the "The Message" video.

The video for N.W.A's "Straight Outta Compton" was more visceral. The raucous clip not only featured the city of Compton getting targeted by police, but also showed group members Ice Cube, Dr. Dre, Eazy-E, MC Ren, and DJ Yella being chased, harassed at gunpoint, and ultimately arrested by the police. The gritty clip presented a seemingly all-out affront by the police against Compton and against N.W.A. The police officers in the video were white and each member of N.W.A was black. It was a visual presentation of the antagonistic relationship between white police and black citizens that led N.W.A to make "Fuck tha Police."

Just as Ice-T had ratcheted up the criminal intensity compared to Schoolly D's music, N.W.A put themselves squarely in the crosshairs of the police, the government, and the overall oppressive white American system with the video for "Straight Outta Compton." With the videos for "Colors" and "Straight Outta

OPPOSITE:

Left to right: Warren G, Leslie "Big Lez" Segar, and Kurupt celebrate Big Lez's birthday at the El Rey Theatre in Los Angeles in 1998.

Compton," it was clear that rap music videos had gone from largely benign to confrontational, and thanks to MTV, these videos were now being seen by millions of kids around the country and the world.

The videos had different effects on different segments of the population. "People were able to see, like, 'Damn. We're selling dope here in Chicago, too,'" Compton's Most Wanted front man MC Eiht said. "There were neighborhood dudes everywhere and [getting a video played on *Yo! MTV Raps*] just opened the door for all neighborhood dudes to connect on our level."

Yo! MTV Raps exposed its viewing audience to the gang, drug, and crime culture. For the first time, millions of white fans could listen to rap and watch rap music videos created by artists from the ghettos of the United States without leaving the comfort of their homes. There was no need to wade into the Bronx, Brooklyn, or Los Angeles to experience rap; it was being broadcast into households across the country. For most viewers, the videos for Ice-T's gang treatise "Colors" and N.W.A's abrasive "Straight Outta Compton" were among their first audio and visual insights into the world of the gang-riddled streets of Los Angeles, the epicenter of gangster rap.

This was a significant step in the development of rap music and hip-hop culture, because before *Yo! MTV Raps* hit the airwaves, only Whodini, Run-DMC, LL Cool J, the Fat Boys, and Beastie Boys were among the rap acts to appear for any meaningful amount of time on television, in print, in movies, and on the radio. And even when these acts enjoyed mainstream coverage, they were typically framed as part of a new fad: rap music.

But another common bond between all these acts was simple and obvious: All of them were from New York. Rap was created in New York, the labels releasing rap were mostly based in New York, and the artists releasing material were mostly from New York. Perhaps unintentionally, but definitely significantly, *Yo! MTV Raps* showed, for the first time, that rap was being produced in more places than just the Empire State.

With MTV's early support of Southern California's Ice-T, King Tee, N.W.A, and Eazy-E; Philadelphia's Schoolly D, Steady B, and D.J. Jazzy Jeff & The Fresh Prince; Miami's 2 Live Crew; Seattle's Sir Mix-a-Lot; and Oakland's Too $hort, among others, rap fans got to experience what artists from different parts of the country looked and sounded like.

"That was the first place where people from New York could see what was going on in Texas," *Yo! MTV Raps* producer Todd 1 said. "People from Texas could see what's going on in Miami. People from Miami could see what was going on in California."

"They were programming a video channel that was more popular than radio," LaSalle said. "That's where you went to see hits—and breaking stuff, too. *Yo! MTV Raps* was definitely breaking the new rap."

"Every record that I saw on *Yo! MTV Raps*, I went and bought it as a fan," said DJ Quik, who later signed to Profile Records. "This was a product for sale, and it was good? Build it, they will come. I went and bought it."

But with that power came pressure. *Yo! MTV Raps* banned N.W.A's "Straight Outta Compton" video, succumbing to the pressure from police organizations, politicians, and others due to N.W.A's "Fuck tha Police." But the show also gave Ice-T, N.W.A, and other rappers something more valuable, something that went beyond video exposure. It gave them the opportunity to speak on camera. For the first time, rappers were being interviewed on television on a consistent basis and were becoming more than pictures on album covers or in urban zines. They were now people with thoughts, ideas, and personalities beyond the music. Through interviews with Ice-T, N.W.A, and others, the predominantly white audience was able to experience firsthand the intelligence and insight rappers used while explaining the sobering realities depicted in their music.

"The videos made those guys, made that movement," the D.O.C. said. "When Eazy got on TV, you couldn't deny it. The guy was so charismatic, and his look was so cool, and his swag was so dope. And the music was fuckin' great."

In Fab 5 Freddy, the rappers also got an interviewer with a rap pedigree who was at least sympathetic to—and always supportive of—the opinions and perspectives the artists presented. Hard-hitting journalism this was not, but the average viewer was still learning more about the artist than they ever had before.

Furthermore, even though he was part of hip-hop culture (he released the oft-sampled "Change the Beat" single with Beside in 1981), given Fab 5 Freddy's art background, he was more worldly than many of the artists he was interviewing. In many ways, he was the Gertrude Stein of rap, with *Yo! MTV Raps* being equivalent, in a sense, to her Paris salon, where great creative minds would mix, mingle, and cross-pollinate ideas, perspectives, and art. Like Stein, he was a host and champion who used his influence to get the artists a seat at the table.

"Every generation has that one place where everything cool happens," radio personality Miss Info said. "That's where you find out what you're supposed to like, whether it was *American Bandstand* or *Solid Gold* or *Soul Train*. And that's what *Yo! MTV Raps* was for us."

For gangster rap, in particular, casting Fab 5 Freddy was also significant. He was from Brooklyn, not Los Angeles. Interviewing artists from Southern

California provided him with the opportunity, much like the overwhelming majority of the *Yo! MTV Raps* viewers, to see, experience, and learn about something he had little knowledge of: the urban Los Angeles experience and its gang culture, lowriders, and swap meets.

Thus, Fab 5 Freddy's interviews with gangster rappers often were, in a sense, like first dates. There wasn't a lot of deep conversation transpiring. It was more about getting to know the artists, even though, in the case of Ice-T and N.W.A, they had been releasing successful material for more than a year before their interviews.

"The whole L.A. vibe was kind of new," the D.O.C. said. "The look, the way they walked and talked, and the things that they said, all that shit was brand-new. So, it kind of swept through the country just like crack did."

During an April 1989 interview, N.W.A took Fab 5 Freddy to the Compton Fashion Center, a flea market, also known as a swap meet. Having N.W.A members as tour guides provided a look into the group's world. Eazy-E said that that's where the group picked up their sunglasses (Locs), shirts, and Levi's. When Fab 5 Freddy asked Dr. Dre to name the most incredible thing he'd ever gotten at the Compton Fashion Center, he responded by saying, "Females."

As the group rode on the flatbed of a truck from Compton to Venice Beach, Fab 5 Freddy asked Ice Cube to speak about the violence consuming the Los Angeles metropolitan area. "After a lot of people saw *Colors*, they thought L.A.'s just all violent," Ice Cube said. "That's not true. Yes, it is some hard parts, but then again there is some good parts. But I like to say, 'When a brother kills a brotherman, the only people that's happy is the other man [a white man].'"

Although N.W.A was quickly gaining a reputation as profane, anti–law enforcement, misogynistic, and violent, Ice Cube's comment showed that there was more to the group's music than just blind rage. Perspective, passion, and pain informed N.W.A's music and *Yo! MTV Raps* viewers got to watch Ice Cube defend and present his city on his terms.

"It brought you into their world and it let you see rap from a real organic standpoint and how the artists actually embodied the hoods that they came from and the reason why the music is the way it is," said EST, front man of Philadelphia rap group Three Times Dope. "It was the show to be on if you were in hip-hop at all."

During a different 1989 interview with Fab 5 Freddy, Ice Cube provided context for his lyrical stylings. He mentioned that he listened to the Last Poets and Gil Scott-Heron, spoken-word artists from the sixties and seventies whose black nationalist material and social commentary predated, directly influenced, and was sampled by scores of rap artists. The Last Poets, for instance, filled their

1970 self-titled album with spirited spoken-word poetry that championed the need for radical change in the black community ("Run, Nigger") and a proactive stance to initiate said change ("Niggers Are Scared of Revolution"). For his part, Gil Scott-Heron's 1970 album, *Small Talk at 125th and Lenox*, featured songs that traced the evolution of the way blacks were perceived in America, from "darkie" to "slave" to "nigger" to the assassinations of Malcolm X and Dr. Martin Luther King Jr. ("Evolution [And Flashback]"). "They give us the flavor so we know what to talk about," Ice Cube said. "We know what people like."

> *"Every generation has that one place where everything cool happens. . . . That's what* Yo! MTV Raps *was for us."*
>
> **MISS INFO**

And what they liked was the gangster rap lifestyle they saw portrayed in the videos *Yo! MTV Raps* played. In addition to bringing awareness to gang culture, the program helped spread it, giving light to a secret society of sorts.

"It really felt like you were getting a bird's-eye view on the back of somebody's motorcycle or the back seat of somebody's lowrider rolling down the street dodging bullets, catching how it's really going down," said Leslie "Big Lez" Segar, a host of BET's *Rap City* video program from 1993 to 2000. "All the things you read in the paper and all the things you see on TV, even though they edit and gloss over it, what gangster rap did was it gave you a front-row seat to what was happening. So you almost felt like you lived on the block in Watts, that you can't be sitting on your porch because you're about to duck bullets if a car driving by too slow was about to roll up on you. You kind of felt like you were in the video with them."

But seeing something and living it are two dramatically different things. Wearing a cowboy hat does not make someone a cowboy.

"It got those dudes in Kansas and North Dakota, where they had never known about gangbanging and colors, now you're starting to see kids wearing Raiders jackets and hats and rags," MC Eiht said. "Sets that are from Compton, you're seeing them all the way out in South Dakota and Wisconsin. . . . Everything was secretive until we started rapping and *Yo! MTV Raps* started putting our videos up so everybody could relate to what we were talking about because a lot of people didn't understand what was going on. They'd hear a record and, 'Oh. They're shooting each other.' 'Why he got on red?' 'Why he got on blue?' I always

FAB FIVE FREDDY

The New York hip-hop ...eer was involved in the genre's growth ...oughout New York City and, eventual-...the world. His early work as a rapper ...released the song "Change the Beat" ...embarked upon the first European ...hop tour in 1982) and visual artist (he ...oduced the white downtown art scene ...he black uptown graffiti world) led to ...work, most notably as an actor and ...ducer on the seminal 1983 hip-hop film ...*d Style*. The *Yo! MTV Raps* card used an ...rnate appellation.

...ctor Dré and Ed Lover (and ...Money): Doctor Dré and T-Money ...ned their stripes as college radio hosts ...as members of the rap group Original ...ncept, which released *Straight From ... Basement Of Kooley High!* with Def ...n Recordings in 1988. Ed Lover was a ...mber of the rap group No Face before ...ing the *Yo! MTV Raps* fold.

tried to incorporate what was going on with the gang-banging in my videos. It gave people a way to symbol-ize [identify] with us."

Seeing gangbanging portrayed in rap videos gave millions of fans around the country a look at a lifestyle they were utterly unfamiliar with. Ironically, one of Gil Scott-Heron's most famous works was "The Revolution Will Not Be Televised," a 1970 selection in which the New York–based artist railed against the corporatized, romanticized, and whitewashed version of America often presented on television and in the media. Gil Scott-Heron ends the song by saying "The revolution will not be televised. . . . The revolution will be live."

Yo! MTV Raps wasn't live, but it was revolutionary in many ways. In March 1989, it graduated from its initial weekend slot and began airing Monday through Saturday, with weekday duties being handled by New York DJ Doctor Dré (not to be confused with N.W.A's Dr. Dre) and comedic-minded hip-hop fan and security guard Ed Lover. Unlike Fab 5 Freddy, who showcased his swagger during his screen time, Doctor Dré and Ed Lover (and occasional special guest host T-Money) brought a balance of rap knowledge and levity to the program through their routines, skits, and slapstick interactions.

The additional programming time gave rap expo-nentially more viewers, offered a new voice to the voiceless, and provided a visual look into some of Amer-ica's most overlooked communities courtesy of some of its most articulate and informed spokesmen.

"It really was an ambassadorship for hip-hop to main-stream America," author, screenwriter, and pioneering rap journalist Nelson George said of *Yo! MTV Raps*.

Chilli, of R&B trio TLC, added: "To have a show that showed some love for rap like that, I just thought that was the greatest thing they've ever done on that net-work."

Almost overnight, *Yo! MTV Raps* had supplanted radio in the rap world. "*Yo! MTV Raps* enabled me to reach the masses of other project, neighborhood, wannabe gangbanger, and gangbanger type of dudes because we didn't have no outlet," MC Eiht said. "On the West Coast, we had KDAY, they played a little Eazy-E, a little Compton's Most Wanted, but being able to go nationwide as far as a video was concerned, it enabled smalltime Compton's Most Wanted to be internationally known because *Yo! MTV Raps* was everywhere. . . . It just catapulted us from being local heroes to national gangbang rappers, or gangster rappers is what people wanted to call it. It enabled us to connect with those dudes in Chicago, Brooklyn, Bronx, down South in Florida, the Atlantas and the Texases. Wherever dudes congregated and called themselves that, they were able to now see [people just like them on television]."

The dirty secret of black urban American life was now, for the first time, being seen and heard by millions of fans, black and white alike. Rap had always been competitive, and *Yo! MTV Raps* gave rappers an extra incentive to deliver their best material. On the one hand, it provided a platform to showcase the best artists, the rappers with the most revered rhymes, the artists with the best music, and the acts with the most remarkable videos. The exposure it provided also helped a handful of rappers become rich and famous. On the other hand, *Yo! MTV Raps* was a tremendous marketing tool to sell a lifestyle to hundreds of thousands of fans who—especially if they were black—remained poor, oppressed, and subject to wanton harassment and police brutality. The handful of rappers who became rich and famous had just moved up several tax brackets.

Furthermore, gangster rap was being seen and heard at a time when American culture was shifting from reading and listening in order to digest its information to getting it by watching television. Viewers were now aware of what was happening in poor diverse neighborhoods. In 1988, Chuck D famously said, "Rap is black America's TV station." If so, then *Yo! MTV Raps* was akin to its nightly news, a snapshot of the most pressing issues of the day.

The rappers took full advantage of the platform, too. In an interview during one of N.W.A's *Yo! MTV Raps* appearances in 1989, Dr. Dre taunted the group's detractors while likely energizing fans who rallied behind the group's explicit material. "People been sweating us for our lyrics and stuff like that," the rapper-producer told Fab 5 Freddy. "We figured since they sweated us, we're gonna make the next album worse."

The next N.W.A album, though, would not feature one of the group's most significant members. He was the only member who wasn't from Compton, and he was about to show the world that he knew how to survive in South Central.

Ice Cube:
"A Gangsta's Fairytale"

IN 1989, URBAN AMERICA AND THE WORLD WERE FALLING DEEPER INTO CHAOS.

As former director of central intelligence and vice president George H. W. Bush was sworn into office as president, America's inner cities continued to disintegrate, thanks in large part to Reaganomics. At the same time, US politicians and their wives continued to rail against the lyrics of gangster rappers. The Lockerbie bombing of Pan Am Flight 103 claimed two hundred and seventy lives and the Exxon Valdez oil spill polluted Alaska's Prince William Sound with two hundred and seventy thousand barrels of crude oil. The savings and loan crisis erupted, costing taxpayers more than $160 billion—and their life savings in many cases. In Tiananmen Square, one million Chinese protesters stood up against their oppressive government's violence and demanded a better democracy, while President Bush invaded Panama to capture and arrest de facto leader Manuel Noriega. Many people watched these events unfold live on CNN,

1990
Key Rap Releases

1. Ice Cube's *Ameri-KKKa's Most Wanted* album

2. Public Enemy's *Fear of a Black Planet* album

3. MC Hammer's "U Can't Touch This" single

US President

George H.W. Bush

Something Else

East and West Germany reunified.

a 24/7 news network that was the go-to channel for nonstop coverage of the world in chaos.

The threat of violence had firmly ensnared black neighborhoods across America, and it seemed that crisis followed crisis. In the Bronx, a five-year-old kindergarten student was found at school in possession of a handgun. In Miami, riots rocked the city after a police officer shot and killed a twenty-four-year-old unarmed black man.

Meanwhile, in South Central Los Angeles, preteens and teenagers joined gangs at an alarming rate in order to survive the urban decay and violence on the streets. Gangs grew more powerful and more violent due to an unprecedented influx of drugs and money spurred in part by the fallout of Reaganomics, which left ghetto America in a frighteningly vulnerable state. Economic and educational resources were becoming increasingly scarce while alcohol, drugs, and guns were becoming more readily available.

For the young people growing up in this chaotic environment, it meant ditching collared shirts and slacks for the gang uniform of a Pendleton shirt, Levi's 501 jeans, Chuck Taylors (with your gang name on the tongue), a hair net, braids, and a golfer hat. On the one hand, the change in attire put their lives at risk, but on the other hand, it provided them with a form of brotherhood and safety largely absent from their lives.

San Diego gangster rapper Mitchy Slick had been gang affiliated for more than half of his fifteen years in 1989. He remembers the chaos and desperation of those days. "People in impoverished situations, they're going to look to each other for help. They're going to come together. . . .When I was coming up, they didn't have no gang intervention. It wasn't no, 'Don't wear these colors to school.'"

At the same time, Ice-T, thirty-one, scored his third consecutive gold album with *The Iceberg/Freedom of Speech . . . Just Watch What You Say!*, and the Ghetto Boys changed their lineup, adding eighteen-year-old Scarface to the mix. The result was a surge in popularity for the group in addition to Texas being put on the gangster rap map. Meanwhile, Eazy-E, now twenty-five years old, was touring the country with N.W.A, and the group was on their way to being the first gangster rap group certified platinum with a million records sold. Inspired by their surroundings, this handful of artists provided a voice to the millions of blacks suffering through poverty, oppression, and a lack of equal access to America's vast economic and social resources. For the artists and listeners alike, there was a sort of cathartic experience in creating and consuming the music. It was a way to connect on a visceral level like never before.

But as select rappers were escaping from the type of poverty they rapped about, a new problem emerged at one of rap's most successful upstart labels. Despite its commercial success, all was not well at Eazy-E's Ruthless Records. Ice Cube had grown disillusioned with what he thought was a massive underpayment for his services. After refusing to sign a contract and accept a check for his past work as a writer and performer on Eazy-E's *Eazy-Duz-It* and N.W.A's *Straight Outta Compton* albums, Ice Cube left N.W.A during the height of the group's popularity. In respect to where the group was in their career arc, it was akin to John Lennon or Paul McCartney leaving the Beatles after the release of *Sgt. Pepper's Lonely Hearts Club Band*.

Ice Cube and Eazy-E may have been from the hood, but they were now part of the legit world of the music business. Not having contracts signed at the beginning of their relationship was a big misstep that manager Jerry Heller should have known could, and would, come back to haunt Eazy-E, as it gave Ice Cube a chance to escape what he saw as an unfair deal.

As he worked through the dissolution of his relationship with Eazy-E, Ruthless Records, and Jerry Heller, Ice Cube sought counsel from the group's publicist. "Pat Charbonnet was very instrumental in me recognizing that the situation with Ruthless and Jerry Heller just wasn't right," Ice Cube said. "Just by her being so smart about the business, I ended up naming her my manager, and the first person she went to was [Priority Records co-owner] Bryan Turner. She said: 'Cube's solo. You want to give him a deal? Or, if not, we're going to go get it somewhere else.' So he stepped up, and I'm glad he did."

Although Ice Cube often conceptualized N.W.A's thematic direction and had

RUTHLESS RECORDS STRIKES GOLD & PLATINUM

J.J. Fad, *Supersonic*, June 27, 1988, Gold album, September 30, 1988

Eazy-E, *Eazy-Duz-It*, November 23, 1988, Gold album, February 15, 1989 (Platinum, June 1, 1989, Double platinum, September 1, 1992)

N.W.A, *Straight Outta Compton*, August 8, 1988 (initial version), Gold album, April 13, 1989 (Platinum, July 18, 1989, Double platinum, March 27, 1992, Triple Platinum, November 11, 2015)

the idea for the group's landmark "Fuck tha Police," many fans and industry insiders viewed him as just another member of N.W.A and little else.

"I don't think anyone knew what they were losing when [Ice Cube left Ruthless]," the D.O.C. said. "I didn't even really give it a whole lot of thought because I was thinking about my shit. But when he left, the spirit of that group was gone."

That's because Ice Cube was N.W.A's "lyricizer," as Eazy-E repeatedly put it to the press. He was the artist whose words and song ideas helped define N.W.A's early music. Eazy-E was the group's "conceptualizer," and Dr. Dre its "musicalizer."

Eazy-E was also the highest-profile member of N.W.A, and Ruthless Records was his company. He was the one with the solo project, *Eazy-Duz-It*, an album that was selling as robustly as N.W.A's *Straight Outta Compton*. *Eazy-Duz-It* was certified gold in February 1989. Thus, Eazy-E was the star of N.W.A, a king among kings in the richest talent pool in rap history. Dr. Dre was positioned as the crew's second star thanks to his musical genius, proficient production, and his visibility from rapping on the N.W.A single "Express Yourself," which had gotten extensive play on *Yo! MTV Raps*.

As word spread that Ice Cube had left N.W.A, rap insiders and casual fans alike had a number of concerns about his career given N.W.A's potency as a group. Ice Cube was now without Eazy-E, MC Ren, and Dr. Dre to share the verbal and lyrical load. Furthermore, the Dr. Dre–produced *No One Can Do It Better* from the D.O.C. and "No More Lies" from singer Michel'le were certified gold in 1989. It appeared that Ice Cube would suffer without the benefit of Dr. Dre's (and DJ Yella's) production prowess and the industry clout Ruthless Records had amassed by that point.

"[Ice Cube] had to set out to prove that he was one of the most important parts of this fuckin' band," DJ Quik said.

Although Ice Cube and Dr. Dre wanted to work together on Ice Cube's solo album, it was blocked. "Jerry Heller vetoed that," Ice Cube said. "So since he vetoed that shit—and I'm pretty sure Eazy didn't want Dre to do it. But Dre did want to do it. We gotta put that on record. Dre wanted to do my record, but it was just too crazy with the breakup of [N.W.A]. The breakup snowballed into some shit."

Other things were snowballing, too. As gangster rap started to tighten its grip on the creative and sonic direction of rap, an explosion of conscious rap occurred in New York. The pro-black work of Public Enemy and the now-politically minded work of Boogie Down Productions helped lead the charge. Several other voices were also making a dent in the rap marketplace, many of them from the New York metropolitan area. Long Island, New York, trio De La Soul delivered what

PRIORITY
R E C O R D S ®

Priority Records, Inc.
6430 Sunset Boulevard
Hollywood, California 90028
(213) 467-0151

Telex 9102406248 (PRI LSA)
Telecopier (213) 856-8796

"EAZY-DUZ-IT" GOES GOLD!

In recent months, the myth that radical innovation and commercial success are incompatible has been exploded by such unconventional success stories as Tracy Chapman, Guns N' Roses, Terence Trent D'Arby and Metallica. Like those artists, hardcore Los Angeles rapper Eric "Eazy-E" Wright (who records for Ruthless/Priority as both a solo artist and as a member of N.W.A.) is showing that selling records isn't necessarily synonymous with selling out. Eazy's debut solo album, "Eazy-Duz-It" -- a brutally realistic effort abounding with graphic descriptions of the type of drug dealing and violence he was exposed to growing up in L.A.'s Compton ghetto -- has been certfied gold by the Recording Industry Association of America (RIAA) for sales exceeding 500,000 units. The album shipped on November 24.

When Priority President Bryan Turner signed Eazy and N.W.A. last year, he felt that giving the b-boys complete artistic control was essential. "Eazy-E, Tracy Chapman and Guns N' Roses are all disparate musically," Turner explains, "but they're all saying something significant and telling their stories in an uncompromising way. A heavy metal street guy like Axl Rose and a formerly disadvantaged girl like Tracy are reiterating what they've experienced -- and that's what Eazy is doing as well. Here's a guy who used to deal drugs and would still be dealing drugs -- or dead -- if he wasn't rapping. What right would I have to censor what he wanted to say? So I played a passive role in determining the actual content of Eazy's record."

Meanwhile, N.W.A.'s equally hard-hitting "Straight Outta Compton" album, which shipped on February 10, is almost four-fifths of the way to gold status with sales that are just under 400,000 units.

FOR MORE INFORMATION, CALL (800) 235-2300 / (213) 467-0151

Pat Charbonnet / Alyssa Pisano

AS N.W.A AND Eazy-E began dominating rap in general and gangster rap in particular, Eazy-E's *Eazy-Duz-It* album was flying off record store racks. In this undated press release from Priority Records, the material contained on the debut collection from the Compton, California, rapper-businessman was positioned by Priority in the same creative category as the work of acclaimed superstars Tracy Chapman and Guns N' Roses.

Foreshadowing the pro freedom of speech stance Priority Records would take with N.W.A, Ice-T, and Paris, among others, label president Bryan Turner also celebrated his willingness to allow Eazy-E to deliver music detailing what the release calls "the type of drug dealing and violence he was exposed to growing up in L.A.'s Compton ghetto." Turner added: "What right would I have to censor what he wanted to say?"

It's also noteworthy that the commercial success of N.W.A's *Straight Outta Compton* album is tacked on to this press release as a footnote.

was deemed a hippy take on rap, but their *3 Feet High and Rising* showed remarkable range with a deft mix of social commentary, humor, and esoteric lyrics. Revered Long Island hardcore rap duo EPMD released its second collection with *Unfinished Business*. And esteemed Brooklyn lyricist Big Daddy Kane released his acclaimed second album, *It's a Big Daddy Thing*, a well-rounded album full of boasts, social commentary, and sexually driven lyrics. EPMD's, De La Soul's, and Big Daddy Kane's albums all went gold within six months.

Black women also began to get noticed in rap. The second album from Brooklyn's MC Lyte, *Eyes on This*, was embraced for its no-nonsense lyrics about love and conflict, while Newark, New Jersey, rapper-singer Queen Latifah delivered largely upbeat and regularly Afrocentric tunes on her debut album, *All Hail the Queen*.

Similarly, white rappers had a minor breakthrough of sorts with Beastie Boys' second album, *Paul's Boutique*. Produced by former college radio DJs the Dust Brothers, it was Beastie Boys' first album in three years, and was rife with obscure samples and witty wordplay, and it enjoyed massive critical acclaim. Also, *The Cactus Album* from 3rd Bass earned credibility and accolades in the black male–dominated rap universe thanks to the New York rap group's lyricism and material with De La Soul producer Prince Paul and Public Enemy producers Eric "Vietnam" Sadler and brothers Hank and Keith Shocklee.

DELICIOUS VINYL

AS GANGSTER RAP gained momentum, Los Angeles rap got a pop jolt thanks to Delicious Vinyl. Founded by Los Angeles DJs Michael Ross and Matt Dike, the imprint scored huge commercial and crossover success in 1988 with Tone Lōc's "Wild Thing" and followed it up a year later with "Funky Cold Medina." Both of Tone Lōc's breakthrough singles were cowritten by fellow Delicious Vinyl artist Young MC. In 1989, Young MC scored his own pop hit with "Bust a Move." These often playful and decidedly ungangster songs sold more than two million copies collectively and set Delicious Vinyl up as a musical foil to the type of music Ice-T, N.W.A, Eazy-E, and Ice Cube were making. The imprint enjoyed subsequent success with Def Jef, the Pharcyde, and Masta Ace Incorporated.

Meanwhile, Los Angeles rap got a decidedly commercial and lighthearted make-over thanks to the success of Tone Lōc's blockbuster "Wild Thing" and "Funky Cold Medina" singles, as well as Young MC's smash party track "Bust a Move." Rap was proving that it was no longer a minor movement, but rather a robust musical genre with many influences by artists emerging from an increasing number of states and from an expanding range of racial and economic backgrounds.

As the rap world continued developing in scope, beginning to reach new and different audiences, Ice Cube began focusing on his solo album. Bolstered by its creative explosion in 1988 and 1989, rap had taken on a heightened sense of purpose coupled with a seething dynamic rage. These changes were thanks, in large part, to Ice Cube's work on N.W.A's material, as well as the work of Ice-T, Public Enemy, and Boogie Down Productions. Ice Cube's insight into contemporary urban distress proved invaluable for the South Central rapper. His profound and incendiary work was rife with rhymes about social injustice and the harsh realities of gang-infested street culture, qualities that had impressed a number of rap industry insiders.

When Ice Cube decided to work on his solo album, he went with members of his new crew, the Lench Mob, to New York to seek out the services of New York producer Sam Sever, best known for his work with 3rd Bass, who recorded for rap industry stalwart Def Jam Recordings. While waiting in the label's offices for Sever to show, Ice Cube saw Chuck D in the hallway. They had a conversation, which led to Ice Cube's appearance on "Burn Hollywood Burn," a cut from Public Enemy's 1990 *Fear of a Black Planet*, which also featured Big Daddy Kane. The selection bashed the Hollywood shuffle that the film industry forced black

THE BOMB SQUAD

BEST KNOWN FOR their work with Public Enemy and later Ice Cube, the Bomb Squad (original core members Hank Shocklee, Keith Shocklee, Carlton "Chuck D" Ridenhour, and Eric "Vietnam" Sadler) worked collectively and individually on a gaggle of other projects, including material with Doug E. Fresh and the Get Fresh Crew, Slick Rick, LL Cool J, 3rd Bass, and Bell Biv Devoe. As sampling became prohibitive because of cost and clearance issues, the Bomb Squad evolved with the addition of Gary "G-Wiz" Rinaldo and the departure of the Shocklees and Sadler. Sample-based music was replaced by computers and keyboard-generated sonics.

actors, actresses, and creatives to endure by offering them little more than demeaning or stereotypical roles.

While in the studio working on "Burn Hollywood Burn," Ice Cube told the Bomb Squad about his fallout with N.W.A and that he had come to New York to work on his album, a fact Ice Cube said had drawn snickers from N.W.A. "Something in [Hank Shocklee's] eyes turned on, like, 'They laughed?'" Ice Cube said. "I said, 'Yeah.' He said, 'We'll do your whole album if you want us to.'"

This exchange produced one of the most noteworthy collaborations in rap history. Given rap's short history at that time and the concentration of artists in New York, there hadn't been much collaboration between artists and producers from different cities. LL Cool J's *Bigger and Deffer* was an early exception. It was produced by LL Cool J and the L.A. Posse, a crew whose members included DJ Pooh (longtime King Tee collaborator and later Ice Cube collaborator) and Bobby "Bobcat" Erving (a member of Uncle Jamm's Army).

Just two years earlier, in 1987, producers had been largely unknown entities in the rap world and in the larger music industry. By contrast, when Ice Cube started working on *AmeriKKKa's Most Wanted* in 1989, Public Enemy was becoming one of music's most acclaimed groups, thanks in part to their raucous, distinctively assembled production, a kind of aural assault punctuated by hard-hitting percussion, sirens, and political speeches.

AmeriKKKa's Most Wanted brought the Bomb Squad's riotous sounds to Ice Cube's blistering lyrics, while the funk-based production from the Lench Mob member and Dr. Dre's cousin Sir Jinx gave much of the album a West Coast sonic feeling. The Bomb Squad and Sir Jinx worked in tandem to create a distinctive muscular aural presence by merging two of the most dominant sounds in rap: Public Enemy's cut-and-paste organized chaos and a funk-driven sensibility via Sir Jinx.

Given his split with N.W.A, there was tremendous pressure on Ice Cube to deliver. With the hype N.W.A had generated, Ice Cube knew that *AmeriKKKa's Most Wanted* had to feature rhymes and concepts more insightful, provocative, and memorable than the ones from *Straight Outta Compton* and *Eazy-Duz-It*. He started with the spelling of the album title. Ice Cube was inspired by popular television program *America's Most Wanted*. Debuting in February 1988, the show profiled criminals on the run and encouraged viewers to call into the program toll-free in order to help bring criminals to justice. Ice Cube changed the spelling of *America* to reflect his opinion of the country during Reaganomics. "Spelling it like that made the record political," he said, "and not just dismissed as a gangsta record."

"I thought it was very bold," said Yo-Yo, Ice Cube's female protégé who made her debut on *AmeriKKKa's Most Wanted*. "America was in a crisis at that time. We were just getting out of the batterram, with the police coming into people's homes using this military device in the urban community, from [N.W.A] having all that controversy with 'Fuck tha Police,' even [Ice Cube] leaving N.W.A."

Lyrically, Ice Cube leaned on a lesson he'd learned from Dr. Dre while working with him at Ruthless Records: Either shock people or make them laugh. He stuck to that winning formula, building upon it and merging the imaginative storytelling abilities of Slick Rick and the XXX-rated raunch of Too $hort with the political insight of Public Enemy's Chuck D in a way that removed any doubt about his artistic acumen.

> ### "America was in a crisis at that time. We were just getting out of the batterram, with the police coming into people's homes . . ."
> **YO-YO**

It was hailed as a masterpiece, and with good reason. Ice Cube put his artistry on full display throughout *AmeriKKKa's Most Wanted*. The album starts off with "Better Off Dead," essentially a skit in which Ice Cube gets executed via the electric chair while in prison. It then kicks into high gear with the first bona fide song, "The Nigga Ya Love to Hate." After opening the first verse saying that he's tired of being treated like a stepchild, he goes on to blast black people who give only a token allegiance to Africanism. Then he takes aim at critics trying to silence his brand of rap.

They say we promote gangs and drugs / You wanna sweep a nigga like me up under the rug / Kicking shit called street knowledge / Why more niggas in the pen than in college? / Because of that line I might be your cellmate / That's from the nigga ya love to hate

For the "The Nigga Ya Love to Hate" hook, Ice Cube took the unorthodox step of having a chorus of people chant "Fuck you, Ice Cube!" followed by a male voice accusing him of not doing anything positive for the black community. After the second verse, the "Fuck you, Ice Cube!" chorus returns and is followed by an animated woman berating Ice Cube for calling women "bitches" and proclaiming that she does not fit the bill.

It was an unprecedented move. True, UTFO let women diss them during the "Roxanne, Roxanne" era in the mideighties and N.W.A and Too $hort featured women checking them on their songs in the late eighties, but male-female tension in the hypermasculine rap world was to be expected, especially when it was being framed by alpha males who typically got the best of the women with whom they were arguing.

What Ice Cube did, on the other hand, was shocking, strident, and extraordinary. To be the best rapper from the most acclaimed gangster rap group and to have a woman diss you and to diss yourself on your own song by having a chorus of people scream "Fuck you, Ice Cube!" was remarkable. By dissing himself on record before N.W.A or anyone else could, Ice Cube was letting the world know that he was aware of the doubters eager to take shots at his solo career and his departure from rap's most significant group. It was a revolutionary move that rallied rap listeners behind Ice Cube's music.

Not everyone thought Ice Cube should be disparaging himself on his own song, though. "That was a big argument between us, about should somebody say 'fuck you' to themselves on their own record," Ice Cube said. "I remember [Sir] Jinx not really wanting to do that. He had his reasons, because he was in the inner thing with me and N.W.A. [Dr.] Dre is his cousin. He didn't think it was cool, at the time, to do that, and I was like, 'Man, it's the perfect time.'"

This was the first song most people heard from Ice Cube's solo album. The California rapper came out swinging, verbally dismissing his detractors, mocking America's bicentennial, and calling out fake black nationalists and sham black cultural fixtures. Before the song concludes, Ice Cube also disses *Soul Train* and *The Arsenio Hall Show*, two vaunted staples of black television programming. Cultural icons took Ice Cube's swing soundly on the chin.

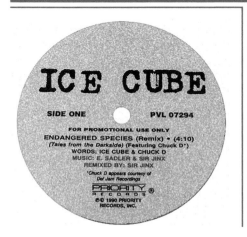

SIR JINX

The cousin of Dr. Dre, Sir Jinx introduced Ice Cube to Dr. Dre and became integral to the early portion of Ice Cube's career, helping produce and shape the sound of Ice Cube's debut album, *AmeriKKKa's Most Wanted*. Sir Jinx continued working with Ice Cube for several years and also collaborated extensively with Yo-Yo, WC and the Maad Circle, Kool G Rap & DJ Polo, and Xzibit, among others.

As he had done while in N.W.A, Ice Cube was eager to examine and highlight the strife between racial and social classes. "In my music, when we talk about race, I give it to everybody," Ice Cube said. "Nobody really gets away clean—not black people, women, Mexicans, whites, Koreans. All races get it, because all races deserve it [because of] what's going on."

Although he was sometimes painted as anti–law enforcement, antiwhite, and anti-establishment, Ice Cube was also anti–police brutality, antiracism, and anti-oppression. This distinction may have been lost on some, but it endeared him to both black and white fans, who embraced Ice Cube as a premier rap talent who presented the positive and the negative, the celebratory and the abhorrent, all in one.

Case in point: "A Gangsta's Fairytale," an explicit reimagining of a number of classic fairy tales that Ice Cube had originally written for Eazy-E and repurposed for himself. In the song's intro, a kid asks him to stop rapping about "the bitches and the niggas" and implores him to rap about the kids. Ice Cube obliges. But instead of the G-rated, good-natured stories of Jack and Jill, Cinderella, and Little Red Riding Hood, these same characters were involved in drug use, gang-banging, drive-by shootings, and prostitution, among other illegal activities. Consider the X-rated revision of the Jack and Jill adventure:

Down on Sesame Street, the dope spot / There he saw the lady who lived in a shoe / Sold dope out the front, in the back, marijuana grew

"A Gangsta's Fairytale" producer Eric "Vietnam" Sadler recalls loving the song, even though his wife took objection as soon as the song's intro was finished. "After the part where the kid starts talking about 'the kids,' my wife said, 'Oh, you're going to hell for that one,'" Sadler said with a laugh. "And I said, 'Yeah, it kinda feels like that.'"

For his part, Ice Cube said that the blend of gangsterism and humor he injects into his music is similar to the balance every person struggles with. "We've all got a dark side and a light side. I don't know too many people that don't love to laugh, and I don't know too many people that don't have those places in themselves. It's a crazy combination that works, like chicken and waffles. When you look at it from the outside, it isn't supposed to work. But when you put it together, it works."

Unfortunately, the social and economic conditions that inspired Ice Cube to write "Endangered Species (Tales from the Darkside)," a collaboration with Public Enemy rapper Chuck D, remained rampant. The cut opens with a faux news broadcast in which the female reporter notes that young black teens have been added to the endangered species list. No efforts, she notes, have been made to preserve the black people because, as one official said, "They make good game."

As he had done on N.W.A's "Fuck tha Police," Ice Cube bemoaned police brutality against blacks on this track. One of his lines played off the Los Angeles Police Department's motto, "To protect and to serve."

They kill ten of me to get the job correct / To serve, protect, and break a nigga's neck

Ice Cube looked at the black existence in America as a rigged game, complete with temptation at virtually every turn. "I feel it is a trap," he said. "I feel it's just all geared to get us drugged out, in the penitentiary, to get us shot—to kill you or to lock you up, to cause misery. The ghetto is a nigga trap. They make it look easier, but as soon as you take the cheese, here they come and your ass is locked up. It's bait. There's bait out there for you."

The bait, all too often, resulted in a stay behind bars, as evidenced by the staggering incarceration rates for young black men in America. A 2013 report from the Sentencing Project stated that one in three black men will go to prison at some point in his life. Ice Cube references being incarcerated in several *AmeriKKKa's Most Wanted* songs, including "Once Upon a Time in the Projects." Here, he goes to a girl's house with the hopes of taking her out. But what should have been a routine stop goes horribly wrong as the girl's mother ends up being a cocaine dealer and the house gets raided as Ice Cube's character is about to leave. Although his character was innocent and beats the case, he still spends two weeks behind bars.

Ice Cube's character in "Once Upon a Time in the Projects" realizes he has gotten himself into a bad situation and tries to vacate the premises. His character on *AmeriKKKa's Most Wanted*'s title track is a criminal but still meets the same fate. In that song, he puts himself in a bad situation by robbing a white man. After he sees himself on the news, his character ends up in the penitentiary, noting that police only pursued him once he robbed a white man. It was the type of imprecise justice—laws being enforced arbitrarily, but always if the victim is a white person—that Ice Cube railed against in his music and warned his listeners about.

"I've always tried to do songs where I want motherfuckers to think before they end up in the pen," Ice Cube said. "I want them to put it all together before that happens to them because those motherfuckers will keep you for years. It ain't no bullshit. They ain't playing. Some stupid little shit will fuck around and have you gone for years. If I can get people to think about that . . . I want people to think. It's easier to think about legal ways to make money than it is [to think about] illegal ways. There's more legal ways to make money out here than there is illegal ways to make money."

On *AmeriKKKa's Most Wanted*, Ice Cube also wanted to show that he viewed women as more than just a temptation or trouble. He was cognizant that "I Ain't

GANGSTA BOO ROSE TO prominence in the mid-1990s as a member of Three 6 Mafia. The Queen of Memphis names her favorite female gangster rappers.

Bo$$. She had a bob. She used to a wear a vest and Locs. She had the record "Deeper," but I was a little young back then.

The Lady Of Rage. First of all, I thought her afro puffs were sick as shit. She was the female of the West Coast at that time rockin' out with all those dudes, the Death Row shit, like, "Who the fuck is this?" She was a taller, bigger chick snapping like that with two fuckin' afro puffs in her hair. That's bad-ass, and she was killing it on all the tracks that she got on, so I just respected that about her. That name, too, The Lady Of Rage, like, "I'm the lady of this fuckin' rage, this fuckin' fire. I'm the lady of this shit. The anger, the rage, the destruction, it's all me. Come fuck with me if you want to, and get your ass fucked up."

Gangsta Boo. I'm the first female rapper that made it out of Memphis and that was with a multiplatinum group. I stood out not even trying to stand out. I listen to my old stuff and be like, 'Damn, dude, I was like fourteen years old snapping like that.' The raps that I wrote when I was fourteen is how bitches sound now. That's just amazing to me. So, that's the good in me. I gave a lot of the youth their sound.

Mia X. Mia was an inspiration. She was the mother of Southern gangster rap. She was much older than me, so when I did come out doing my thang, I show love to the motherfuckas that's older than me, that got a little more experience. She reminded me of me. She was the only female, before [Master] P started signing other women, in a clique full of dudes as gangster as No Limit. It was very inspiring to see

a female rip it with a whole bunch of dudes with no problem, and killin' half of 'em on their own tracks. That's gangster.

La Chat. To me, La Chat is like ratchet, the ratchet everybody is being now. She was before her time. She's got gold teeth, and those are her permanent gold teeth. It's something about permanent gold teeth on females I think is the most gangster, hoodish shit ever. And, she's not doing it for a gimmick. That's who she is, and I think that's dope.

"IT'S A MAN'S WORLD"

YO-YO PARLAYED HER powerful performance on Ice Cube's "It's a Man's World" into a successful career that jumpstarted with 1991's *Make Way for the Motherlode* and its singles "Stompin' to tha 90's" and "You Can't Play with My Yo-Yo," the latter of which featured Ice Cube. Even though she was affiliated with Ice Cube and was from Los Angeles, she was not a gangster rapper, a reality that took on additional meaning with the emergence of female gangster rapper Bo$$ in 1993.

"At the beginning, I thought it was just like a fantasy until they started blaspheming Bo$$ for not being a real gangster chick," Yo-Yo said. "Then I went into a shell. I started hiding, like 'Oh my God. I'm not really a gangster chick, and here are these journalists calling me a gangster,' so I went into hiding. I was like, 'Oh, god. I have to perpetrate who I really was.' It was hard for me to say that I really didn't live a gangster life."

In addition to impacting her personal life, the gangster rap stigma affected her musical trajectory.

"Creatively, it opened my eyes and it started letting me see what the real world was all about and how hip-hop was really affecting the community," she said. "All those years that I told journalists I wasn't a role model, I started thinking, 'Well maybe I am.' I never knew that lyrics had power, and I started realizing how powerful lyrics in hip-hop was. I was introduced to a new reality. I was realizing that there were ghettos in every community. I was realizing that dark skin[ned blacks] didn't like light skin[ned blacks], and that society was pinning brown against the black. I started seeing that the political figures had a monetary gain and that people of power had influence [in that rift]."

tha 1" from N.W.A's *Straight Outta Compton* and his N.W.A single "A Bitch Iz A Bitch"— explicit songs where Ice Cube illustrated that he wasn't going to cater to money-hungry females, regardless of how attractive they might be—had created an antiwoman identity around his raps. He saw this as an opportunity. With that in mind, he recorded "It's a Man's World," on which he introduced his Los Angeles–based female protégé Yo-Yo and gave her the platform to respond to his assertion at the top of the song that women were only good for fulfilling his sexual needs. Yo-Yo took full advantage:

Yo-Yo's not a ho or a whore / And if that's what you're here for / Exit through the door

It's noteworthy that the hypermasculine, alpha-male Ice Cube let a female rapper diss him on his own album. "I felt like if we did a song where we were battling—she was talking shit about me, I was talking shit about her— that she would be looked at as a top-tier rapper, like Queen Latifah or Salt-N-Pepa," Ice Cube said. "I didn't want her to have to struggle from the bottom up."

Pomona, California, rapper, singer, G-Funk practitioner, and former Ruthless Records recording artist Kokane also believes Ice Cube looked at Eazy-E's business blueprint when selecting Yo-Yo.

"Ice Cube knew why there was a Ruthless Records in the first place," Kokane said. "J.J. Fad was a woman group that actually broke in the door for *Straight Outta Compton*. From that aspect, he was already seasoned, like 'I'm going to get me a tight-ass female, and she's gonna be dope like me,' and he found the right fit. Ice Cube knew that Yo-Yo could identify with women [that are] in the hood, the women [that have] got their own shit. It was empowerment for women, especially women of color."

By dissing himself on "The Nigga Ya Love to Hate," partnering with Chuck D on "Endangered Species (Tales from the Darkside)," reworking nursery rhymes into XXX-rated adventures on "A Gangsta's Fairytale," introducing his new crew on "Rollin' Wit the Lench Mob," and letting a female insult him on "It's a Man's World," Ice Cube pulled off a remarkable feat. He left rap's hottest group and became, arguably, the best and most important solo rapper of the time. Ice Cube wanted to make music his way, regardless of the consequences.

"I'm pretty sure it's turned some people off," he said. "What I'm saying is being recorded. I don't take that lightly. I take that as an opportunity because that's going to be here when I'm gone. So I feel like I've got to speak on that, or really, what am I rapping about? If I'm not rapping about shit that affects us all, what really am I rapping about? I say what I feel. It's that simple. I say what I feel. I can gain a fan and lose a fan in the same verse. I say what I gotta say and let the chips fall where they may."

Ice Cube bet on himself and was rewarded with a platinum plaque and the start of one of the most successful careers in music history, one that melded the gangster rap world of N.W.A with the political work of Public Enemy. *AmeriKKKa's Most Wanted* offered a brilliant balance of street-centered insight and big-picture commentary accented by a masterful blend of violence and humor, reverence and rage. It was also a manifesto of a black man standing on his own by escaping America's oppressive cultural system through his art and his beliefs—as well as Ice Cube's exit from Eazy-E's Ruthless Records.

"You could tell that N.W.A had not made Ice Cube," DJ Quik said.

Stylistically, Ice Cube was backed by riotous music. More than any other rap album before it, *AmeriKKKa's Most Wanted* was a groundbreaking mélange of East and West Coast sonics that moved the genre into new aural territory and showed what rap could be when it combined sounds from different regions.

AmeriKKKa's Most Wanted also put N.W.A on notice: Ice Cube could stand on his own and excel while doing so.

"He was a strong-minded, powerful African American dude," the D.O.C. said. "He walked out holding his nuts and he believed in what he was doing. It wasn't just for blowing his horn, or riding any particular bandwagon, or doing something so he could label it this or label it that. That's how he felt, and I was 1,000 percent with it."

Even as Ice Cube's solo career was gaining steam, gangster rap was about to get a grisly makeover, thanks to a group of self-proclaimed madmen.

GHETTO BOYS

CAR FREAK

CAR FREAK

GHETTO BOYS

5th Ward Chronicle

Ghetto Boys Making Trouble

MAKING TROUBLE

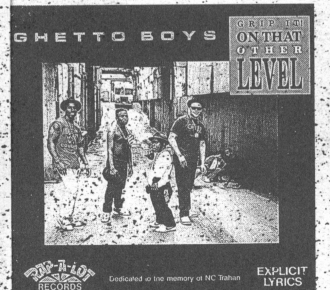

GHETTO BOYS

GRIP IT!
ON THAT
OTHER
LEVEL

RAP-A-LOT
RECORDS

Dedicated to the memory of NC Trahan

EXPLICIT
LYRICS

THE GETO BOYS

PARENTAL
ADVISORY
EXPLICIT CONTENT

CH. 6

"Say Hello to My Little Friends": Gangster Rap Meets Scarface and the Geto Boys

OPPOSITE:
The Geto Boys went from independent to infamous.

In August, the Federal Bureau of Investigation said that the number of violent crimes reported nationwide in 1988 was 1.56 million, an increase of 5.5 percent from the previous year and an all-time high. This represented increases in aggravated assaults, robberies, murders, and rapes. Nearly half of the 18,269 murder victims in 1988 were black, meaning that blacks were being killed at a rate that was more than four times what it should have been relative to their percentage of the US population.

These sobering statistics helped fuel the steady growth of gangster rap. As Ice-T, N.W.A, and Ice Cube were changing the direction of rap in Los Angeles, another rap entrepreneur was making moves in Houston. James Prince (also known as J. Prince, Lil' J, or J), a used-car salesman, had founded Rap-A-Lot Records in 1986 with the intention of becoming a major player in the emerging rap world.

1990
Key Rap Releases

1. A Tribe Called Quest's *People's Instinctive Travels and the Paths of Rhythm* album

2. Vanilla Ice's "Ice Ice Baby" single

3. Digital Underground's "The Humpty Dance" single

US President

George H.W. Bush

Something Else

Nelson Mandela was released after twenty-seven years behind bars.

The Texas businessman's debut group proved to be his most significant. Originally called the Ghetto Boys, Rap-A-Lot Records' flagship crew initially consisted of rappers Raheem, K9 (Sir Rap-A-Lot), and Sire Juke Box. Scarface, who had yet to join the outfit, remembers their first release, "Car Freak," as being one of Houston's first rap releases.

Although gangster rap from Los Angeles, in particular, was steadily becoming more prominent, the majority of rap was still coming from New York, its birthplace. "Everything else was coming from New York, and the stuff that was coming out of Houston sounded so far behind, it was like Cracker Jack rap—just super-simple rhymes not saying shit that [could] have been printed on the back of a pack of some kiddie snacks," Scarface said. "'Car Freak' wasn't crazy, but it gave J something to build on."

A savvy businessman with a talent for marketing, J. Prince was modeling his fledgling imprint on two of rap's premier talents of the era: LL Cool J and Run-DMC. Raheem, who left the Ghetto Boys after "Car Freak" to embark upon a solo career, was the LL Cool J equivalent, even going so far as to appear on the cover of his *The Vigilante* album in 1988 wearing a red Kangol hat, LL Cool J's signature choice of headgear at the time.

On their debut album, 1988's *Making Trouble*, the Ghetto Boys (now composed of Sire Juke Box, Prince Johnny C, and DJ Ready Red, and featuring dancer Bushwick Bill) rapped in a bombastic tag-team style similar to the one Run-DMC employed. Musically, the production on the early Ghetto Boys material was often bare-bones and percussion-driven with a smattering of rock guitars thrown into the mix. Lyrically, the rhymes were neither distinctive nor memorable. AllMusic called the album "clunky and derivative."

Thus, rather than making a name for itself by bringing a new perspective and energy to rap, it was as if Rap-A-Lot Records was merely making its own versions of material patterned after that of rappers who were already successful. Raheem, for his part, was talented and enjoyed regional success with his singles "Dance Floor" and "The Vigilante," but he didn't break through as a solo artist, at least in part because his sound wasn't particularly distinctive and he was viewed by those outside of the region as an LL Cool J knockoff.

But J. Prince had a plan for the Ghetto Boys. In 1972, the funk and soul band War had released the album *The World Is a Ghetto*. J. Prince, embracing a belief similar to the one presented by the album's title, determined that kids in the ghetto needed a group to represent them, to talk how they talked, to articulate what they felt. These kids were downtrodden, and J. Prince was looking for a crew of artists to execute his vision.

SETTING THE SCENE
(AS OF 1990)

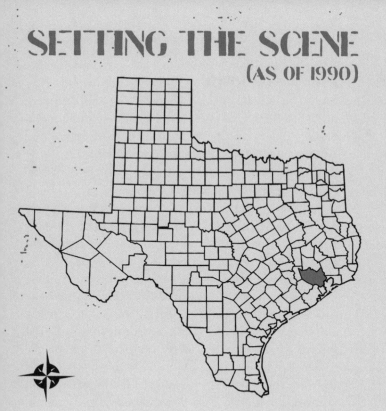

PHYSICAL LOCATION: Houston

POPULATION: 1.6 million

BLACK PEOPLE LIVING IN HOUSTON: 448,000

HISPANIC OR LATINO PEOPLE LIVING IN HOUSTON: 451,000

WHITE PEOPLE LIVING IN HOUSTON: 662,000

ASIAN PEOPLE LIVING IN HOUSTON: 67,000

OTHER: 3,000

MURDER RATE AMONG MAJOR CITIES: No. 6

LOCAL POLITICS: Houston hosted the sixteenth annual G7 Summit. The leaders of Canada, France, Germany, Italy, Japan, the United Kingdom, and the United States attended the forum. Topics discussed at the event included narcotics, the environment, and Third World debt.

POLICE: In 1990, Elizabeth Watson became Houston's first female police chief.

Not believing the existing members of the Ghetto Boys could implement his concept, J. Prince revamped the group's lineup. Bushwick Bill, who has dwarfism and who had been a Ghetto Boys dancer, was already in the fold, and J. Prince signed Golden Gloves boxer-rapper Willie D after he won a string of rap battles at Houston's Rhinestone Wrangler nightclub. Scarface, who originally recorded as DJ Akshen and changed his name in honor of the title character of the 1983 film starring Al Pacino, earned a spot at the label after battling Ghetto Boys member K9, who happened to be J. Prince's brother. After losing to Scarface, K9 was no longer in his brother's flagship group. With holdover DJ Ready Red, the new lineup of the Ghetto Boys was set: rappers Scarface, Willie D, and Bushwick Bill and producer DJ Ready Red.

After the success of Schoolly D, Ice-T, Boogie Down Productions, and N.W.A, all of whom had sold hundreds of thousands of records rife with talk of guns, illicit sex, and violence, the underground rap world was ravenous for more. Given that no Houston rap act had made either a critical or a commercial dent in the rap world (and because of the bland fare on their debut album), the Ghetto

SCARFACE'S INFLUENCE ON GANGSTER RAP

SCARFACE MAY HAVE had more effect on rap than any other film. The 1983 movie starring Al Pacino traces Cuban immigrant Tony Montana's rise from a petty drug dealer to kingpin status. Montana's rise to power, his code of ethics, his street savvy, and his memorable lines appealed to members of the rap world, who felt they could identify with the character's hopes, dreams, ambitions, and struggles. Albums from the Geto Boys, Scarface, and others liberally used *Scarface*'s theme music and score, and made several of Montana's catchphrases ("Say hello to my little friend" and "All I have in this world is my balls and my word, and I don't break them for no one") famous by incorporating them into several songs and choruses.

Boys was an unlikely group to push gangster rap forward. But where *Making Trouble* contained mostly typical rap bluster on such songs as "You Ain't Nothin'" and "I Run This," and featured relatively tame lyrics about robbery on the title track, the new cast of the Ghetto Boys infused extreme levels of violence, paranoia, sex, drugs, and profanity into their next project, 1989's *Grip It! On That Other Level*.

Whereas much of the music and lyrics on *Making Trouble* is quaint, *Grip It! On That Other Level* was anything but. The album's sonics were forceful and the rhymes ribald, rambunctious, and rancorous. *Grip It! On That Other Level* also featured sound bites from Al Pacino's portrayal of crime lord Tony Montana in *Scarface* woven into the fabric of several songs throughout the album, mainly his yelling "Fuck you, man" and "I'll bury those cockroaches" in his faux Cuban accent.

On "Do It Like a G.O.," *Grip It! On That Other Level*'s opening track, J. Prince (going as Lil' J) appears on a conference call with Willie D and Scarface and laments that he's tired of being disrespected as a black businessman and that he won't sell out. J. Prince then orders the group to take it to "the other level of the game."

The Ghetto Boys did not disappoint. On "Do It Like a G.O.," Willie D boldly took the unprecedented step of dissing the rap industry elite, all of whom were located in New York at the time:

> *The East Coast ain't playin' our songs / I wanna know what the hell's goin' on . . . Everybody know New York is where it began / So let the ego shit end*

Willie D's comments would be akin to a child talking back to their parents for the first time. All the emerging labels putting out rap music (Def Jam Recordings, Jive Records, Tommy Boy Music, Profile Records, Select Records, Next Plateau Records, and Cold Chillin' Records, as well as Sleeping Bag Records and its sublabel Fresh Records) were located in New York, save for the rising Los Angeles–based Priority Records. The men running rap labels had been largely content with signing and working with local talent up to this point. The rap business had also been fighting the larger music industry to get exposure in the mainstream press and on the radio, with little success. Things were changing, though, thanks to the fledgling *Yo! MTV Raps*.

The motto of the prominent New York–based hip-hop awareness organization Universal Zulu Nation was "peace, unity, love, and having fun." But with rappers starting to sell hundreds of thousands of singles and albums, and the exposure *Yo! MTV Raps* offered, Willie D was speaking for every American city that wanted in to the rap game. They felt they had been marginalized by being denied a legitimate opportunity due to rap's xenophobic nature. Essentially, if you weren't from New York, you didn't matter to the New York rap crowd, which drove much of the national market.

Thus, it was a bold, risky move for Rap-A-Lot to stick its neck out in the ultra-insular rap world, which had been slow to develop artists of note hailing from beyond New York's five boroughs during its first decade on record, by calling them on it.

In one of his verses on the song, Scarface announced one of the Ghetto Boys' roadblocks:

Black radio is being disowned / Not by the other race, but its own / A lot of bullshit records make hits / Because the radio is all about politics

In general, rap had enjoyed little radio exposure up to 1989, other than Los Angeles rap radio station KDAY and specialty rap shows in major markets such as New York and Philadelphia. That didn't appear to matter to the Ghetto Boys.

"DO IT LIKE A G.O."

Two main versions of the song "Do It Like a G.O." were released by Rap-A-Lot Records in 1989. One appears on the Ghetto Boys' *Grip It! On That Other Level* album with raps from Willie D, Scarface, Bushwick Bill, and DJ Ready Red. The other version of the song was included on Willie D's *Controversy* album, which was also released in 1989 and features Sire Juke Box and Prince Johnny C rapping virtually the same lyrics as the ones Scarface and Bushwick Bill use on the other version of the cut.

BLACK OWNED, AND PROUD OF IT

IN THE LATE 1980s and early 1990s, a wave of Southern, black-owned record companies emerged, including Luther Campbell's Luke Skyywalker in Miami and James "J. Prince's" Rap-A-Lot Records in Houston. Their success paved the way for Tony Draper's Suave House Records in Houston; Master P's No Limit Records, first in California and then in Louisiana; and Three 6 Mafia's Hypnotize Minds. Each imprint released gangster rap material, though they didn't all focus exclusively on the genre. What each company did do, though, was bring a street-based way of operating to the music business.

"We all have a street element because we come from a street element," said Tony Draper, whose company released gold and platinum projects from 8Ball & MJG. "We were all already of the mindset of spending our own, owning our own. So by the time we did a deal with any major label, we had already sold hundreds of thousands of records through our one-stop distributors. So, when we'd come to New York and see the people we used to admire on TV and they had nothing – no money, no ownership of anything – we were like, 'Yo. That's not what it is. That was never impressive to us.' I think that we had a different mindset coming from a street element, but being educated enough to convert a street element into a real form of business."

To paraphrase President George W. Bush, a fellow Texan, more than a decade later, the Ghetto Boys and Rap-A-Lot Records had adopted the mindset that either you were with them, or you were against them—that is, with the enemy. And the Ghetto Boys' enemy was anyone who didn't support rap or, more particularly, didn't support the Ghetto Boys.

The power of "Do It Like a G.O." continued as Willie D claimed that blacks were being taken advantage of in the drug game and Bushwick Bill warned that the street life resulted in either death or incarceration—the latter situation also typically resulted in your woman quickly and happily finding another man. For his part, Scarface detailed how racism impacted the school system:

> Whites get more funds from the state / And this is why minorities learn so late

This institutional and financial racism has a trickle-down effect, one not lost on Bushwick Bill during his take on the evolution of black people in America:

> Our ancestors were killed at will / Bought and sold like a used automobile / We fought so blacks could exist / Now we're killin' one another, ain't that a bitch

On "Do It Like a G.O.," the newly revamped Ghetto Boys demonstrated that their aggressiveness knew no limits and that the group was more than willing to take on any opponent, whether it be the rap gatekeepers, black radio stations, the school system, the black urban community, or the white power structure.

Rap-A-Lot Records owner James Prince also wanted to make sure his presence was felt on "Do It Like a G.O." In the cut's intro, Prince mentioned the frustration he faced as a black businessman trying to make his mark in the rap world. As the song concludes, he takes a phone call from the president of White Owned Records, who gives him two choices. One: Keep your boys quiet or else. The other: Keep a five percent stake in his own company and become rich in fifteen years, but White Owned Records would own ninety-five percent of Rap-A-Lot. J. Prince's response: "Man, fuck you."

For the disenfranchised black audience J. Prince was targeting, cursing out a white man offering him a substandard business deal established him as a sort of mythical figure, a businessman ready to go to war with the powers that be for what he believed in.

"It was easy to relate to because their stories mirrored our stories at that same time," DJ Quik said. "They made it cool to be from Down South."

Much of the rest of *Grip It! On That Other Level* set J. Prince and the Ghetto Boys up for both success and war. The album's second song, "Gangster of Love," was one of the most sexually explicit rap songs ever released at that point. Prior to "Gangster of Love," Too $hort released songs such as "The Bitch Sucks Dick," "Blow Job Betty," and "Freaky Tales," while the 2 Live Crew built their brand on such selections as "We Want Some Pussy," "Do Wah Diddy," and "One and One."

Schoolly D ("Mr. Big Dick") and Ice-T ("Girls L.G.B.N.A.F.") also had overtly sexual songs that graphically discussed sex and/or sex acts, but the Ghetto Boys ratcheted up the stakes with "Gangster of Love." In the first verse, Willie D rapped that he would kick a girl's ass if she messed with him, while Bushwick Bill expressed his affinity for having sex with his girl's friend

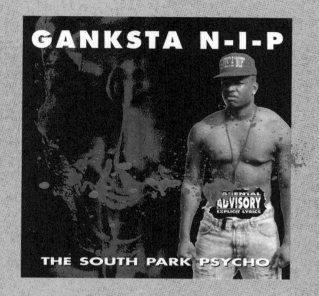

RAP-A-LOT RECORDS' MOST GRUESOME ALBUMS AND SONGS

THE GETO BOYS and fellow Rap-A-Lot Records act Ganksta N-I-P have released some of rap's most grisly material. In 1991, Ganksta N-I-P wrote the song "Chuckie" for Bushwick Bill. The song appears on the Geto Boys' 1991 album, *We Can't Be Stopped*, and features Bushwick Bill imagining himself as the horror movie character Chuckie and slicing up someone's nieces into eighty-eight pieces and putting severed heads with knives in them into mailboxes. "It scared the bejesus out of me," DJ Quik said. For his part, Ganksta N-I-P pioneered the horrorcore rap subgenre with his *The South Park Psycho* album in 1992. It features the Houston rapper detailing his violent, murderous, and sometimes cannibalistic ways.

and watching them have sex with each other. He also boasted that he would readily have sex with his girlfriend's mother if she gave him the opportunity.

But what made the Ghetto Boys different from their sex rap predecessors was their willingness to include violence as a consequence for sexual disobedience or for lying about being pregnant. Willie D rapped about Ms. P, a woman who lied and said he had gotten her pregnant. After saying that he drugged "her little ass like a motherfucking horse," he upped the ante even more.

> *I'll kick a bitch smack dead in the ass if she ever say we / Made a kid when I make it / I'll grab her by her motherfucking neck and try to break it / 'Cause I know I wore a fucking glove*

Willie D continued his verbal assault against "no-good women" on "Let a Ho Be a Ho." With the sound of a cash register ringing throughout the guitar-accented track, Willie D rapped about how men fall in love with women who have sex with as many men as possible. In the fourth verse, he rapped about having sex with a woman, arranging a threesome with a second woman, and then realizing that they stole his wallet once he drops them off. Rather than get upset, though, he laughs it off because he is able to have sex with the women whenever he likes. He also made a point to say that he'd never buy a woman jewelry, makeup, or food, among other things.

The rap community had taken issue with LL Cool J's 1987 song "I Need Love," which was the first popular rap love song. A sizable segment of the rap world was turned off by what it perceived to be LL Cool J's sellout attempt to appeal to women with a song it deemed soft, especially after he had gone to such lengths to prove his status as a hardcore rapper. By contrast, two years later, the Ghetto Boys were making antilove songs. They were promoting a combination of sex and violence in ways that separated them from other gangster rappers.

The menacing music wasn't limited to just a few other selections from *Grip It! On That Other Level*. The album also featured Willie D and Bushwick Bill rapping about beating up anyone (including women) who didn't support the Ghetto Boys ("Read These Nikes"), Bushwick Bill claiming that his dwarfism would not impede his ability to "fuck you up like a goddamn accident" ("Size Ain't Shit"), and Scarface relaying a story about how he killed twenty men who tried to ambush him and a cop who tried to stop his escape ("Life in the Fast Lane").

The album's final cut, however, took the violence to a grisly place. The macabre "Mind of a Lunatic" featured Bushwick Bill, Scarface, and Willie D rapping about their homicidal tendencies and their respective bloodlusts. The song unfolded more like a horror movie than either the shoot-outs of N.W.A's most brazen moments or even the rest of *Grip It! On That Other Level* had.

THE MANY LOOKS OF THE GETO BOYS

Scarface, Bushwick Bill, and Willie D are the core members of the Geto Boys, but none of them appear on all of the group's albums. Here's a look at the many incarnations of the Geto Boys.

Making Trouble (1988). Members: Sire Juke Box, Prince Johnny C, and DJ Ready Red

Grip It! On That Other Level (1989). Members: Scarface, Willie D, Bushwick Bill, and DJ Ready Red

The Geto Boys (1990). Members: Scarface, Willie D, Bushwick Bill, and DJ Ready Red

We Can't Be Stopped (1991). Members: Scarface, Willie D, and Bushwick Bill

Till Death Do Us Part (1993). Members: Scarface, Bushwick Bill, and Big Mike

The Resurrection (1996). Members: Scarface, Willie D, Bushwick Bill

Da Good da Bad & da Ugly (1998). Members: Scarface and Willie D

The Foundation (2005). Members: Scarface, Willie D, and Bushwick Bill

RAP-A-LOT RECORDS' OTHER NOTEWORTHY ACTS

Convicts. The duo's self-titled 1991 album would be their only LP, but Big Mike later became a member of the Geto Boys and a gold-certified solo artist, while Mr. 3-2 released solo material and formed the group Blac Monks.

Big Mike. After one album with the Geto Boys, Big Mike became a solo rap star, releasing his *Somethin' Serious* in 1994.

CJ Mac. Going as Mad CJ Mac at the time, the rugged gangster rapper gave the imprint a Los Angeles presence with his *True Game* album in 1995.

Do or Die. The smooth-flowing, tongue-twisting Chicago trio of Belo (aka Belo Zero), N.A.R.D., and AK released a string of platinum and gold albums starting with their 1996 single "Po Pimp" from their *Picture This* album. The group also gave the imprint a foothold in the Midwest.

Devin the Dude. A member of Rap-A-Lot group Odd Squad, Devin the Dude is a pioneering blues rapper whose whimsical, self-deprecating rhymes are among the genre's funniest. Devin the Dude later collaborated with Dr. Dre, Snoop Dogg, 8Ball, Nas, OutKast's André 3000, Lil Wayne, and others.

On the two opening verses of "Mind of a Lunatic," Bushwick Bill added a new wrinkle to murder on a rap record. He started the song by rapping that he's paranoid, sweating, and craving sex. Then his thoughts turn murderous.

The sight of blood excites me, shoot you in the head / Sit down, and watch you bleed to death / I hear the sound of your last breath

During the rest of the verse, Bushwick Bill returns to reality but has flashes of Jason, the killer from the *Friday the 13th* horror film franchise.

In the second verse, Bushwick Bill acts on his thoughts:

Looking through her window, now my body is warm / She's naked, and I'm a peeping Tom / Her body's beautiful, so I'm thinking rape / Shouldn't have had her curtains open, see that's her fate

He then raps about snatching her as she leaves her house, dragging her back in the house, raping her at knifepoint, and then killing her. As the police arrive, his verse ends, leaving the aftermath of his actions a mystery.

But with his verses on "Mind of a Lunatic," Bushwick Bill took rap to a new place. His crime was not a response to oppression, racism, a slight, a drug deal gone bad, or a gang problem. He made killing impersonal, something he was compelled to do. It was because he was a self-proclaimed lunatic. The subsequent verses from Scarface and Willie D were brazen, but far less savage than those of Bushwick Bill.

Grip It! On That Other Level was produced by DJ Ready Red, Doug King, J. Smith, John Bido, and Prince Johnny C. Unlike the uninspired beats on much of *Making Trouble*, the sonics on *Grip It! On That Other Level* accented and enhanced the words of the Ghetto Boys. "Do It Like a G.O." sizzled with aggressive percussion, while the rugged scratching on "Size Ain't Shit" added a rough texture to Bushwick Bill's threats. The ominous horns and guitar on "Mind of a Lunatic" accentuated the tortured rhymes of Bushwick Bill, Scarface, and Willie D.

As *Grip It! On That Other Level* gained traction in the South and Midwest through influential mom-and-pop retailers, it also earned an important fan. Producer Rick Rubin became enamored with the album. Rubin had partnered with Russell Simmons for Def Jam Recordings, which the pair launched from Rubin's New York University dorm room in 1984. During the next several years, Rubin produced material from many of rap's biggest artists, including Run-DMC, LL Cool J, and Beastie Boys.

After establishing himself as a premier producer and rock and rap talent scout, Rubin left Def Jam in 1988 over creative differences, moved to Los Angeles, and launched his Def American Recordings with major label Geffen Records. Rubin worked out a deal with J. Prince to make the newly rechristened group the Geto Boys the first rap faction at Rubin's new company.

Given that *Grip It! On That Other Level* had only been distributed independently through J. Prince's channels, Rubin and J. Prince decided to revamp the album rather than record an entirely new project. Rubin kept ten *Grip It! On That Other Level* songs for what would be *The Geto Boys* album. He had the Geto Boys rewrite and rerecord some of their verses and changed the music on some of the tracks. They also dropped the songs "Seek and Destroy" and "No Sell Out" from the album while adding "F#@* 'Em," which opened the album in spectacularly controversial fashion, taking aim at people who doubted the group's staying power or their willingness to push lyrical boundaries. In short, they targeted anyone they thought was against their kind of rap.

The real challenge, though, came with "Mind of a Lunatic," which had gone from ending *Grip It! On That Other Level* to prime placement as track three on *The Geto Boys*. The song also became more gruesome thanks to reworked lyrics and to new, more menacing deliveries from Bushwick Bill, Scarface, and Willie D. Bushwick Bill was now virtually screaming his verses, making his new lyrics all the more frightening.

She begged me not to kill her, I gave her a rose / Then slit her throat and watched her shake till her eyes closed / Had sex with the corpse before I left her / And drew my name on the wall like Helter Skelter

The new lyrics evoked the image of the Manson Family's crime and murder spree in the sixties, in which leader Charles Manson envisioned an impending apocalypse he called "Helter Skelter." The name came from the title of a popular song by the Beatles and referred to a child's slide on a playground. During their murder spree, members of the Manson Family also used their victims' blood to write words and images, including *Helter Skelter*, on the walls.

Scarface's lyrics had also taken on a more sinister dimension.

I sit alone in my four-cornered room staring at candles / Dreaming of the people I've dismantled / I close my eyes and in the circle appears / The images of sons of bitches that I murdered

"It was so fuckin' out there," DJ Quik said. "Scarface's words, he sounded like a real funeral-home curator."

In defending his lyrics, Bushwick Bill said that the Geto Boys' material was based on actual events and other forms of entertainment. "This is the reality I've seen on the news and around me growing up: *[The] Texas Chainsaw Massacre* and Freddy Krueger," Bushwick Bill said. "When I turn on the TV, there's always someone getting raped, someone getting killed."

This new form of reality rap had a major champion in Rubin, and with the type of trailblazing rap he coveted releasing, Rubin was planning on making a grand reintroduction to the rap world with *The Geto Boys*. But after hearing the album and facing pushback when the Terre Haute, Indiana–based Digital Audio Disc Corporation, which was contracted to make the CD version of *The Geto Boys*, refused to manufacture the album because of its content, Geffen Records executives declined to release *The Geto Boys* and terminated their manufacturing and distribution deal with Rubin's Def American Recordings.

Geffen Records released a statement about its decision that was printed in the *New York Times*. "While it is not imperative that lyrical expressions of even our own Geffen artists reflect the personal values of Geffen Records, the extent to which *The Geto Boys* album glamorizes and possibly endorses violence, racism and misogyny compels us to encourage Def American to select a distributor with a greater affinity for this musical expression."

Scarface found the move and the label's position perplexing given the success Geffen was having with X-rated comic Andrew Dice Clay (a Def American artist, no less) and rock group Guns N' Roses. The former cursed ad nauseam, while the latter was fronted by politically incorrect singer Axl Rose who lamented about "immigrants and faggots" on his group's song "One In A Million."

"Axl Rose was running around singing about all of the heroin and easy pussy he was getting, chasing death in the alleys of Los Angeles, and somehow that was okay," Scarface said, "but those same stories told from our perspective were somehow a problem."

Rubin, though, understood why Geffen executives declined to release the project. "I don't think [some people at Geffen] like the record very much, and I can understand why," he said. "I don't think it's unreasonable for anyone not to like it."

Nonetheless, Rubin was able to find an outlet for *The Geto Boys*. Eventually released in 1990 by Rap-A-Lot Records in conjunction with Rick Rubin's Def American Recordings and WEA Manufacturing (whose parent company, Warner Bros., also owned Geffen at the time, ironically), the album came with a sticker on the cover with the following warning: "Def American Recordings is opposed to censorship. Our manufacturer and distributor, however, do not condone or endorse the content of this recording, which they find violent, sexist, racist, and indecent."

> *"It was so fuckin' out there. Scarface's words, he sounded like a real funeral-home curator."*
>
> **DJ QUIK**

Scarface said Geffen's trepidation was about more than the content of the work. "If you ask me, Geffen just didn't want to see a bunch of niggas make some real money. When you think about all of the shit that we went through just trying to find a place to put our music, it's hard not to see that shit as what I really think it was: active discrimination. We were entertainers just like the rest of them."

But when two Dodge City, Kansas, teens were charged with killing a man in 1990, their defense placed blame on the Geto Boys. The teens' lawyer claimed that the kids were temporarily hypnotized by the Geto Boys' songs. Just as the Beatles had come under scrutiny because of the Manson Family's appropriation of their "Helter Skelter" song and rock group Judas Priest had been sued in 1985 after two men entered a suicide pact and shot themselves after getting intoxicated and listening to the band's *Stained Class* album, a rap group now found themselves on trial for what their music purportedly encouraged their listeners to do. The jury in the Geto Boys' case didn't accept the defense, but the Parents Music Resource Center (PMRC) blasted the rappers for music it deemed inappropriate.

Perhaps in part due to the media firestorm surrounding *The Geto Boys*, it failed to go gold, selling fewer than five hundred thousand copies. The Geto Boys' next album, though, would be the group's most successful. It also arrived the year that gangster rap exploded in popularity thanks to a series of high-profile albums and movies.

Gangster Rap Is the Name

OPPOSITE:

DJ Quik became one of rap's most popular acts in 1991. The Compton rapper-producer is shown here performing at 92.3 The Beat's Summer Jam at Irvine Meadows Amphitheater in Irvine, California, on August 8, 1999.

IN AN ATTEMPT TO KEEP THEIR NAME CIRCULATING AFTER ICE CUBE'S SUCCESSFUL SOLO DEBUT, N.W.A RELEASED THEIR *100 MILES AND RUNNIN'* EP ON AUGUST 14, 1990.

But where Ice Cube did not address the departure on his first post-N.W.A project, Dr. Dre took two thinly veiled shots at Ice Cube and his exit from the group on *100 Miles And Runnin'*. On the EP's title track, Dre rapped:

Started with five and, yo, one couldn't take it / So now there's four cause the fifth couldn't make it

Then, on "Real Niggaz," Dr. Dre compares Ice Cube to the most infamous traitor in American history.

We started out with too much cargo / So I'm glad we got rid of Benedict Arnold

Although these are minor slights when weighed against rap's typically overly macho posturing, N.W.A's disses on *100 Miles And Runnin'* nonetheless fanned

1991
Key Rap Releases ◄

1. N.W.A's *efiL4zaggiN* album

2. Geto Boys' "Mind Playing Tricks on Me" single

3. Ice Cube's *Death Certificate* album

US President ◄

George H.W. Bush

Something Else ◄

LAPD officers beat unarmed black motorist Rodney King.

the flames for the next round of material. Ice Cube returned with his *Kill at Will* EP on December 18, 1990, but he remained silent about N.W.A. Instead, he focused on the rash of deaths in black urban America ("Dead Homiez") and pushing the genre into new and interesting sonic directions by taking the music of contemporary rappers D-Nice, EPMD, Public Enemy, Digital Underground, LL Cool J, and X Clan and rapping over their signature instrumentals in what could be seen as a precursor to both the mixtape and "mash-up" waves of music that followed more than a decade later ("Jackin' for Beats").

In 1991, as the United States' international military actions were winding down and domestic strife was increasing as America's police force aggressively militarized itself, rap was gaining steam. The Gulf War ended when Iraqi troops retreated and the United States reclaimed control of Kuwait. In the Southern Hemisphere, infamous Columbian drug lord Pablo Escobar gave himself up to police in his homeland. Meanwhile in America, racial tensions between blacks, whites, and the police reached a boiling point when footage of Los Angeles police relentlessly beating black motorist Rodney King was captured by an onlooker and released to the media. This video served as a major piece of evidence that backed the numerous claims of police brutality that hardcore rap acts such as Ice-T, Boogie Down Productions, Public Enemy, N.W.A, and others had been voicing for years.

It was at this moment that gangster rap moved from garnering attention from select segments of the population and the media, as it had done throughout the eighties, to dominating commercial media for the first time.

Even though record companies tended to shy away from releasing material in January and February, because the business typically shuts down during the holidays and doesn't ramp up until the end of January, Profile Records (Run-DMC, Dana Dane, and Rob Base and DJ E-Z Rock) bucked that trend by releasing DJ Quik's *Quik Is the Name* in January 1991. The Compton rapper-producer had been infatuated with music since his adolescence and was drawn to the work of funk and soul artists. He started playing instruments before he hit his teenage years, and he had time to focus on his DJing, rapping, and production prowess after being taken in by mentor, fellow rapper, and Penthouse Players Clique member Tweed Cadillac.

Quik Is the Name, the debut collection from DJ Quik, introduced a new sound and style of gangster rap: a largely relaxed and feel-good one in which the protagonist focused as much on women ("Sweet Black Pussy," "I Got That Feelin'"), getting intoxicated ("Tha Bombudd," "8 Ball"), and having fun ("Tonite") as he did on telling tales about the perils of life growing up in the gang-infested Los Angeles metropolitan area ("Born and Raised in Compton," "Loked Out Hood").

"I just wanted to write these stories that mirrored what I had just seen, but take the sting out of it with a cool voice," DJ Quik said. "It was our neighborhood, what's going on right now just put to a beat."

On "Loked Out Hood," DJ Quik also took a dramatic step by naming specific streets in Compton (Aranbe, Spruce, Maple) that would have signaled to listeners familiar with Los Angeles gang culture that he was a member of the Bloods. Prior to that, DJ Quik's Los Angeles–area forebears (Ice-T, King Tee, N.W.A, Eazy-E) identified and rapped about sections of Los Angeles, but they didn't identify themselves with streets or neighborhoods synonymous with particular gangs. They also made a point to wear neutral colors (eschewing blue and red specifically) in their videos and on their album covers. This tactic kept gang affiliation from being a promotional or marketing tool. It also gave Los Angeles rappers the biggest consumer base from which to draw, as Bloods and Crips would be less likely to support work from a member of a rival gang.

By March 3, 1991, though, the main group of people the urban black community was rallying against was the police, who were caught on tape beating Rodney King. Black American men had been routinely and unjustly targeted and abused by police for well more than a century, a reality all too often met by indifference, at best, by the legal system and law-enforcement agencies. Now there was a video of an unarmed black man getting savagely attacked by police being aired on a seemingly nonstop loop on news outlets. Five days later, *New Jack City* arrived in theaters.

GOOD OL' BOYZ-N-THE-HOOD

THEN-REPUBLICAN SENATE LEADER Bob Dole sent the following invitation to Eric Wright in February 1991: "Elizabeth and I are looking forward to seeing you in Washington on March 18," the senator wrote, inviting Wright to join the Republican senatorial inner circle and to attend "Salute to the Commander in Chief," a Republican luncheon President George H.W. Bush was set to attend.

Dole and his team likely had no idea that Eric Wright was Eazy-E.

A philanthropist who had donated to the City of Hope hospital and Athletes and Entertainers for Kids under his given name, Eazy-E imagined he was invited to the swanky dinner because of his charitable contributions. Intrigued by the opportunity, Eazy-E paid $1,000 for annual dues to the organization and $230 to attend the two-day conference. The N.W.A mastermind—whose group released "Fuck Tha Police"—remained true to form when he showed up for the posh event wearing a Los Angeles Kings hat, a white T-shirt, and a gold and diamond bracelet emblazoned with his rap moniker. The Game was so taken with Eazy-E's infamous White House attire that he later referenced it on his 2005 single "Dreams."

Eazy-E said he would have liked to network at the event, and that he endorsed President Bush. "I do support the president's policy in the Persian Gulf," said the rapper, who was not a Republican and was not registered to vote. "I'm not against anything, really, that he's doing."

Wendy Burnley, the director of communications for the National Republican Senatorial Committee, issued a statement regarding Eazy-E's attendance at the event. "This is clear and convincing evidence of the success of our new Rap-Outreach program. Democrats, eat your hearts out."

The film follows vicious crime lord Nino Brown (Wesley Snipes), who rises to power during the crack epidemic by implementing an expertly efficient, supremely organized, and remarkably ruthless team to manage, distribute, and sell his drugs. The off-kilter undercover police officer charged with ending Brown's run is Scotty Appleton (Ice-T).

New Jack City provided a snapshot of what was happening in black urban communities across the United States and showed how difficult it was for well-intentioned police officers to take on better-funded, better-armed, and particularly savvy drug dealers and their crime syndicates. Yet, in the real-life wake of N.W.A's "Fuck tha Police," the federal government waged a censorship war against N.W.A, the Geto Boys, Ice-T, and others. Hence, by portraying a police officer in a major motion picture, Ice-T was taking a tremendous career risk. He was, in effect, humanizing the police officer, showing that there was more to the story than just black versus white, us against them, and the system against poor black people in America.

Ice-T's *New Jack City* gamble paid off handsomely.

Released by film industry stalwart Warner Bros. Pictures, *New Jack City* appealed to the rap audience thanks to Ice-T's leading role, well-placed cameos from rap industry heavyweights (Fab 5 Freddy, Public Enemy's Flavor Flav), a predominantly black cast, and the quality story, which revered movie critic Roger Ebert trumpeted in his 3.5-out-of-4-star review: "By the end of the film, we have a painful but true portrait of the impact of drugs on this segment of the black community: We see how they're sold, how they're used, how they destroy, what they do to people."

New Jack City peaked at No. 2 at the box office, grossing $47 million against a reported $8.5 million budget. The film also benefitted from a sterling soundtrack anchored by Ice-T's "New Jack Hustler (Nino's Theme)" and Color Me Badd's sensual R&B smash hit "I Wanna Sex You Up."

In signature Ice-T fashion, "New Jack Hustler (Nino's Theme)" showed the criminal underworld from the perspective of those living a life similar to Nino Brown's character in *New Jack City*, but with a dose of compassion and insight into the conflicted minds of some of the men caught up in the drug-dealing lifestyle.

I had nothing, and I wanted it / You had everything, and you flaunted it / Turned the needy into the greedy / With cocaine, my success came speedy / Got me twisted, jammed into a paradox / Every dollar I get, another brother drops / Maybe that's the plan and I don't understand / Goddamn, you got me sinkin' in quicksand / But since I don't know, and I ain't never learned / I gotta get paid, I got money to earn

Released on March 5, 1991, the *New Jack City* soundtrack sold more than one million copies by May 1991, earning platinum status.

BOX-OFFICE PERFORMANCE OF RAP-RELATED FILMS RELEASED THROUGH THE END OF 1991

FILM: Wild Style (1983)
SHOOT LOCATION: New York
BUDGET: N/A
BOX OFFICE: N/A
ROTTEN TOMATOES RATING: 89%

FILM: Krush Groove (1985)
SHOOT LOCATION: Bronx, New York
BUDGET: $3 million (estimated)
BOX OFFICE: $11 million
ROTTEN TOMATOES RATING: 43%

FILM: New Jack City (1991)
SHOOT LOCATION: New York
BUDGET: $8.5 million
BOX OFFICE: $47.6 million
ROTTEN TOMATOES RATING: 77%

FILM: Breakin' (1984)
SHOOT LOCATIONS:
  Los Angeles and Venice
  Beach, California
BUDGET: $1.2 million
BOX OFFICE: $38.7 million
ROTTEN TOMATOES RATING: 43%

FILM: House Party (1990)
SHOOT LOCATION: Los Angeles
BUDGET: $2.5 million (estimated)
BOX OFFICE: $26.3 million
ROTTEN TOMATOES RATING: 96%

FILM: Boyz N the Hood (1991)
SHOOT LOCATIONS: Los Angeles and
  Inglewood, California
BUDGET: $6.5 million (estimated)
BOX OFFICE: $57.5 million
ROTTEN TOMATOES RATING: 96%

May 1991 also saw the release of Ice-T's fourth album, *O.G. Original Gangster.* The LP included "New Jack Hustler (Nino's Theme)," and with the surging popularity of gangster rap, Ice-T released the album's title track as a single with an accompanying video. He then went on to take the groundbreaking step of making a video for every track on the collection, a first in any genre.

With three gold albums, numerous national and international tours, and a burgeoning empire with his Rhyme Syndicate label and management company (which had handled King Tee, WC, and Everlast, among others) under his belt, Ice-T wanted to cement his status as a pioneer with "O.G. Original Gangster," an autobiographical chest-thumping exercise that traces his evolution as a rapper, as well as the entire gangster rap subgenre.

When I wrote about parties, it didn't fit / "6 'N the Mornin'," that was the real shit … When I wrote about parties, someone always died / When I tried to write happy, yo, I knew I lied / 'Cause I live a life of crime

America's fascination with a life of crime had been well documented throughout the years, as evidenced by the country's affinity for organized crime beginning

GANGSTER RAP ALBUMS

Quik Is the Name by DJ Quik
Release date: January 15, 1991
Certified gold: May 30, 1991
Certified platinum: July 26, 1995

New Jack City soundtrack
Release date: March 5, 1991
Certified gold: May 24, 1991
Certified platinum: May 24, 1991

O.G. Original Gangster by Ice-T
Release date: May 14, 1991
Certified gold: July 24, 1991

Efil4Zaggin by N.W.A
Release date: May 29, 1991
Certified gold: August 8, 1991
Certified platinum: August 8, 1991

We Can't Be Stopped by the Geto Boys
Release date: June 29, 1991
Certified gold: September 11, 1991
Certified platinum: February 26, 1992

Boyz N the Hood soundtrack
Release date: July 9, 1991
Certified gold: September 12, 1991

Cypress Hill by Cypress Hill
Release date: August 9, 1991
Certified gold: March 26, 1992
Certified platinum: January 5, 1993
Certified double platinum: May 30, 2000

Mr. Scarface Is Back by Scarface
Release date: October 1, 1991
Certified gold: April 23, 1993

Death Certificate by Ice Cube
Release date: October 21, 1991
Certified gold: December 20, 1991
Certified platinum: December 20, 1991

2Pacalypse Now by 2Pac
Release date: October 28, 1991
Certified gold: April 19, 1995

Juice soundtrack
Release date: December 31, 1991
Certified gold: March 4, 1992

NON–GANGSTER RAP ALBUMS

De La Soul Is Dead by De La Soul
Release date: May 14, 1991
Certified gold: July 18, 1991

**Homebase by D.J. Jazzy Jeff
& The Fresh Prince**
Release date: July 9, 1991
Certified gold: September 19, 1991
Certified platinum: September 19, 1991

A Wolf in Sheep's Clothing by Black Sheep
Release date: August 6, 1991
Certified gold: April 3, 1992

Naughty by Nature by Naughty by Nature
Release date: September 3, 1991
Certified gold: November 13, 1991
Certified platinum: February 6, 1992

**Sports Weekend (As Nasty as They Wanna
Be Part II) by 2 Live Crew**
Release date: September 23, 1991
Certified gold: April 16, 1992

**The Low End Theory by A Tribe
Called Quest**
Release date: September 24, 1991
Certified gold: February 19, 1992
Certified platinum: February 1, 1995

**Apocalypse 91...The Enemy Strikes Black
by Public Enemy**
Release date: September 27, 1991
Certified gold: November 26, 1991
Certified platinum: November 26, 1991

Bitch Betta Have My Money by AMG
Release date: September 30, 1991
Certified gold: September 28, 1994

Too Legit to Quit by Hammer
Release date: October 28, 1991
Certified gold: January 8, 1992
Certified triple platinum: January 8, 1992

in the thirties, and by the commercial and critical success of such high-profile seventies and eighties films as *The French Connection*, *The Godfather*, *Scarface*, and *Once Upon a Time in America*, among others. But the leading personalities and characters in those organizations and in those films weren't black. *New Jack City*'s success, however, showed that there was a desire to see black characters on both sides of the law in major motion pictures.

Similarly, the success of N.W.A's *Efil4Zaggin* album ("Niggaz 4 Life" spelled backward) demonstrated that the audience for gangster rap was even larger than almost anyone realized. Released on May 28, 1991, the second studio album from N.W.A was its first without Ice Cube (following their extended play project *100 Miles And Runnin'*).

N.W.A, however, was not so courteous on *Efil4Zaggin*. On lead single "Alwayz Into Somethin'," Dr. Dre rapped about going to pick up MC Ren. Dre then hears gunshots, sees someone hopping a fence, and then MC Ren jumps into his Mercedes-Benz. Dre recounts Ren's statement to him.

"Dre, I was speakin' to yo' bitch O'Shea"

O'Shea Jackson is Ice Cube's given name, so in addition to calling Ice Cube Dre's bitch, it is implied that MC Ren had just finished shooting Ice Cube. That wasn't the worst of *Efil4Zaggin*'s Ice Cube bashing, though. In the interlude of the next track of the collection, "Message to B.A.," a series of phone messages are played in which Ice Cube is dissed for not being from Compton (Ice Cube is from South Central Los Angeles but rapped on "Straight Outta Compton") and for jumping on the East Coast rap bandwagon (Ice Cube worked with New York–based producers the Bomb Squad on *AmeriKKKa's Most Wanted*), among other slights. Then MC Ren says: "Yeah, nigga. When we see yo' ass, we gon' cut your hair off and fuck you wit' a broomstick."

With *Efil4Zaggin*, N.W.A was making good on Dr. Dre's 1989 edict to be more violent, more confrontational, and more outrageous than they had been on *Straight Outta Compton*. Just on song titles alone, N.W.A had ratcheted up its potential offensiveness. "Real Niggaz Don't Die," "Niggaz 4 Life," "Real Niggaz," "To Kill a Hooker," "One Less Bitch," "Findum, Fuckum & Flee," and "I'd Rather Fuck You" took sex, violence, and the use of the word *nigga*, and its various incarnations, to new rap levels thanks to Dr. Dre and DJ Yella's searing production and the profanity-saturated lyrics of MC Ren, Eazy-E, and Dr. Dre. There was also "She Swallowed It," the group's sequel to *100 Miles And Runnin'* track "Just Don't Bite It." Both selections were tributes to receiving oral sex that contained instructions for women on how to properly perform fellatio on a man.

Efil4Zaggin may have been lacking the political bite of Ice Cube's *AmeriKKKa's Most Wanted*, but N.W.A's fan base flocked in droves to the record stores to purchase the group's second (and what would be final) studio album. *Efil4Zaggin* entered the Billboard charts as the No. 2 album in the country. The next week, the project made history.

For the first forty-five years of the Billboard charts, album sales were reported on an honor system in which record stores and DJs would name the most popular artists at that time. Naturally, personal whims, biases, and payola likely influenced who a record store representative reported as being popular. But thanks to the advent of SoundScan, which tracked sales by a project's UPC, or bar code, for the first time, tallies from retail outlets became the driving force in creating Billboard charts. Gangster rap wasted no time in showing its power.

On the June 22, 1991, chart, the new Billboard sales system using SoundScan was employed. The No. 1 album in the country during that sales week: N.W.A's *Efil4Zaggin*, becoming the first No. 1 album in the SoundScan era and the first gangster rap album to earn the No. 1 slot on the Billboard 200 chart. By simply measuring the actual sales of albums, N.W.A rose on the charts and outsold every other album in the country, including rock group R.E.M.'s smash *Out of Time* album, which held the No. 1 spot under the old chart system. The popularity of gangster rap was now quantified and verified.

Released on Eazy-E's Ruthless Records/Priority Records, N.W.A's *Efil4Zaggin* showed that independent gangster rap was the bestselling and fastest-selling music in the country.

YO! MTV RAPS = PLATINUM

DJ Quik's first album, 1991's *Quik Is the Name*, sold more than one million copies. He credits the exposure his videos got on *Yo! MTV Raps* for making his collection a brisk seller. "I don't believe for a moment that my debut record would have gone platinum as soon as it did without MTV," DJ Quik said. "At that point, MTV was like Twitter is now to music and to culture. At that time, they were the be all[, end all] in media. That was it."

Soon thereafter, Priority Records enjoyed another breakthrough success. After a messy divorce from Rick Rubin's Def American Recordings and parent company Geffen Records, Rap-A-Lot Records signed a deal to partner with Priority Records for its releases. All was not well with the Geto Boys, however. During a drug- and alcohol-fueled argument with his girlfriend on June 19, 1991, Bushwick Bill begged her to shoot and kill him. She did her best, shooting the rapper in his right eye.

Ever the shrewd businessman, label owner James "J." Prince turned tragedy into triumph. J. Prince had a picture taken of Bushwick Bill on a gurney with fellow Geto Boys members Willie D and Scarface flanking him in a hospital hallway. Bushwick Bill had just emerged from surgery and the graphic image showed his exposed, blood-stained, and severely damaged eye. J. Prince used the image as the cover art of the Geto Boys' next album—their first with Priority Records—1991's *We Can't Be Stopped*.

Released on July 2, 1991, *We Can't Be Stopped* was quickly certified platinum with sales in excess of one million copies. The album also spawned the hit single "Mind Playing Tricks on Me," which became a mainstay on MTV. Scarface's opening lines, which incorporated some of his lyrics from the group's gruesome "Mind of a Lunatic," set the stage for the group's song about paranoia, doubt, and depression. "Mind Playing Tricks on Me" ended up being the Geto Boys' most popular song. Its success, and that of *We Can't Be Stopped* as a whole, again showed that the Geto Boys and gangster rappers could be commercial juggernauts on their own terms.

As gangster rap was finally getting the chart recognition it deserved, it was about to hit another major milestone in film with *Boyz N the Hood*. Released on July 12, 1991, the movie, which stars Ice Cube, Cuba Gooding Jr., and Laurence Fishburne, follows the lives of three young men (an athlete, a scholar, and a gang member) growing up in South Central Los Angeles. The gritty film showed how gangs, guns, and drugs were ravaging Los Angeles, ending the lives of innocents and criminals alike.

Like *New Jack City* before it, *Boyz N the Hood* was a commercial and critical success. It hit No. 3 at the box office, grossing $57 million against a $6.5 million budget, and was nominated for two Academy Awards. John Singleton became the youngest director and the first black person to be nominated for the Academy Award for Best Director. Singleton was also nominated for Best Writing (Screenplay Written Directly for the Screen) for his script.

The *Boyz N the Hood* soundtrack was buoyed by the Ice Cube single "How to Survive in South Central" and the breakthrough single "Growin' Up in the Hood" by Compton's Most Wanted. On the latter, group member MC Eiht rapped in the first person about his exploits growing up with an emotionally distant mother, getting incarcerated, getting released, witnessing the shootings of his brother and mother, and killing the guys who shot his family. Fellow Compton's Most Wanted rapper Tha Chill focused his verses on how the police were trying to arrest him and the community wanted him to set up his drug-dealing business elsewhere. Unlike MC Eiht, though, Tha Chill ends up dead at the end of "Growin' Up in the Hood." The song's visual storytelling style and poignant lyrics showing the pain and struggle of living in the black Los Angeles ghetto resonated with fans. The *Boyz N the Hood* soundtrack went on to sell more than five hundred thousand copies, qualifying it for a gold certification.

"Growin' Up in the Hood" was also featured on Compton's Most Wanted's *Straight Checkn 'Em*, their second studio album. The album arrived in stores on July 16, four days after *Boyz N the Hood* became a box-office sensation.

With the success of King Tee, Eazy-E, N.W.A, DJ Quik, and Compton's Most Wanted, Compton had become one of the most exciting cities in rap. The emergence of DJ Quik and Compton's Most Wanted also showed that the second wave of Compton gangster rap had already arrived.

Gangster rap's next breakthrough and subgenre came from Cypress Hill. The Los Angeles–based trio of rappers, including B-Real and Sen Dog and producer DJ Muggs, was significant for several reasons. For one, none of the members were black Americans. B-Real had a Mexican father and a Cuban mother, while Sen Dog was of Cuban heritage, and DJ Muggs was a New Yorker of Italian and Cuban descent. The group also added a distinctive wrinkle to this brand of hardcore rap, making their affinity for marijuana a hallmark of their music. Cypress Hill's self-titled album was released on August 13, 1991, and featured the pro-weed songs "Light Another," "Stoned Is the Way of the Walk," and "Something for the Blunted," while also championing the group's heritage ("Latin Lingo," "Tres Equis"), their disdain for crooked police ("Pigs"), and their gangster, gun-toting ways ("How I Could Just Kill a Man" [the video featured a cameo from Ice Cube], "Hand on the Pump," "Hole in the Head").

The Geto Boys' Scarface also made gunplay a focal point of his debut solo album, *Mr. Scarface Is Back*. Released on October 1, 1991, the project featured a deep dive into the Houston rapper's murderous mentality. "Mr. Scarface," "Born Killer," and "Murder by Reason of Insanity" detailed Scarface's gruff and violent personality, while "Good Girl Gone Bad" and "A Minute to Pray and a Second to Die" showed his introspective side, framing passionate stories of deceit and revenge against the backdrop of drugs and homicide.

As Scarface was separating himself as the standout rapper of the Geto Boys, Ice Cube made one of the most powerful statements in rap to that point with his conceptually rich *Death Certificate* album, which examined the mental and physical status of blacks in America. The searing collection concludes with "No Vaseline," widely regarded as one of the most potent diss songs in rap history. Ice Cube employed a tactic on "No Vaseline" similar to the one he used on the *AmeriKKKa's Most Wanted* cut "The Nigga Ya Love to Hate," which featured a chorus of people chanting "Fuck you, Ice Cube!" In that instance, he was empowering himself by dissing himself. On "No Vaseline," however, he was about to turn that idea on its head.

Ice Cube starts the song off by playing portions of his work with N.W.A and Eazy-E (including Eazy-E rapping, "Ice Cube writes the rhymes that I say" on "The Boyz-N-The Hood"), as well as the *Efil4Zaggin* cut "Message to B.A." Ice Cube flipped the script, though, by mimicking "Message to B.A." and including sound bites of people dissing Dr. Dre and DJ Yella in particular and N.W.A in general, saying they "ain't shit without Ice Cube."

It's the first verse on "No Vaseline," though, where Ice Cube took rap disses to a new level. He clowns the crew for working with R&B singer Michel'le, who was also Dr. Dre's girlfriend at the time, and for moving out of Compton to a white neighborhood. Ice Cube dismisses DJ Yella's production skills and says Dr. Dre should leave rapping alone and stick to producing. He then accuses Eazy-E of raping Dr. Dre—likely meant to represent the idea that Eazy-E wasn't paying Dr. Dre what he was worth, as was the case with Eazy-E and Ice Cube before Ice Cube's departure from the group.

The second verse is equally arresting. Ice Cube says Eazy-E is financially and literally screwing MC Ren. He then alludes to MC Ren's threat on *Efil4Zaggin*'s "Message to B.A.," that N.W.A was "gon' cut your hair off and fuck you wit' a broomstick."

NEW YORK & CALIFORNIA SENSIBILITIES CLASH

DJ QUIK PROTÉGÉS 2nd II None (Gangsta D and KK) enraged rap purists when they said on *Yo! MTV Raps* that they didn't freestyle. This is an early example of what would be a huge rift between segments of East Coast and West Coast rappers (both DJ Quik and 2nd II None are from Compton), as the New Yorkers felt that the West Coast rappers weren't real MCs and didn't take the craft seriously.

COLLECTING ICE CUBE'S DEATH CERTIFICATES

AMIR RAHIMI DIDN'T just want one copy of Ice Cube's *Death Certificate* album. Instead, the music collector wanted every version of the album ever released. To date, Rahimi has twenty-eight different versions of the LP, and a total of forty-four items related to the LP, which was originally released in 1991.

Rahimi, who started collecting in 2004, when he was twelve, believes *Death Certificate* is the best rap album of all time, that it contains the greatest diss song of all time in "No Vaseline," and that it shows Ice Cube's brilliance as an artist because, among other things, "Color Blind" is the only song on the entire album that features other artists.

"*Death Certificate* features an Ice Cube in his prime talking about a wide range of topics, including, but not limited to, racism, gangs, drugs, STDs, self-improvement," said Rahimi, founder of the Rappin' and Snackin' website.

The Southern California resident, who became obsessed with rap when his friend burned him copies of 2Pac's *Me Against the World* and *Loyal to the Game* albums, looks for new versions of *Death Certificate* in a variety of ways. He asks friends online that have versions he hasn't seen. He checks #DeathCertificate on Instagram, especially around the anniversary of the album's release. He also regularly searches Discogs, an online music database and marketplace.

Among his most cherished editions of *Death Certificate* are a Japanese edition with an obi strip, and a Russian version that features Russian words above the parental advisory label. His favorite, though, is an original pressing of the vinyl version of the album, which is sealed and in mint condition. Rahimi said the album could fetch between $50 and $75.

"For over twenty-five years, it's stayed perfect," Rahimi said. "It's like you picked it off the rack at the store today."

The broomstick fit your ass so perfect / Cut my hair? Naw, cut them balls / 'Cause I heard you like giving up the draws / Gangbanged by your manager, fella

Ice Cube's onslaught continued, saying that N.W.A let a "Jew," ostensibly Jerry Heller, break up his crew in a classic case of divide and conquer.

Eazy-E was Ice Cube's next "No Vaseline" target. In addition to calling him a "house nigga," "half-pint bitch" (Eazy-E was reportedly 5'5"), and a "faggot," he advocated hanging Eazy-E from a tree and lighting him and his Jheri curl on fire.

Ice Cube's rhymes about Jerry Heller were equally sinister.

Get rid of that Devil real simple / Put a bullet in his temple / 'Cause you can't be the Nigga 4 Life crew / With a white Jew telling you what to do

In his memoir fifteen years later, Heller wrote that he was fed up with Ice Cube's disses, which included interviews as well as songs. "I'm tired of your slurs," Heller wrote. "It makes me sick that you exploit the anti-Semitism rampant in the world today just to justify yourself."

In 2015, Ice Cube said he regretted using anti-Jewish language on "No Vaseline." "I didn't know what 'anti-Semitic' meant, until motherfuckers explained why it was just not okay to lump Jerry with anybody cool," Ice Cube said. "But I wasn't like, 'I wanna hurt the whole Jewish race.' I just don't like that motherfucker."

N.W.A, though, did not respond to "No Vaseline." As the last cut on *Death Certificate*, it was an explosive and incongruous end to an album simmering with social commentary and insightful looks at how the American system was failing its black population. "My Summer Vacation" provides a look at how gangs, drugs, and the respective cultures surrounding them spread from Los Angeles to the Midwest. On "A Bird in the Hand," Ice Cube tells the story of a high school graduate and father who, despite earning great grades, doesn't have money for college and doesn't land a job he wanted at AT&T. He ends up working at McDonald's and decides that, given the options he sees for himself, his best course of action is to sell drugs to support his family.

With "Alive on Arrival," Ice Cube raps about going to the hospital with a gunshot wound, being forced to fill out paperwork, getting handcuffed and interrogated by police about the shooting, and waiting more than an hour to be seen by an overworked physician before eventually dying handcuffed to the bed. The death of the "Alive on Arrival" protagonist leads into "Death," the end of the Death Side of *Death Certificate*. The second side, or the Life Side, opens with "The Birth," a signal for the rebirth and the resurrection of the black community.

"I Wanna Kill Sam" features Ice Cube imagining killing Uncle Sam because of the racist and oppressive American system he has created and sustains, while

"Black Korea" lamented black customers being followed and harassed in stores. At the end of the song, Ice Cube said that these types of store owners needed to respect their black patrons. Otherwise, they'd face either a boycott or their businesses burning to the ground. The song was likely inspired, at least in part, by the shooting of Latasha Harlins, a fifteen-year-old black girl who was shot and killed in Los Angeles by Soon Ja Du, a female convenience store owner from South Korea who thought Harlins was attempting to steal a bottle of orange juice from the store. After a physical altercation with Du, Harlins put the juice on the counter and attempted to leave the store. Du shot Harlins in the back of the head, killing her instantly. Du was convicted of voluntary manslaughter and sentenced to five years of probation, four hundred hours of community service, and a five-hundred-dollar fine.

Ice Cube and guest rappers Threat, Kam, WC, Coolio, King Tee, and the Lench Mob's J-Dee also take sobering looks at living the life of a gangbanger on "Color Blind," while Ice Cube points the finger at black America for contributing to its problems on "Us." He cites jealousy, envy, and backstabbing as systemic and crippling issues in the black community. Rather than glorify drug-dealing, Ice Cube condemns the trade, likening drug dealers to the police (they both kill black people in the neighborhood) and blasting them for buying Cadillacs without investing in improving the community.

> *"I'm tired of your slurs. It makes me sick that you exploit the anti-Semitism rampant in the world today just to justify yourself."*
>
> **JERRY HELLER TO ICE CUBE**

> *Exploitin' us like the Caucasians did / For four hundred years, I got four hundred tears / For four hundred peers / Died last year from gang-related crimes / That's why I got gang-related rhymes*

Released on October 29, 1992, Ice Cube's *Death Certificate* album debuted at No. 2 on the Billboard charts, cementing his status as one of rap's most significant and popular artists.

Less than a month later, on November 12, 1992, former Digital Underground dancer and roadie 2Pac released his debut album, *2Pacalypse Now*. 2Pac's album was filled with songs and lyrics about killing police officers, being there for his

OTHER NOTEWORTHY 1991 LPs

Make Way for the Motherlode **by Yo-Yo (March 19).**
The debut album from Ice Cube's female protégé
contained a number of no-nonsense female
empowerment lyrics.

Addictive Hip Hop Muzick **by Who Am I? (July 2).**
The Eazy-E-backed debut album from rapper-singer
Kokane introduced another talented member of
the Ruthless Records roster. He went by Who Am
I? because major label Epic Records didn't want to
release an album by an artist named Kokane.

Vocally Pimpin' **by Above the Law (July 16).** This EP
and its 1992 follow-up, *Black Mafia Life*, laid the sonic
foundation for Dr. Dre's *The Chronic*.

MC Breed & DFC **by MC Breed and DFC (August 13).**
The Flint, Michigan, crew scored a funk-driven hit
with "Ain't No Future in Yo' Frontin'."

Ain't a Damn Thang Changed **by WC and the Maad
Circle (September 17).** Formerly one-half of Low
Profile, WC returned with his new crew, the Maad
Circle. Members included Coolio and WC's late
brother and DJ, Crazy Toones, among others.

A Wolf in Sheep's Clothing **by Black Sheep (October 22).**
The debut album from the New York duo of Dres and
Mista Lawnge contained "U Mean I'm Not," a gangster
rap parody in which a school-aged Dres imagines
himself shooting his sister because she used his
toothbrush, his mother because she messed up his
egg breakfast, and his father after he protested the
events. As he exits his house, Dres cuts the mailman's
throat and then waits for the school bus.

Bitch Betta Have My Money **by AMG (December 3).**
The DJ Quik affiliate delivered a series of clever,
sexually slanted rhymes over funk-drenched beats.

friends at all costs, feeling trapped in the corrupt American justice system, and the far-reaching fallout of preteen pregnancies. Although 2Pac would soon become one of rap's most iconic figures, *2Pacalypse Now* did not gain a large audience, taking three and a half years to go gold.

Also released on November 12 was the first anti–West Coast gangster rap album, Tim Dog's *Penicillin on Wax*. Rather than celebrating the culture, the Bronx, New York–based Ultramagnetic MCs affiliate spent much of the album disparaging gangster rap, particularly the West coast side of it. With "Fuck Compton," Tim Dog dissed the city itself in addition to taking digs at Eazy-E, Ice Cube, and N.W.A. He also boasted of having sex with Michel'le, Dr. Dre's then-fiancée. But Tim Dog took things even further by dissing the West Coast's entire gang culture.

Having that gang war / We want to know what you're fighting for / Fighting over colors? / All that gang shit's for dumb motherfuckers / But you go on thinking you're hard / Come to New York and we'll see who gets robbed

The rest of *Penicillin on Wax* included disses of DJ Quik ("DJ Quick Beat Down"), a talk about dissing Dr. Dre with a Michel'le impersonator ("Michel'le Conversation"), and a song that hinted at the reason Tim Dog may have made "Fuck Compton" and taken his aggressive anti-Compton stance ("I Ain't Havin' It").

Although Ice Cube had collaborated with Public Enemy on *Fear of a Black Planet* and worked with the Bomb Squad on his *AmeriKKKa's Most Wanted*, there was a growing, unspoken tension between artists from the East Coast and artists from the West Coast. Rap started in New York, and for the first time in the genre's history, rappers from the West Coast were the ones selling more records, garnering more media attention, and shaping the culture more than their East Coast contemporaries. It's a phenomenon that got its start with Eazy-E and N.W.A in 1989 and avalanched in 1991 thanks to the commercial success of DJ Quik, N.W.A, Ice-T, Compton's Most Wanted, Cypress Hill, and Ice Cube.

Furthermore, the success of *New Jack City* and *Boyz N the Hood*, as well as the 1990 comedy *House Party* starring lighthearted rap duo Kid 'n Play, ushered in a new era of black cinema, the likes of which had not seen been since blaxploitation.

The year in rap—which concluded with the December 31 release of the soundtrack for *Juice*, the film starring 2Pac in his breakthrough role—had been defined by the expansion and intensification of gangster rap. DJ Quik blended good times, menace, and musicianship in his work, while Ice-T's insightful rhymes and a powerful screen performance showed how the genre's pioneers could achieve longevity. N.W.A took the music to dark, savage places, while Compton's

Most Wanted provided a street-level reporting perspective. Cypress Hill rapped about Los Angeles's drugs, gangs, police, and crime from a Latin perspective, while Ice Cube crystallized the experience of blacks living in the ghettos of America. 2Pac also railed against the American system from a position of outrage and vengeance, while Tim Dog showed that a rift was emerging between New York and Los Angeles artists.

While all these events were significant in their own rights, they were recognized primarily within the emerging rap community and not in the larger musical or cultural scene. Gangster rap's next milestone, however, took the genre to a new place: true mainstream acceptance from the media, radio, and television.

California Dreamin':
The Aftermath

OPPOSITE:
Snoop Dogg (left) and Dr. Dre perform at an N.W.A reunion concert in Los Angeles in March 2000.

During the next few years, material by Eazy-E, the Geto Boys, 2Pac, and others had also decried police brutality and had become fodder for politicians coast to coast. Then, in 1992, President George H. W. Bush said Ice-T's "Cop Killer" with his metal band Body Count was "sick," Vice President Dan Quayle labeled it "obscene," and sixty members of congress deemed it "vile" and "despicable" in a signed letter.

At the same time, one of gangster rap's chief laments made headlines around the world, giving credence to even the most incendiary work of any rap act. Once the acquittal of the four Los Angeles Police Department officers who were video-taped beating unarmed black motorist Rodney King was announced on April 29, 1992, the world saw that the claims gangster rappers made in their music

1992
Key Rap Releases

1. Dr. Dre's *The Chronic* album

2. Das EFX's *Dead Serious* album

3. House Of Pain's "Jump Around" single

US President

George H.W. Bush

Something Else

The European Union (EU) was formed by twelve countries.

were not overblown artistic ploys, as the government, critics, and special-interest groups had all alleged. Rather, the not-guilty verdict was evidence that the reality in black urban America was as sobering and deplorable as rappers proclaimed it to be.

After news of the King verdict spread, Los Angeles erupted into riots, the scale of which had not been seen since the Watts riots in the sixties. Five days of riots rocked the region, leaving sixty-four people dead and more than two thousand injured, and much of the carnage was broadcast live on television. Even though more than 9,800 California National Guard troops were called up to help quell the riots, the ensuing destruction was estimated to top $1 billion, with more than one thousand buildings reportedly damaged during the uprising.

In one fell swoop, the world finally got to see the injustice Ice-T, Eazy-E, N.W.A, the Geto Boys, 2Pac (who filed a 1991 lawsuit against the Oakland PD for police brutality), and others had been rapping about, from the brutal beating of King to the officers getting away with nearly killing him. It was as if one of the stories from a gangster rap album had come to life, although there was no redemption, no measure of satisfaction or revenge enjoyed by the victim in this story. Instead, a black man had been savagely beaten and many of the black neighborhoods of Los Angeles were set ablaze, looted, and destroyed by residents seething in the aftermath of what was seen as yet another case of unchecked police brutality on African Americans.

As the world at large reacted with shock and awe at both the verdict and the ensuing destruction, rap was about to get a musical makeover. N.W.A and Ice Cube had released two of rap's most important albums, *Efil4Zaggin* and *Death Certificate*, respectively, in 1991. N.W.A had also proven that they could thrive without Ice Cube in the fold, as they became the first act to have the No. 1 album in the country in the SoundScan era with *Efil4Zaggin*. But N.W.A had lost a key ingredient with Ice Cube's departure: his unparalleled blend of storytelling, street reporting, and social commentary. The group retained their rage, but they lost much of their poetic perspective. As N.W.A writer and collaborator the D.O.C. said, the group lost their spirit once Ice Cube departed.

Ice Cube, on the other hand, had shown that he remained sharp lyrically, conceptually, and commercially, as *Death Certificate* debuted at No. 2 on the Billboard charts. He had gone from a member of rap's most popular group to, arguably, the best, most popular, and most respected artist in the genre.

Both *Efil4Zaggin* and *Death Certificate* were sonically searing affairs, projects whose aggressive sounds and ribald rhymes made for aural powder kegs, presentations that were both scintillating and stimulating. Each album also sold more than one million copies within weeks, showing that gangster rap was the genre's most popular and dominant form.

While Ice Cube's star was on the rise as a recording artist and actor, thanks to his sophomore album and his acclaimed role in the Academy Award–nominated film *Boyz N the Hood*, Ruthless Records was about to endure its second major loss. Like Ice Cube before him, Dr. Dre left Eazy-E and Ruthless Records over a financial dispute. It was a crushing blow.

Ruthless Records was Eazy-E's company, and he was its mastermind, but Dr. Dre (with significant help from regular production partner DJ Yella) was its musical backbone, the overlord of the label's sound, the go-to producer for Eazy-E, N.W.A, J.J. Fad, the D.O.C., Michel'le, and Above the Law. Dr. Dre felt he was being underpaid, especially given the pivotal role he played as either producer or coproducer of virtually every Ruthless Records project prior to his departure. When Dr. Dre exited, Ruthless Records was without its best rapper (Ice Cube) and rap music's most bankable producer (Dr. Dre).

With the success of *100 Miles And Runnin'* and *Efil4Zaggin*, Ruthless Records showed that it could survive—even thrive—despite the departure of Ice Cube. But losing its in-house producer proved to be a significant and immediate blow. Subsequent releases from MC Ren and Eazy-E were not met with the same fanfare as either Eazy-E's *Eazy-Duz-It* album or N.W.A's previous projects, though they were still commercial successes. MC Ren's *Kizz My Black Azz* EP went platinum less than three months after its June 22, 1992, release, while Eazy-E's *5150: Home 4 tha Sick* EP went gold two months after its December 4, 1992, release.

BODY COUNT'S "COP KILLER": SHOOT THE MESSENGER

In 1992, Ice-T created a tidal wave of controversy with Body Count, his offshoot rock-and-roll group. The group's "Cop Killer" song, which Ice-T sang from the perspective of someone who kills police officers, was protested by police organizations and the National Rifle Association (NRA), among others. In the wake of the controversy and pressure from stock holders, Warner Bros. Records, parent company of Sire Records, which had released all of Ice-T's albums as well as Body Count's self-titled 1992 album, refused to release Ice-T's forthcoming rap album, *Home Invasion*. The Los Angeles rapper and Time Warner parted ways before the end of 1992.

Short for "extended play," an EP is usually less than thirty minutes long and typically costs more than a single but less than an album. It is also worth noting that EPs are counted differently than albums in terms of gold and platinum certifications. For an album to go gold, it needed to sell five hundred thousand units under the original SoundScan configuration. The requirement for an EP to go gold was two hundred and fifty thousand sales. For an album to go platinum, it needed to sell one million units. For an EP, the sales had to exceed five hundred thousand.

While still impressive in their own rights, the sales for MC Ren's and Eazy-E's EPs showed the relative lack of urgency fans had for purchasing Ruthless Records projects now that Dr. Dre was no longer in charge of the sonics.

As MC Ren and Eazy-E were busy promoting their respective 1992 projects, Dr. Dre spent the year preparing for his reintroduction to the music scene. Just as Ice Cube had done, his first move post–Ruthless Records was significant.

Dr. Dre returned to the music scene in 1992 with a menacing new business partner in Marion "Suge" Knight and the blockbuster single "Deep Cover," the title track for the Laurence Fishburne movie *Deep Cover*, which was released on April 15, 1992. In the film, Fishburne portrays a police officer who is recruited by the DEA to infiltrate a drug-smuggling operation.

On the song "Deep Cover," Dr. Dre raps about being a police officer going undercover. He also featured his new protégé, Snoop Doggy Dogg, an aspiring rapper and gangbanger who was friends with rapper-producer Warren G, who is Dr. Dre's stepbrother. On "Deep Cover," Snoop Dogg, as he's now known, raps about being a dealer who the cops want to turn into a snitch and exploit, though he ultimately refuses their overtures.

In the chorus, Snoop Dogg drops the phrase that made the song significant: "187 on an undercover cop." The call for a "187" denotes a murder in the California Penal Code. Dr. Dre had gone from N.W.A's "Fuck tha Police" to "Deep Cover," which detailed the murder of undercover police officers. The track's thunderous bass, menacing sounds, and mid-tempo speed combined for a stark departure from N.W.A's often riotous soundbeds.

Deep Cover director Bill Duke said that he wanted to work with Dr. Dre given his résumé, and that he was looking for a new sound and lyrics with meaning for the song's title track, a song that would augment and enrich the film. Duke said Dr. Dre's "Deep Cover" met all those requirements, and that Snoop Dogg's lyrics were—and remain—particularly poignant.

"I understood the feelings that he had, particularly at the time, because there were a lot of things going on in our streets where young men, particularly black

"COP KILLER" TIMELINE

1990. Body Count writes "Cop Killer" but doesn't record it.

Summer 1991. Body Count performs their "Cop Killer" song to little fanfare during the national Lollapalooza tour.

Fall/Winter 1991. Body Count records their self-titled debut album, including "Cop Killer."

March 1992. Body Count releases their eponymous album.

June 1992. Vice President Dan Quayle calls the song "obscene." A week later, President George H. W. Bush says it is "sick" to make music glorifying the killing of police officers; Combined Law Enforcement Associations of Texas (CLEAT) calls for a boycott of all Time Warner Inc. products because of "Cop Killer"; Time Warner co-CEO Gerald M. Levin writes an editorial in the *Wall Street Journal* defending the release of "Cop Killer."

July 1992. Actor Charlton Heston reads some of the lyrics to "Cop Killer" and "KKK Bitch," also from the Body Count album, at the Time Warner Inc. shareholders meeting, saying that he condemns the officials responsible for releasing Body Count's album.

August 1992. Body Count's self-titled album is certified gold, with more than five hundred thousand units sold; More than one thousand record stores pull the Body Count album from their shelves.

January 1993. Time Warner Inc. subsidiary Warner Bros. Records announces that Ice-T and Body Count have been released from their respective contracts with the label.

men, were being killed," Bill Duke said. "And there are unfortunate parallels to today. Some things have changed, some things have not. But those guys represented a voice at that time, of the street and the frustration of the street at that particular time. It was something that I think fit well with the film."

With one song, Dr. Dre had effectively distanced himself from Eazy-E and Ruthless Records and established himself as a viable solo artist with a new protégé in tow. Similar to what Ice Cube had done with *AmeriKKKa's Most Wanted*, "Deep Cover" signaled a rebirth for Dr. Dre, a new beginning with a new crew. Ice Cube had the Lench Mob post–Ruthless Records. For Dr. Dre, it was Death Row Records.

Dr. Dre's partner at Death Row Records was former security guard Suge Knight, who was also close with and the manager of the D.O.C., Dr. Dre's long-time friend and collaborator from Ruthless Records' early days. Having Knight and the D.O.C. in his corner was one of the reasons Dr. Dre was willing and able to leave Ruthless Records.

Death Row needed clearance for Dr. Dre to be able to work, as he was still technically signed to Eazy-E's Ruthless Records. Unlike Ice Cube, Dr. Dre had signed a contract with the company and was still obligated to record for the imprint. Knight decided Dr. Dre, the D.O.C., and Michel'le no longer needed to be bound by their Ruthless Records contracts and set up a meeting in late 1991 where he either threatened (according to a forthcoming lawsuit) or had his henchmen beat up Eazy-E (as depicted in the 2015 film *Straight Outta Compton*). Either way, Eazy-E agreed that night to release Dr. Dre, the D.O.C., and Michel'le from their Ruthless Records deals.

In October 1992, Eazy-E sued Sony Music Entertainment, Death Row Records, Solar Records, and others for racketeering, extortion, and money laundering. The suit alleged that Eazy-E signed the agreement under duress when he was confronted by Knight and a cadre of baseball bat–wielding thugs. Sony Music, which released the *Deep Cover* soundtrack in conjunction with Solar Records, was set to sign Death Row Records and initially backed Solar Records and Death Row Records publicly in the Eazy-E lawsuit.

"Launching a lawsuit with a publicity campaign is a clear indication that the plaintiffs are pursuing an agenda other than the legal adjudication of their claim," Sony said in an October 15, 1992, statement. "As far as we are concerned, we look forward to a full and fair review of the facts. . . . We are confident that Sony Music executives acted at all times lawfully, ethically, and with sound business judgment."

But Sony quickly reneged on its potential partnership with Death Row Records. However, the fledgling label rebounded nicely.

Thanks to Dr. Dre's impeccable musical pedigree and remarkable sales history, Death Row Records found a significant business partner in Jimmy Iovine, producer for John Lennon, Stevie Nicks, Tom Petty, and others. Iovine and partner Ted Field had launched their Interscope Records company in 1990 and had enjoyed success with rock bands Primus and Helmet; ska group No Doubt; and pop rappers Gerardo and Marky Mark and the Funky Bunch. Thus, Iovine supplied Death Row with something Ruthless didn't have: a true music industry power-broker backing the business. Jerry Heller knew the business. Jimmy Iovine, by comparison, *was* the business.

Despite their respective successes at the time, Death Row and Interscope were both in need of a partnership. Death Row was mired in the aftermath of its Ruthless Records lawsuit, while Interscope was enjoying hits but not enough success to sustain itself.

Given Dr. Dre's muddied contractual status, Priority Records, Ruthless Records' partner for N.W.A material, worked out a deal in which Priority would distribute Dr. Dre's forthcoming debut album. Also, as part of the settlement from the lawsuit he filed against Death Row Records, Eazy-E would get paid from Dr. Dre's forthcoming record sales, a fact that made Dr. Dre's departure a bit less painful for Eazy-E.

"I had Dre signed as an exclusive producer and exclusive artist," Eazy-E said during a 1993 interview on *The Arsenio Hall Show*. "So when Dre tried to make his deal over at Interscope, I was included for the next six years."

Eazy-E's business acumen was again on display, as he was rewarded handsomely as part of Dr. Dre's debut album, *The Chronic*. Released on December 15, 1992, *The Chronic* was an artistic milestone and a commercial juggernaut, selling more than three million copies in a year. It also changed the sound and the direction of rap as a whole, and gangster rap in particular.

JIMMY IOVINE: ROCK AND RAP RINGMASTER

After twenty years of working with some of the biggest names in rock (John Lennon, Bruce Springsteen, Patti Smith, Stevie Nicks) as a recording engineer and producer, Jimmy Iovine founded Interscope Records in 1990. In 1992, he partnered with Dr. Dre and established a relationship with the rapper-producer that continues today. Through their partnership, they've released albums from such artists as Snoop Dogg, Eminem, 50 Cent, and Kendrick Lamar. Outside of their music relationship, they also partnered on Beats Electronics.

DR. DRE'S *THE CHRONIC* may have been the most popular weed-related rap project, but several other rappers also made marijuana a major part of their respective brands prior to the arrival of *The Chronic*. Philadelphia's Schoolly D rapped about smoking weed in 1985 on his landmark gangster rap single "P.S.K. What Does It Mean?" and named his 1988 album *Smoke Some Kill*. During the next decade, rap's relationship with marijuana blossomed. Better known for his pop hits "Wild Thing" and "Funky Cold Medina," Los Angeles rapper Tone Lōc had the weed song "Cheeba Cheeba" on his 1989 album, *Lōc-ed After Dark*. In 1991, DJ Quik and Cypress Hill made ganja a focus of some of their music. Compton's DJ Quik dedicated "Tha Bombudd," a reggae-inspired cut from his platinum 1991 album, *Quik Is the Name*, to his affinity for marijuana. Los Angeles's Cypress Hill made weed a focus of several songs on their eponymous debut album. "Ultraviolet Dreams" was an interlude that championed smoking, while "Light Another" celebrated getting high. "Stoned Is the Way of the Walk" and "Something for the Blunted" contained similar themes. The latter also featured a sample of Schoolly D celebrating cheeba on his 1986 single "Saturday Night." In 1992, Newark, New Jersey, rapper Redman delivered instructions for joint preparation with "How to Roll a Blunt." A year later, Dr. Dre named his debut album, 1992's *The Chronic*, after particularly potent marijuana.

Prior to *The Chronic*, gangster rap—and a lot of other popular rap at the time, from Public Enemy and Redman to Das EFX and Ice Cube—was typically some combination of aggressive, loud, and angry.

The Chronic changed rap's sound with its funk-inspired production. EPMD, Eazy-E, N.W.A, Ice Cube, MC Breed, and others had used funk music in their work prior to *The Chronic*, but they used the hard-hitting claps, the aggressive synthesizers, and the heavy, muddy bass as the foundation for their own sonic platters. Dr. Dre, on the other hand, crafted laid-back soundscapes that borrowed from the same batch of artists (including George Clinton aka Parliament or Funkadelic) as EPMD, Eazy-E, and Ice Cube, but he flipped the sound into something less abrasive and more digestible to the average consumer. Unlike much of the rest of gangster rap, which was rugged, several of the key songs on *The Chronic* were smooth, almost inviting.

Similarly, Dr. Dre had traded the gruff, menacing type of delivery he flexed on much of N.W.A's material for an almost sanguine style, a delivery that was still muscular and powerful, but much less aggressive. For his part, Snoop Doggy Dogg, who appeared on more than half of *The Chronic*'s fifteen songs, rapped in a silky style that had lost the angst he'd displayed on "Deep Cover."

One such track was the lead single, "Nuthin' But a 'G' Thang." The song, which builds its groove off Leon Haywood's "I Want'a Do Something Freaky to You," arrived with a chilled-out sonic sound, ditching the menace of the ghetto streets and swapping that type of presentation for the feel-good vibes of a summer barbecue. (Maybe not coincidentally, the "Nuthin' But a 'G' Thang" video featured Dr. Dre, Snoop Dogg, the D.O.C, and the rest of the Death Row Records crew at a barbecue, but one where the grill masters prepared food with guns in their waistbands and women got their tops pulled off while playing volleyball.) It all set the scene of a family environment, but one where women and weed were in abundance, as was the threat of potential life-ending violence.

The new sound was so starkly different, so mesmerizing, that it was instantly recognized as a line of sonic demarcation. "We made records during the crack era, [when] everything was hyped up, sped up, and zoned out," Public Enemy's Chuck D said. "Dre came with "'G" Thang' and slowed the whole genre down. He took hip-hop from the crack era to the weed era."

From the title of *The Chronic*, itself a reference to potent weed, to Dr. Dre imploring listeners "take a toke, but don't choke," marijuana references were part and parcel of this album. Snoop Dogg peppered his lyrics with pimp and sex rhymes, while Dr. Dre ends "Nuthin' But a 'G' Thang" with a verse where he disses Ice Cube ("Mobbin' like a motherfucker, but I ain't lynchin'," a shot at Ice Cube and his Lench Mob collective) and warns his detractors that he's carrying a gun, and that he isn't afraid to either use it or to smack the suckers in his path.

Although there were plenty of gangster rhymes—violence, firearms, drugs, and sex—they were, for the first time here, delivered in a warm, seductive package.

Another *The Chronic* single, "Let Me Ride," turned the same trick. With a beat taken from two Parliament songs, its warbling keys from "Mothership Connection (Star Child)" and the celebratory chants from "Swing Down, Sweet Chariot," Dr. Dre made his raps about being sweated by a guy with a TEC-9 and his willingness to use his own gun sound almost peaceful. It's a great example of not *what* you say, but *how* you say it.

Dr. Dre rapped in a laid-back tone on the song, and the cut's video also took things back by showing Los Angeles's old-school car culture. Dr. Dre peppers his

N.W.A: THE SPLINTER EFFECT

N.W.A went through a number of lineup changes during their brief lifetime. Here's the who, what, when, where, and why.

Arabian Prince. The rapper-producer left the group in 1988 before the release of *Straight Outta Compton*. He did not agree with the gangster lyrics and imagery the group employed and wanted to remain focused on the electro music he'd been making before N.W.A. He appeared on "Something 2 Dance 2," a dancy and incongruous end to *Straight Outta Compton*.

Ice Cube. The South Central Los Angeles rapper left N.W.A while touring in support of Eazy-E's *Eazy-Duz-It* and N.W.A's *Straight Outta Compton* albums. He declined to sign the contract offered to him, deeming the remuneration inadequate given his contributions as a writer and performer on both albums. Today, he stands as one of the most successful rappers and actors in entertainment history.

Dr. Dre. The rapper-producer left Ruthless Records in 1991 after the release of N.W.A's second studio album, *Efil4Zaggin*. Like Ice Cube, Dr. Dre did not feel as though he was being compensated fairly for his work with the label. He and business partner Marion "Suge" Knight launched Death Row Records. Its first release was Dr. Dre's revered *The Chronic* album.

MC Ren. Eazy-E's longtime friend remained on Ruthless Records after the breakup of N.W.A and stayed after Eazy-E died in 1995 due to complications from AIDS. The Compton rapper released three albums and one EP on the label, including the platinum *Kizz My Black Azz* EP in 1992. His run with the label ended after the 1998 album, *Ruthless for Life*.

DJ Yella. Rather than joining longtime producing partner Dr. Dre at Death Row Records, DJ Yella remained with Eazy-E and Ruthless Records. He produced for Ruthless acts Eazy-E, Bone Thugs-N-Harmony, and Menajahtwa after Dr. Dre's departure. DJ Yella left the imprint after Eazy-E's death. Billed as Yella, he released one album, 1996's *One Mo Nigga ta Go*.

*Snoop Dogg. Released in 1999 on the *Next Friday* soundtrack, "Chin Check" represented a quasi-reunion for N.W.A. Snoop Dogg replaced the late Eazy-E on the song, which was produced by Dr. Dre and does not include contributions from DJ Yella. Talk of an N.W.A reunion album with Snoop Dogg in the fold gained momentum after the release of "Chin Check," but the project failed to materialize.

raps with mentions of cruising through the streets in his '64 Chevrolet Impala. For a music and culture that was typically defined by lyrical references to things that were new and flashy, Dr. Dre flipped the script by focusing on classic cars.

Dr. Dre took another significant stance on "Let Me Ride." On the song's second verse, the N.W.A alumnus also rebelled against the type of politically minded, socially aware, "conscious" rap that was prominent in New York in the late eighties and early nineties thanks to such groups as Public Enemy, Boogie Down Productions, and X Clan.

No medallions, dreadlocks, or black fists / It's just that gangsta glare / With gangsta raps / That gangsta shit makes a gangs of snaps

> ## *"Dre came with "'G' Thang' and slowed the whole genre down. He took hip-hop from the crack era to the weed era."*
>
> **CHUCK D**

The conscious rappers of the era wore medallions featuring the image of Africa on them. Some sported dreadlocks as a nod to their ancestral roots and had raised their fists in videos and photographs as an homage to the Black Power salute conducted by black athletes Tommie Smith and John Carlos at the 1968 Olympics. With "Let Me Ride," Dr. Dre let listeners know he was about gangsterism, not pushing a social or political agenda.

Throughout most of *The Chronic*, Dr. Dre's agenda was weed, women, and taking out the competition. He and Snoop Doggy Dogg made the latter their focus on "__ wit Dre Day (And Everybody's Celebratin')" and its accompanying video, which featured caricatures of the people Dr. Dre and Snoop Dogg targeted in their lyrics.

On the first verse, Dr. Dre targets former friend and collaborator Eazy-E, while Snoop Doggy Dogg blasts Tim Dog, whose 1991 song "Fuck Compton" was an indictment of West Coast gangster rap, not just rappers from Compton. On the third verse, Dr. Dre and Snoop Doggy Dogg alternate lyrics dissing 2 Live Crew's Luke Skyywalker (whom they felt had dissed gangster rappers on his 1992 "Fakin' Like Gangsters" song), Eazy-E, and Ice Cube. As much as it was a diss song, it was also a line in the sand, one that said that Dr. Dre had a new crew and wasn't worried about either his past allegiances or new rivals. They were all dismissed quickly, without hesitation, and humorously in the song's video.

The heavy funk elements on "__ wit Dre Day (And Everybody's Celebratin')" were borrowed from Funkadelic's "(Not Just) Knee Deep," George Clinton's "Atomic Dog," and Tom Browne's "Funkin' for Jamaica (N.Y.)." But where the original songs were lively cuts, "__ wit Dre Day (And Everybody's Celebratin')" was a slow, heavy track complete with thick bass. It was a song to nod and bob your head to, not one to get hyped to.

Other songs from *The Chronic*, though, were much more lively and sounded like conventional confrontational gangster rap. "The Day the Niggaz Took Over," for instance, was a reaction to the acquittal of the four Los Angeles Police Department officers in the Rodney King case. The song's ominous bassline and sinister sonics would have fit in nicely on N.W.A's *Efil4Zaggin*. Instead of sharing mic time with N.W.A's Eazy-E and MC Ren, however, "The Day the Niggaz Took Over" featured Dr. Dre rapping with some of his new partners in rhyme: Snoop Doggy Dogg, Dat Nigga Daz (now known as Daz Dillinger or simply Daz), and RBX.

The infusion of new talent was a hallmark of *The Chronic*, including Snoop Doggy Dogg's appearances on singles "Nuthin' But a 'G' Thang," "Let Me Ride," and "__ wit Dre Day (And Everybody's Celebratin')," as well as album cuts such as "The Day the Niggaz Took Over" and "The Chronic (Intro)." But it didn't stop there. Philadelphia transplant Kurupt delivered lyrically dexterous gangster raps on "Stranded on Death Row" and "Lyrical Gangbang."

There was also another noteworthy voice in the mix: the Lady of Rage. Where Yo-Yo had been more of a sassy, no-nonsense female artist backed by Ice Cube, the Lady of Rage was a hardcore female rapper whose lyrics on "Stranded on Death Row" included her referring to herself as a "lyrical murderer," loading her AK-47 assault rifle, and dropping 187 references.

Even though the Lady of Rage presented herself as just one of the guys, guns and all, her presence on *The Chronic* was distinctive. These lines from "Stranded on Death Row" illustrate Rage's tough talk, as well as her lyrical prowess.

On all counts, let the ball bounce where it may / It's just another clip into my AK / Buck 'em down with my underground tactics / Facts and stacks of clips on my mattress

"It added balance and she was spittin'," Dr. Dre collaborator and fellow rapper-producer Hi-Tek said. "She was spittin' just as hard as any dude on the album. You've got to have a lady soldier in the camp. . . . For them to start competing against the dudes neck and neck, [it's] like what Nicki Minaj is doing now. [Minaj] found her voice, and she learned how to project her voice, and that's why she's winning. Rage was the same way. If you're around people like Dre, Snoop, Kurupt, and Daz, you can't do nothing but be dope."

DOING NUMBERS WITH THE D.O.C.

ONE OF THE D.O.C.'s biggest singles as a solo artist was "It's Funky Enough." Dr. Dre's lead single from *The Chronic* was "Nuthin' But a 'G' Thang." Both songs start similarly. The D.O.C.'s song begins with the artist rapping, "One and in comes the two to the three and four." The first verse of Dr. Dre's tune arrives courtesy of guest vocalist Snoop Dogg, who starts the record with "One, two, three, and to the four." The similarity is thanks to the work of the D.O.C., who worked with and wrote for several artists with Dr. Dre while they were both signed to Ruthless Records. Their partnership continued once Death Row Records launched and includes the D.O.C.'s writing work throughout *The Chronic*.

"When we were writing 'Nuthin' But a "G" Thang,' if there was a first lesson, that song was the first lesson," the D.O.C. says. "It was the first real writing session where I had Snoop all to myself and we could sit down and construct it. I told him to think about ['It's Funky Enough'], and when he started writing his verses, you could tell he was listening to what I told him, because he went right back to it.

"I had told him that the most important lines in any song are the first one and the last one," the D.O.C. added. "This is me talking to Dogg. 'When you start a song, Snoop, you only have five to seven seconds to grab 'em and make 'em want to sing the song along with you. That means the line has to be catchy and cool, and something to where when they hear it the first time, they want to say it along with you the second time.' I said, 'Think about my song, "One and in comes the two,"' and I said, 'That's simple for most people, because they know what's going to come next. Then you have to make the last line something to where they remember you. So when they get to that last line, everybody wants to say it.' So he goes upstairs and he writes, and when he came back down and started spittin', sure enough, that's the way he started the song. By the time we got to the end of the song, I told him to put my name in it because that was the only way I got my shine at the end. He put my name in the record, which pissed Dre the fuck off, but that was the only way I got mine, which was to slip my name into joints when I'm writing it. I don't know why Dre didn't like it, but he didn't like it. I told him that if you say my name in the song, the camera got to hit me at some point."

RIGHT:

Kurupt raps live on the air
on 92.3 The Beat in Los
Angeles in April 1998.

When looking back at *The Chronic*, Hi-Tek recalled that Dr. Dre benefitted from working with emerging talent. "He feeds off of young energy," said Hi-Tek, who became a staff producer at Dr. Dre's Aftermath Entertainment in 2003. "He feeds off the young artists. Us as producers, we can't do it without those artists. We look at those artists as instruments, basically. They're like an extra instrument. They're like another saxophone, piano, and here comes these vocals and these pictures that they paint."

The artists also benefitted greatly from Dr. Dre's tutelage and coaching. "People you never heard about just became instant stars just like that," Hi-Tek said.

Indeed, the rap world became enthralled with the new voices showcased on *The Chronic*. Snoop Doggy Dogg's languid delivery made his vocals stand out in rap's hypermasculine jousting, while Kurupt brought an energetic, East Coast style of rap to a decidedly West Coast rap camp. RBX rhymed with a scholarly tone at times, yet never lost his angst. The Lady of Rage offered a hardcore female perspective and a stern, no-nonsense feminine attitude to the "Death Row Inmates," as they came to be known.

Rappers had collaborated with one another on songs and albums, but *The Chronic* was as much a showcase for all of Death Row Records as it was for

Dr. Dre, the solo artist. Snoop Doggy Dogg was clearly Dr. Dre's right-hand man, but Kurupt, Daz, RBX, the Lady of Rage, and the other Death Row acts showcased on *The Chronic* now had a built-in fan base eager to hear their solo material. By allowing his pupils to shine, Dr. Dre became more respected as an artist and producer than ever before.

The Chronic's new sound for gangster rap, delivered by production maverick Dr. Dre and aided by his new batch of protégés, proved to be a mesmerizing elixir for a large group of people who had either mostly dismissed rap, gangster or otherwise, or ignored it completely. Although the album's lyrics remained as abrasive as ever, the vibe of the songs made them come off as less threatening and, thus, more appealing to a wider range of people, namely cultural tastemakers beyond the rap world.

In fact, the mainstream-media praise of *The Chronic* created a watershed moment for rap and gangster rap. Even with all the same elements that writers, listeners, critics, and the government had just bemoaned on albums from Ice-T, N.W.A, and the Geto Boys—violence, drug use, gangbanging, misogyny, profanity—*The Chronic* is one of the most acclaimed releases in music history, earning a spot on *Rolling Stone*'s 500 Greatest Albums of All Time list, as well as on *Spin*'s "90 Greatest Albums of the '90s" and *Time*'s "All-TIME 100 Albums."

Artists hold Dr. Dre's debut solo album in equally rarified air, comparing it to some of the most acclaimed projects in music history. "*The Chronic* is still the hip-hop equivalent of Stevie Wonder's *Songs in the Key of Life*," Kanye West said. "It's the benchmark you measure your album against if you're serious."

"*The Chronic*," adds Hi-Tek, "was just a testimony to what I wanted to be as a producer. There's nothing I could ever hear in Dre's production that was a mistake. Everything was flawless."

The Chronic became a faster-selling, better-selling, and more-acclaimed album than anything that Ice-T, Eazy-E, N.W.A, or the Geto Boys had released. Its success showed that gangster rap was still ascending creatively, commercially, and critically.

And while it may have been Dr. Dre's album, *The Chronic* wasn't just a Dr. Dre coronation. The vocal star of the show is arguably Snoop Doggy Dogg, who delivered a remarkable appearance on "Deep Cover" and was then featured on each of the singles and videos from *The Chronic*. The Long Beach rapper's subsequent debut album made history, making him both famous and infamous.

A Doggy Dogg World

In New York, a van parked beneath the North Tower of the World Trade Center exploded, killing six people and injuring more than one thousand others. A fifty-one-day standoff between the government and the Branch Davidians, led by David Koresh, ended with the death of six Davidians and four Bureau of Alcohol, Tobacco, Firearms and Explosives (ATF) agents during a raid on the group's Waco, Texas, compound. A subsequent fire on the grounds killed an additional seventy-six people. Rodney King, the unarmed black motorist whose beating was captured on video and broadcast around the world, testified at the federal trial of the four Los Angeles police officers accused of violating his civil rights. Officers Stacey Koon and Laurence Powell were each sentenced to thirty months in prison for violating King's civil rights.

When William "Bill" Jefferson Clinton was sworn in as president, the world appeared ready for change. The start of Clinton's presidency ended the twelve-year Ronald Reagan–George H. W. Bush era, which was defined, in part, by an

OPPOSITE:
Snoop Dogg on the set of his
Da Game of Life short film in
Los Angeles in July 1998.

1993
Key Rap Releases

1. Snoop Doggy Dogg's *Doggystyle* album

2. Wu-Tang Clan's *Enter The Wu-Tang (36 Chambers)* album

3. Cypress Hill's "Insane in the Brain" single

US President

Bill Clinton

Something Else

Oslo Peace Accords were signed.

explosion of inner-city drugs, violence, and incarceration. In an attempt to appeal to a new and diverse section of the American public, Clinton famously played the saxophone on *The Arsenio Hall Show* in the run-up to his election. Thus, Clinton was able to play up being younger and more in touch with the people than the stiff, paternal vibes of Reagan and Bush. He was even labeled by some as "the first black president." When he took office, Clinton was deemed more affable than his predecessors, which endeared him to a younger demographic, one that wanted change.

The rap world was also going through a major change in 1993 thanks to Dr. Dre's genre-shifting *The Chronic*. It replaced menacing gangster rap with a more relaxed, inviting incarnation of the genre, making it more palatable for a bigger audience.

Yet as dramatic as Dr. Dre's *The Chronic* was sonically for gangster rap, it also delivered a number of other landmark achievements. It showed that, in less than a decade, Dr. Dre could move from one record company to another and make each one dramatically more successful than the one before it. He had done so with World Class Wreckin' Cru in the mideighties, with Ruthless Records in the late eighties and early nineties, and with his own Death Row Records in 1992.

With *The Chronic*, Dr. Dre was now a better-selling artist than Eazy-E, N.W.A, and Ice Cube, more than doubling the sales of any artist he'd ever produced. The rapper-producer was now a bona fide star in his own right.

Yet *The Chronic* was also remarkable for the way in which Dr. Dre shared the spotlight. The Compton musical visionary introduced a wave of new artists and featured them on several songs each. Though the idea of featuring affiliated acts wasn't new to rap. In fact, there were two main ways rappers were featured on one another's songs prior to *The Chronic*.

The first way was for an artist to feature other members of their crews on songs with them. This type of collaboration gained steam in 1987 and 1988. Dana Dane and his producer, Hurby "Luv Bug" Azor, engaged in tag-team rhyming on "We Wanna Party," a cut from the Brooklyn rapper's gold-certified 1987 album, *Dana Dane with Fame*. Another early example was Marley Marl's landmark 1988 single "The Symphony," which featured Masta Ace, Craig G, Kool G Rap, and Big Daddy Kane, members of his Juice Crew stable of artists. "The Symphony" stands in rap lore as the first "posse cut" and is widely revered as the best by many rap scholars.

On the gangster rap side of things, in 1988 Eazy-E featured fellow N.W.A member MC Ren on "2 Hard Mutha's" on his *Eazy-Duz-It* LP, while N.W.A featured the D.O.C. on "Parental Discretion Iz Advised," a *Straight Outta Compton* cut. Dr. Dre and Yella produced both of these songs. Fellow Compton rap artist

King Tee featured raps from his producer, DJ Pooh, on several cuts from his 1988 album, *Act a Fool*.

The other way rappers collaborated with other acts was to feature artists outside of their immediate circles on their material. This type of collaboration became popular in 1988 and 1989. Too $hort featured Rappin' 4-Tay and Danger Zone on "Don't Fight the Feelin'," a song from his double-platinum album *Life Is... Too $hort*. Another early example arrived in 1989 when Big Daddy Kane featured Nice & Smooth on his "Pimpin' Ain't Easy," which appeared on his gold *It's a Big Daddy Thing* LP. A year later, Public Enemy featured Ice Cube and Big Daddy Kane on "Burn Hollywood Burn," a single from their platinum *Fear of a Black Planet* album.

But these types of songs were still the exception rather than the rule, even though they were becoming increasingly popular by the time Dr. Dre released *The Chronic* in 1992. True, DJ Quik had taken things a step further by featuring protégés AMG and 2nd II None on a couple of songs each on his 1991 *Quik Is the Name*, but those were album cuts.

Then Dr. Dre changed the way rap albums are put together and artists are promoted. Dr. Dre put Snoop Dogg on more than half of *The Chronic*'s songs and, more importantly, on his singles, the biggest, most promoted songs on *The Chronic*, as well as the pre–*The Chronic* Dr. Dre single "Deep Cover." By default, Snoop Dogg had a massive built-in audience. He had, indeed, become the hottest rapper in the world without having released an album of his own.

Creatively, Snoop Dogg felt free as he worked on his debut album. "I had no concerns of what I was supposed to be," Snoop Dogg said. "It was carefree. I was

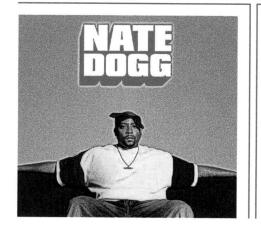

NATE DOGG: R&G (RHYTHM & GANGSTER)

Nate Dogg played a minimal role on Dr. Dre's *The Chronic*, crooning on the outro of "Deeez Nuuuts." The Long Beach singer also appeared on only one *Doggystyle* song, "Aint No Fun (If The Homies Cant Have None)," but that track became an underground favorite and set up Nate Dogg's career. He sang like a gangster rapper and was one of the most prolific and in-demand singers in rap history. He released several solo albums and appeared on dozens of songs with everyone from Warren G and Dr. Dre to Eminem and Fabolous.

MUSICAL MARTIAL ARTS

AS THE MOST prominent collaborator on Dr. Dre's *The Chronic*, Snoop Dogg got to work with a wide range of artists, including Daz Dillinger, Kurupt, Nate Dogg, RBX, and the Lady of Rage. Here, Snoop Dogg likens their recording sessions to martial-arts training.

"Having all those artists on all those records, it was like a karate movie," Snoop Dogg said. "Imagine Bruce Lee, Chow Yun-fat, Jet Li, Jim Kelly, Ong-Bak, Bolo [Yeung], and [the] Five Fingers of Death, all these badass karate motherfuckas all in one motion picture fighting to get on one song. There's only three, sometimes four, verses on a song, and I just named about eight muthafuckas, so when you've got that kind of sorcery going down, steel sharpening steel and the best swinging and with no egos and no attitudes, you're in a battle.

"I come from battle rap, so I wanted the best muthafuckas around me, and when I was able to bring Kurupt, bring RBX, that was me bringing muthafuckas that was better than me or who were pushing me to a level where I had to be better than them. It forced us all to give our all when Dre was giving us the best music in the world to complement that with the best lyrics, the best flow, the best everything.

"[Dr. Dre's *The Chronic* single] 'Let Me Ride,' for example, RBX wrote the first verse. Snoop Dogg wrote the second verse. RBX and Snoop wrote the third verse together. But you wouldn't know that if I didn't tell you that. That's because me and RBX, we're cousins. We battled our whole life, and I could never beat him. But when we're battling on this song, whose verse is the dopest? It don't matter. Dre won a Grammy for it, so we both win. Despite me never winning a Grammy with seventeen nominations [as of the writing of this book], that moment right there solidifies that my karate is black-belt material."

back in the studio making some more music. This time, it's my record. Same energy. Same everything. I don't have an on/off switch, or a medium. I've got a 'Go.' My shit is just go, and that's what it was. That's why the transformation was so easy to go from *The Chronic* to my record. You never heard the same rhymes, the same styles. You never heard that, because I was an MC. I was lyrical, so when you load up, I'm ready to go. It wasn't like I was like, 'Oh. I've got to make this record better than *The Chronic*.' That expectation wasn't on my shoulders because I didn't give a fuck."

But the run-up to the album was clouded with uncertainty regarding Snoop Dogg's life and career. On August 25, 1993, Snoop Dogg was allegedly driving a Jeep in the Palms section on the West Side of Los Angeles. The people in the Jeep purportedly got into a heated exchange with Philip Woldemariam, a gang member. After originally leaving the scene, the Jeep later returned. A passenger in the Jeep then shot Woldemariam, and the twenty-five-year-old died soon thereafter.

Snoop Dogg turned himself in to police on September 4, a day after he presented the winner of the rhythm-and-blues category of the MTV Video Music Awards. Snoop Dogg and his passengers told police that Woldemariam approached their vehicle brandishing a firearm, which led one of Snoop Dogg's passengers, who told police that he was the rapper's bodyguard, to fire several shots at Woldemariam. According to Detective David Straky, other witnesses said Woldemariam did not have a gun. David Kenner, Snoop Dogg's attorney, said that Woldemariam had been threatening the rapper for three months prior to the shooting.

"This shooting was the result of self-defense following a series of assaults and threats against Snoop," Kenner said.

Snoop Dogg was released on bail on September 4 under charges of first- and second-degree murder. He was eventually found not guilty.

OPPOSITE:

Dr. Dre (left) and Snoop Dogg created music in the early 1990s in a way Snoop likens to martial arts training.

DAVID KENNER

David Kenner was longtime legal counsel to Suge Knight and Death Row Records, representing both for several years and for several high-profile cases. The criminal defense attorney handled Snoop Dogg's murder case and became Death Row's main lawyer in 1994. Among the other cases he handled was a 1996 conflict of interest case for Knight. The label executive signed the teenage daughter of prosecutor Lawrence M. Longo to a Death Row Records recording contract while Longo was supervising Knight's probation.

JOE COOL: DOGGY ART

A CRACK ADDICT who was also smoking sherm, Darryl "Joe Cool" Daniel was encouraged by his cousin Snoop Dogg to get off drugs. Snoop Dogg wanted his cousin to be sober, and he also said he had an assignment for Joe Cool. He wanted him to draw the cover art for his *Doggystyle* album. After discussing Dr. Dre's concept for the cover with Snoop Dogg, Joe Cool delivered the now iconic artwork.

Joe Cool remembers Snoop Dogg discussing the cover during an interview on *The Arsenio Hall Show*. "Arsenio said, 'Who drew this?'" Joe Cool said. "And Snoop said, 'My cousin Joe Cool did that.' When he said that, I almost passed out. I was there with him when he did the interview. I was there with him. I'm like, 'Oh wow.' Everybody was clapping and shit. 'Woo woo,' all that, like damn. They clapping 'cause I drew this shit. He said, 'My cousin drew that, you know, my cousin Darryl "Joe Cool."' I'm like, 'Wow. He said my name to Arsenio.'"

Legal problems notwithstanding, Snoop Dogg was riding high on the success of *The Chronic*. He established himself as a solo star with the October 1993 release of "Who Am I (What's My Name)?" The single was as much a coronation of Snoop Dogg as the new face of rap in general and gangster rap specifically as it was a celebration of Snoop Dogg himself. The song's hook featured a chorus of people singing "Snoop Doggy Dogg" similar in tone and feel to George Clinton's "Atomic Dog," which "Who Am I (What's My Name)?" sampled. So although the Long Beach, California, rapper started off his first verse talking about how he was selling cocaine, how he was willing to put money in on buying weed with his friends, and why he wasn't hesitant to shoot someone, the song's up-tempo, funky vibe made it all sound deliberately fun and celebratory.

Like "Nuthin' But a 'G' Thang" and "Let Me Ride" before it, "Who Am I (What's My Name)?" was a new chapter in gangster rap. It was feel-good gangster rap starring Snoop Dogg. Even though the sound and feel of the music played a major role in how the music was received, Snoop Dogg's voice, delivery, and demeanor also played a huge part in his popularity.

Schoolly D, Ice-T, and the members of N.W.A were often brash and aggressive, typically rapping with what sounded like a snarl. By contrast, Snoop Dogg delivered his rhymes in a calm, laid-back, and comforting manner chock-full of charisma and with only a smidgeon of menace. It was as if a friend had pulled you to the side to have a private conservation. "Snoop brought the smooth gangster style to the game," longtime collaborator Warren G said.

With "Who Am I (What's My Name)?"

taking the music world by storm and Snoop Dogg facing murder charges, there was significant buzz for his November 1993 release, *Doggystyle*.

"Snoop Dogg is an amazing artist, and his album is by far the most anticipated rap album in years," said Jon Shecter, then-editor of the *Source* magazine, the leading rap magazine at the time. According to Shecter, Snoop Dogg being charged with murder would "only make the record blow up even bigger because it will generate even more curiosity among those who have never heard of him."

Consumers showed just how much they wanted *Doggystyle*. The Dr. Dre–produced album made history by being the first debut album to enter the Billboard charts at No. 1. Despite never having released an album, Snoop Dogg had the bestselling album in music the first week *Doggystyle* arrived in stores.

Doggystyle also earned another far more dubious distinction. It was the first time that an artist had been indicted for murder while he had the No. 1 album in the country. Snoop Dogg's popularity and his legal status led *Newsweek* to put him on the cover of its November 29, 1993, issue with the headline: "when is rap 2 violent?"

Even as *Doggystyle* dominated the album charts and the pop-culture consciousness, "Who Am I (What's My Name)?" was also enjoying tremendous success. The Dr. Dre–produced song hit No. 1 on Billboard's Hot Rap Songs chart and No. 8 on Billboard's Hot 100 chart the week of January 1, 1994, meaning it was the eighth most popular song that week in any genre of music, not just rap.

HOLY SKIT

GROWING UP IN Long Beach, California, Snoop Dogg studied the work of the members of N.W.A, who hailed from nearby Compton. When Snoop Dogg started making his own music with N.W.A's sonic architect Dr. Dre, he wanted to incorporate a key component of what he loved about the group's material.

"Remember, we was fans of N.W.A," Snoop Dogg said. "So anything we seen or heard them do, we'd always say, 'Dre. How come we ain't got no commercials?' That's when we came up with [*The Chronic* skit] 'The $20 Sack Pyramid.' Me, D.O.C., and Warren G, we was like, 'Fuck it. Let's come up with our own *The $25,000 Pyramid*,' because that was a show that we all liked and we all knew it to be funny if we put the right shit in there.

"Then on the [*The Chronic* skit] 'Deeez Nuuuts,' we was doing that shit all the time. A nigga would call, and we'd do that. Then when it came to my record, I was into the pimpin', so I took a scene from *The Mack* where a nigga said, 'Nigga, your bitch chose me.' It was certain shit that was fly to me that I was able to get off on my records and there was certain shit that was funny and fly to me that I was able to get off on Dre's record.

"With [the intro to *The Chronic* song] 'Lil' Ghetto Boy,' I had just gotten out of jail, and me and my homie [and fellow Long Beach rapper Lil] 1/2 Dead, it was like a real story to me, but it was like I was able to get this off on [Dr. Dre's] shit and have fun, so when it was time for me to do my record, naturally [Dr. Dre] was going to give me the same energy, 'cause I had gave him all of mine.

"Adding that humor showed that we were human, that we had a funny side. We had a serious side, a hard side. Motherfuckas always say that Snoop Dogg could have been a comedian if he wouldn't have been a rapper. That's some of the elements we're able to show through the music we make, that we can have fun while keeping it gangster."

As "Who Am I (What's My Name)?" was dominating the charts, Snoop Dogg released his second mammoth *Doggystyle* single, "Gin and Juice." Arriving in January 1994, the song became the first smash party gangster rap single. On the cut, Snoop Dogg rapped about having a house party because his parents weren't home, smoking weed, and sipping on gin and juice. It was the life of a gangster—sans the violence—an oasis (of sorts) amid the chaos consuming the content of virtually every other gangster rap song up to that point.

The song's video also added some levity to the visual side of gangster rap. Prior to the party in the video, Snoop Dogg gets his hair done, navigates a fight between two girls, and attends a drive-in movie with Tha Dogg Pound rap crew. The party goes a little too well and swells to the front yard as his parents return. Off-screen, his father fires some gunshots, and people start streaming out of the house, including several topless girls.

Whereas most gangster rap videos that came before "Gin and Juice" showed the dark side of the hood, this clip showed an abundance of drinking, partying, sex, games, and dancing before Snoop Dogg's parents showed up. It looked as if it could have been a house/college frat party in any corner of the country.

Snoop Dogg was reaching a key demographic, the casual (often) white rap fan with plenty of disposable income. By 1994, rap music had been recorded for fifteen years, and some of the stigma surrounding the genre was starting to wear off. Snoop was a perfect blend of street, cool, and fun, a combination that appealed to a universal audience. He wasn't viewed as menacing or anti-white like other gangster rappers, though his lyrics suggested he should definitely be looked at as the former. Snoop Dogg was just plain cool.

> *"When you load up, I'm ready to go. It wasn't like I was like, 'Oh. I've got to make this record better than* **The Chronic.** *'That expectation wasn't on my shoulders because I didn't give a fuck."*
>
> **SNOOP DOGG**

"What makes him so special is that he's just so personable," the D.O.C. said. "Not to mention the guy's got swag out of this world."

"Snoop is like your cool nephew or your cool uncle," DJ Quik said. "He's like the one that, if a fight started, he ain't even gonna flinch. He's got some Bruce Lee shit going on with him, but he's like a pimp, too."

Snoop Dogg was indeed more complicated than his persona made him seem, and there were other parts of himself that he wanted to share with the world. With "Doggy Dogg World," for instance, Snoop Dogg did what Dr. Dre had done for him: showcased his friends on one of his major songs. Fellow Death Row Records artists Tha Dogg Pound (Daz and Kurupt) were featured on the tune, which also included crooning from seventies R&B group the Dramatics. The silky smooth song was a showcase for Snoop Dogg to diss both people biting his style and no-good women. For their part, Kurupt and Daz alternated between trumpeting their gangster ways, disparaging women, and indulging in chronic.

The song's video, though, provided many young rap fans their first look at the pimp and player lifestyle previously memorialized by the blaxploitation films of the seventies and eighties. Snoop Dogg, Daz, Kurupt, and the Dramatics perform in the video at a throwback nightclub modeled to look like a seventies hotspot. The stars of the video wore flamboyant suits, flashy brimmed hats, and other seventies regalia. Snoop Dogg even adopted another alias for his "character," billing himself in the video as Silky Slim, a player who always has five women on his arm. Kurupt doubled as Small Change Willy from Philly, while Daz was Sugafoot, and Dr. Dre was Fortieth St. Black.

The rest of the video was equally retro. Actor Antonio Fargas was cast as Huggy Bear, reprising his role as the flashy-dressed character from the popular seventies show *Starsky & Hutch*, while blaxploitation star Fred Williamson appeared as the Hammer, a nod to his career as a hard-hitting professional football player and to the title character of his 1972 film *Hammer*. Other black seventies film and television stars, including Rudy Ray Moore (*Dolemite*), Pam Grier (*Foxy Brown*), Max Julien (*The Mack*), and Ron O'Neal (*Super Fly*), also made cameos in the video.

Too $hort, Ice-T, Ice Cube, and others had rapped about pimps, players, and macks, but given Snoop Dogg's visibility at the time the video for "Doggy Dogg World" was released, it was a watershed moment for the popularity of the pimp and player lifestyle that Snoop Dogg had grown up admiring.

"It was the beautiful women, the outfits," Snoop Dogg said. "The way they dress, the cars, the money. It was just the whole persona and knowing you look good and when you look good, it feels good to look good. It makes you feel a little better.

"It's a way of life and it's a statement," Snoop Dogg added. "When you can get fly with yourself and have some women behind you to accessorize that, make it look real good and play it out to the fullest, that's a good feeling. A lot of us rappers came up in an era where we've seen it and we wanted to do it. Now that we can do it, some of us will do it."

Beyond shifting the vibe and the look of rap in general and gangster rap specifically, with *Doggystyle* Snoop Dogg made something popular that was once taboo. Prior to *Doggystyle*, in rap, "biting"—or using someone else's material, style, or lyrics—was among the worst things a rapper could do. A rapper was supposed to strive to be original, different, and distinctive at all times.

However, Snoop Dogg became all those things when he went against the grain and covered Doug E. Fresh and MC Ricky D's landmark 1985 single "La Di Da Di." For *Doggystyle*'s "Lodi Dodi," Snoop Dogg slightly reworked the original tale and applied it to himself, updating the cologne from Polo to Cool Water and the shoes from Bally to Chucks, among other things.

Snoop Dogg knew covering a song might be criticized by the rap community and others, so he addressed any doubters in the song's intro and referred to MC Ricky D as Slick Rick, the moniker the rapper used after recording "La Di Da Di."

Gotta say what's up to my nigga Slick Rick / For those that don't like it, eat a dick / But for those who with me, sing that shit

Unlike other rappers, who were seemingly obsessed with all things new, Snoop Dogg felt it was important for rappers to acknowledge their musical forefathers.

"We have to be more leaders to show homage, to hug each other and to say to each other, 'Yo, your shit's dope, cuz. You're bad,'" Snoop Dogg said. "That's always been my thing. . . . I never had that problem of telling a nigga that they was dope. It didn't bother me because I felt like, in the game that we're playing, if I play at my highest level, y'all can't fuck with me, so it don't hurt me to give you a compliment. And I like playing with niggas that push me. I started off with Dr. Dre and the D.O.C., the baddest motherfuckers in the game. There wasn't nothing better than that when I got in the game, besides Ice Cube."

With its initial buzz and the additional push from radio and videos, *Doggystyle* became one of the bestselling rap albums of all time, moving more than four million copies in less than seven months. It also stands as a watershed rap release.

"Snoop is classic," said the Game, the Compton rapper and fellow Dr. Dre protégé whose debut album was released more than eleven years after Snoop Dogg's debut project. "*Doggystyle*, that was the only album he needed to solidify him in West Coast gangster rap forever."

Given *Doggystyle*'s popularity, Snoop Dogg was an in-demand performer at music industry events, including awards shows. The rapper blurred the lines

AN ALTERNATE SLAUGHTAHOUSE

WHEN BROOKLYN RAPPER Masta Ace appeared on Marley Marl's 1988 landmark posse cut "The Symphony," a high-energy song with top-tier lyricism from Big Daddy Kane, Kool G Rap, and Craig G, being aligned with established rap figures seemed to have his career on a fast track to success.

But when labelmate and comedic rapper Biz Markie was a no-show to a subsequent recording session, Masta Ace decided to impersonate Biz Markie on his "Me and the Biz" single, the first release from Masta Ace's debut album, 1990's *Take a Look Around*. The song was panned and Masta Ace caught a lot of flak for what people perceived to be a novelty record. While much of the rest of *Take a Look Around* was simmering with insightful social commentary, strong storytelling, and impressive wordplay, it failed to gain much commercial traction.

The rap world had changed dramatically as Masta Ace prepared to work on his second album. N.W.A had become a dominant force with a far-reaching influence. "It wasn't just West Coast rap, because New York was on that, too," Masta Ace said. "Dudes [in New York] were rhyming about wearing Timberlands, drinking forties, guns, and just taking it to this real negative direction.

"They [gangster rap albums] were being purchased in places in America you would have never thought people were listening to this stuff," Masta Ace continued. "The middle of America, the red states, the suburbs of America, all these white kids were growing up listening to this and maybe didn't know anything about Boogie Down Productions or Run-DMC or anything that came before it, but they gravitated to this music and that kind of became the prevailing sound of what people associated with hip-hop music, even though there was a lot more to hip-hop music. But as soon as it crossed into the living rooms of America, the white living rooms of America, it turned into this other phenomenon, and it kind of took over for a long period of time."

With the rap world evolving, Masta Ace changed creative course with his own material.

"I wanted to come back and do the hardest album I could do," Masta Ace said. "I looked at the landscape and I said that, 'It appears that people probably think the only way to do a super-hard album is to rap about gangster stuff or guns, rap about drinking and smoking and partying, and shooting people that get in your way.' My goal was to make the hardest album I could do without falling into any of those typical patterns that I felt every other artist was doing at the time."

Flanked by a new crew of artists, he returned rechristened as the leader of Masta Ace Incorporated. The group's 1993 album, *SlaughtaHouse*, took aim at hardcore rap and the artists who espoused violence for the sake of violence, as well as the companies who clamored for that type of material. The album is a stark look at the impact violence and violent imagery was having on rap consumers and the communities in which they lived. "A Walk Thru The Valley" features Ace wondering what goes through the mind of a black man when he's about to shoot another black man, while on "Late Model Sedan," he laments feeling like he needs to carry a gun, saying that he ought to be safe in a black neighborhood. The title track features material from faux rappers "MC Negro" and "Ignant MC," who are celebrating their imaginary *Brains on the Sidewalk* album.

"That was really the hardest, most underground, most grimiest record that I've done," Masta Ace said. "I went out of my way on that album to point out that I didn't have a gun, that I wasn't smoking weed, I wasn't drinking forties, but that this was hardcore hip-hop."

between art and reality when he performed the *Doggystyle* song "Murder Was the Case" at the September 8, 1994, MTV Video Music Awards. The song begins with Snoop Dogg getting shot. As he lies on the ground bleeding to death, he makes a deal with the Devil so that he can see the birth of his child. He wakes up from a coma, lives like a baller, and buys his mother a Mercedes-Benz and his girlfriend a Jaguar. But then he gets incarcerated and sees one of his friends get stabbed in the neck.

At the end of his "Murder Was the Case" performance at the MTV Video Music Awards, Snoop Dogg said, "I'm innocent. I'm innocent," which is not on the album version of the song and was taken as commentary about his ongoing murder case.

The following month, Death Row Records also took the innovative step (in the rap world, at least) of releasing a *Murder Was the Case* short film and soundtrack. Rock acts such as the Beatles and the Monkees starred in their own feature films in the sixties, but rappers had yet to have similar productions. At eighteen minutes long, *Murder Was the Case* closely followed the storyline of the song. A remixed version of the cut appeared on the soundtrack.

"I was always with trying different shit," Snoop Dogg said. "Even when I tried 'Murder Was the Case,' that was me wanting to make a song about actually visualizing death and being able to come back from that, just having a crazy thought in my head and wanting to try that."

The *Murder Was the Case* soundtrack became the third consecutive blockbuster release for Dr. Dre, Snoop Dogg, and Death Row Records. The soundtrack

THA DOGG POUND: DOGG FOOD FOR THOUGHT
After being showcased alongside Daz and Kurupt on Dr. Dre's *The Chronic*, Snoop Dogg kept Tha Dogg Pound members and the rest of the Death Row Records roster in the mix on *Doggystyle*. Daz and Kurupt were key players on the LP, appearing on "Doggy Dogg World," among other cuts. Daz also contributed backing vocals on "Gin and Juice" and "Murder Was the Case," while Kurupt appeared on fan favorite "Aint No Fun (If The Homies Cant Have None)" with Nate Dogg and Warren G.

featured several notable tracks. Most prominent was "Natural Born Killaz," which reunited Dr. Dre and Ice Cube. It was the first time the two rappers had worked on or appeared on a song together since Ice Cube left Ruthless Records five years prior.

The soundtrack also featured Tha Dogg Pound's "What Would U Do?" The propulsive first cut from Daz and Kurupt as a standalone entity established them as a duo to watch. The song also gained additional exposure from its inclusion on the soundtrack for Oliver Stone's 1994 film *Natural Born Killers*, which starred Woody Harrelson and Juliette Lewis as a pair of serial murderers who are glorified by the media as they carry out their crimes and try to evade capture by the police.

DJ Quik's freshly minted relationship with Death Row Records was also showcased on the *Murder Was the Case* soundtrack. He was being managed by Death Row co-owner Suge Knight at the time, and his "Dollars & Sense" song was featured on the collection. On this track, DJ Quik dissed Compton's Most Wanted rapper MC Eiht and made bold declarations of his membership in the Tree Top Pirus, a Compton-based Bloods gang. From his disses of MC Eiht, which included saying he dropped the *g* from his name because he wasn't a G (gangster), to his flaunting his gang ties and his affiliation with Death Row Records, DJ Quik created waves with "Dollars & Sense."

With the attention *Murder Was the Case* was generating, it became a brisk seller, moving more than two million units in its first two months in stores and another million over the next six months.

But while gangbanging on wax was proving to be incredibly profitable, gangbanging in the streets was becoming an epidemic that was spreading beyond Los Angeles to other major cities throughout the country.

Bangin on Wax:
There Goes the Neighborhood

IN JANUARY 1993, THE LOS ANGELES COUNTY CORONER'S OFFICE RELEASED A REPORT SAYING THAT 1992 WAS THE DEADLIEST YEAR IN THE COUNTY'S HISTORY.

OPPOSITE:

CJ Mac (left) and WC attend a party in Los Angeles in May 1998.

The year had seen a stunning 2,589 homicides, with 517 of those murders in July and August alone. The LAPD said that about one-third of those homicides were gang-related and that homicide rates had increased about 8 percent from 1991. This dramatic uptick in violence was not isolated and was seen throughout the United States and was showing no signs of slowing down.

Newsworthy violence wasn't limited to the streets of L.A. President Clinton, for instance, ordered a missile strike in the Al Mansour district of Baghdad, Iraq, because of the assassination attempt purported Iraqi agents had made on Clinton's predecessor, George H. W. Bush. Also in 1993, disgruntled housewife Lorena Bobbitt cut off the penis of her husband, John Wayne Bobbitt, in Manassas,

1993
Key Rap Releases

1. A Tribe Called Quest's *Midnight Marauders* album

2. Onyx's "Slam" single

3. Naughty By Nature's "Hip Hop Hooray" single

US President

Bill Clinton

Something Else

South Africa approved a new democratic constitution.

Virginia, while he slept. She asserted that he had raped her earlier that night; she was later found not guilty.

With crime exploding in both the United States as a whole (1993 was the peak of gun homicide rates) and in the Los Angeles metropolitan area, the music being made by L.A.'s most vulnerable inhabitants had become firmly entrenched in the musical lexicon of the early to midnineties. By that time, gangster rap had made substantial inroads in movies and in popular culture while also seeping into mainstream America. But a new wrinkle to the movement was about to materialize.

Back in 1988, the movie *Colors* showcased the emergence of the Los Angeles–based Bloods and Crips, two collectives of gangs that had a stranglehold on black urban life in Los Angeles throughout the seventies and eighties. The Crips emerged first, rising to prominence in the seventies wearing blue, at least in part, to honor the memory of an early Crips member who wore a blue bandana. Born a few years later, the Bloods were formed as a way for the members to protect themselves against the Crips. The Bloods' symbolic color of choice was red.

Ice-T's song "Colors," the title track to the film, featured the rapper explaining the mentality of the Los Angeles gangbanger, examining the world from both the perspective of a gangbanger who had dedicated himself to the lifestyle and from the perspective of someone who is urging people not to join gangs.

Nevertheless, there was still a separation between the gangs themselves and the artists, at least in public. Even though Ice-T, King Tee, and the members of N.W.A (Eazy-E, Ice Cube, Dr. Dre, MC Ren, and DJ Yella) were from Crips neighborhoods, none of them typically wore the gang's signature blue clothing or bandanas. These artists often wore black on their album covers, in their videos, and in their promotional photographs.

Indeed, the first wave of Los Angeles street rappers remained largely neutral image-wise in the eighties and early nineties, seemingly keeping specific gang affiliations out of the music. It was a conscious decision, one that was rooted in both safety and business.

"If you wore blue, then you ain't finna attract nothing but Crips," Compton's Most Wanted rapper MC Eiht, a Crip who initially followed the same code, said. "Now the Bloods ain't finna buy your music. You wear red all the time, now the Crips ain't gonna buy your music. You ain't gonna attract nothing but Bloods. Wearing black is neutral, so where you can be there and have Bloods here, Crips there, hustlers there, and to them you're not choosing a side.

"[With] N.W.A, everybody knew Eazy[-E] was Crippin'," MC Eiht continued. "Everybody knew [MC] Ren was a Crip. They knew [Dr.] Dre was where he was from and knew [Ice] Cube lived where he's from. Wearing black neutralizes us. So when we've got to do a show in an all Blood neighborhood, we're really not getting up under a lot of niggas' skin—all they gotta do is stare at blue all day on stage. You have to know shit like that."

Even though the public at large was not familiar with the specific neighborhoods the rappers they were listening to called home, many of their fellow Los Angeles artists and consumers were. That made wearing neutral colors and not promoting gang ties prudent.

"I already know where you're from, but when you're finna throw it in my face, you're irritating me and I don't want to buy your record," MC Eiht said. "That's why I would never do that. I would never get on records and go, 'I'm a Crip,' get in videos and wear blue rags. I might have worn a blue hat or whatever, but you try to be [neutral]. Like a lot of times when I would go on tour, it would be black T-shirts, black jeans, black shoes, black Raider[s] hat. Black, black, black. Gray, gray, gray. You try to be neutral, because you don't know where you're going. You don't know what they about and you're still an artist."

In 1990, the West Coast Rap All-Stars, a mixture of Crips and nonaffiliated rappers, released the song "We're All in the Same Gang." The song was a one-off that featured West Coast rappers King Tee, Body & Soul, Def Jef, Tone Lōc, Above the Law, N.W.A, Digital Underground, Young MC, Ice-T, Oaktown's 357,

A NEW PRIORITY

PRIORITY RECORDS ESTABLISHED itself as a haven for gangster rap in the late eighties through its partnership with Ruthless Records for Eazy-E's and N.W.A's material. In the early nineties, it became a bastion for established artists seeking creative freedom. When Ice-T was released from his recording contract with Sire Records due to the controversy surrounding the "Cop Killer" song from his rock group Body Count, he found a welcome home with Priority Records, which released his next two albums, 1993's *Home Invasion* and 1996's *VI: Return of the Real*. Similarly, when Tommy Boy Music balked at releasing Paris's *Sleeping with the Enemy* album because of the song "Bush Killa," which advocated the assassination of President George H. W. Bush, the San Francisco rapper partnered with Priority Records for his 1994 album, *Guerrilla Funk*.

TIMELINE OF THE BANDANA

1745–55. The Hindi word can be traced back to the eighteenth century.

1776. A bandana with an image of George Washington riding a horse became a popular item.

1900s. Bandanas become wildly popular thanks to cowboy movies in which the actors pulled bandanas over their mouths and noses to protect their identities and to avoid breathing in dirt and dust while they were tending to their cattle.

1930s. Miners use red bandanas to cover their mouths and noses from dust and dirt. Hobos tied bandanas to sticks and used them to hold their belongings.

1940s. Women begin using bandanas to tie their hair back.

1980s. The Bloods and the Crips become infamous for their affinities for red and blue bandanas, aka rags, respectively.

MC Hammer, J.J. Fad, and Eazy-E, as well as chanteuse Michel'le, voicing their concern about violence in the streets and gang violence in particular.

The video for "We're All in the Same Gang" featured a storyline in which a child hid in a car and saw his older brother get shot in a gang-related shoot-out. The clip features the shooters and the victims wearing their respective colors, an obvious nod to the gang warfare the song was trying to curtail.

One rapper notable for his absence on "We're All in the Same Gang" was Ice Cube, who had left N.W.A at this point. For his part, though, Ice Cube was chronicling the ravages of the gang epidemic in his own way.

On *Death Certificate*, his acclaimed 1991 album, Ice Cube delivered "My Summer Vacation," a song that tells the story of a group of Los Angeles gang members who move to St. Louis in order to run their drug-dealing operation without the concern of rival gangs, the police, and others familiar with their business. He points out that by dressing in khakis and wearing their typical Los Angeles style of clothing, these gang members go unnoticed by the police. Eventually, the people in their St. Louis neighborhood begin to look up to them, adopt their colors and gang terminology, and start claiming affiliation with Los Angeles–based gangs to which they have no legitimate connection. This lead to deadly violence that stemmed from turf wars that were happening thousands of miles away.

But where Ice Cube rapped a story based on what was happening in the streets, DJ Quik chronicled his experiences while touring on his 1992 song "Jus Lyke Compton," a cut from his gold *Way 2 Fonky* album. DJ Quik, who made a subtle nod to his Bloods affiliation on the *Way 2 Fonky* album cover by wearing a black jacket with red lettering, raps on "Jus Lyke Compton" about seeing Bloods and Crips fighting in St. Louis, San Antonio, and Denver and how the gangs' portrayals in film had affected people around the country.

They need to stop watching that Colors *and* Boyz N the Hood / *Too busy claimin' 60s, trying to be raw / And never ever seen the Shaw*

The "Shaw," or the Crenshaw area of Los Angeles, was a popular cruising area and is near the home of the Rollin 60s Neighborhood Crips, one of the most prominent factions of the Crips. Like Ice Cube, DJ Quik was fully aware that Los Angeles gang culture had spread far beyond Southern California.

Although he doesn't mention it in the song, DJ Quik said that the way he and his roadies represented the Bloods during his tours to promote *Quik Is the Name* did not sit well with the Crips members in the audiences at his shows.

"Some of the Crips in some of the places I was going kind of wasn't having it," DJ Quik said. "Me being as naive as I was to the fact that gangbanging did just go a little bit farther than California."

The overt discussion of gangs and rappers as gangbangers got a transformative jolt in 1993 with the release of *Bangin on Wax*. The album came from a group that billed themselves as the Bloods & Crips, which was a largely nondescript collection of rappers. With the creation of this group came a striking pledge of allegiance between the two most prominent gangs in Los Angeles. Songs such as "Piru Love" and "Crippin' Ain't Easy" gave the Bloods and Crips, respectively, platforms to promote their sets.

Peaking at No. 86 on the Billboard Top 200 chart in May 1993, *Bangin on Wax* gave a sonic jolt to listeners beyond Southern California, providing them information about the Bloods and Crips and how they operated.

"In Los Angeles, the streets definitely set the tone of the hip-hop music," said CJ Mac, who worked extensively with WC and released his 1999 album, *Platinum Game*, through Mack 10's Hoo-Bangin' Records imprint. "Our gang culture, it goes back since the sixties."

DEE BARNES REFLECTS ON MAKING "WE'RE ALL IN THE SAME GANG"

WHEN DEE BARNES MOVED to Los Angeles from New York in 1986, she got a crash course in Southern California's street gangs. "I learned immediately I can't go here, I can't wear this color," said Barnes, one-half of rap duo Body & Soul with partner-in-rhyme Rose. "These were rules given to me as I got off the plane from cousins of mine."

The type of violence exacted by Los Angeles gangs took Barnes aback. In New York, gang members also fought, but usually with their fists or in brawls. By contrast, Southern California gangs were much more violent and willing to use guns to settle their disputes.

As she adjusted to life on the West Coast, Barnes and Rose earned a buzz for their music. After considering signing to Eazy-E's Ruthless Records, Body & Soul signed with Delicious Vinyl, then home to Tone Lōc and Young MC, among others. In 1990, Barnes and Rose were approached by Michael Concepcion to appear on "We're All in the Same Gang," a song from The West Coast Rap All-Stars. Concepcion was the executive producer of the song (and the group's subsequent compilation), as well as a godfather of Los Angeles gangsters.

Body & Soul were excited to be featured on the song with Ice-T, N.W.A, King Tee, Digital Underground, MC Hammer, Young MC, Tone Lōc, Def Jef, and Above The Law, as well as such fellow female artists Michel'le, J.J. Fad, and Oaktown's 357. Barnes and Rose took a particular approach with their verse.

"Body & Soul wanted to talk about how women factor into gang activity," Barnes said. "We knew a lot of single mothers were raising gang members, and that gangs were a family outside of their family. A lot of these were single parent homes, mostly the mothers with no fathers in the house, so we knew that the gang members gravitated toward this, some voluntarily. Some were forced into the gang and jumped into the gang, and had no choice basically because you lived in that neighborhood. It was a boy's club, or a man's club. They were the only type of men that they had any type reference to, so we were trying to come from the angle of how mothers play a role in it. That's why we talked about being good mothers since birth and teaching your children to fight and win for the right reasons."

Once the song was done, the artists reassembled to film the song's video in Nickerson Gardens, located in the Watts neighborhood of Los Angeles. At the time, it was a place people didn't want to go to because of safety concerns, even during the day.

Through Concepcion, though, the video brought valuable resources to the community, Barnes said. Food, sneakers, and backpacks with school supplies were provided to local residents courtesy of Reebok, among other companies. The artists also interacted with locals who happened upon on the set. By connecting with Watts residents, the artists and the video production staff were able to foster goodwill in an area where outsiders were typically greeted with suspicion.

Nonetheless, extra, and unconventional, security measures were taken to keep everyone safe. "I'm not talking about cops," Barnes said. "We had gangs policing gangs, OGs policing the younger ones. Everybody was strapped. There were so many guns there, it was ridiculous. Here we are doing a song about peace and stop the violence, and everybody had a gun."

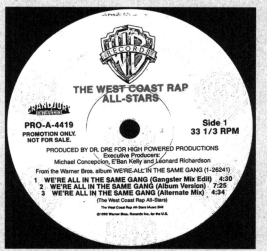

In addition to performances from the artists, the storyline of the "We're All in the Same Gang" video follows a child who unwittingly gets thrust into gang activity because of his older brother. The child wants to hang out with his older brother, sneaks into the back seat of his car, and waits in the car while his older brother meets with fellow gang members in a house. As the child waits for his brother to return, members of a rival gang approach the house, and shoot and kill the child's brother.

In the video's concluding scenes, the child ends up in the crosshairs of a potential shootout at his basketball game between the gang members who killed his brother and his brother's friend. The gang member who shot the child's brother recognizes the child from the earlier shooting, and drops his weapon as he signals for his fellow gang members to do the same. As is the case with the song's lyrics, the "We're All in the Same Gang" video illustrates how gangbanging affects the lives of the gang members and their families.

The song was an unofficial companion piece of sorts to the Stop the Violence Movement's "Self Destruction," which was released in 1988. It featured such New York artists as KRS-One, Public Enemy, Heavy D, D-Nice, Doug E. Fresh, Just-Ice, and Kool Moe Dee admonishing black on black crime, as well as bad decision-making and the media for perpetrating a negative perception of black people. Like "Self Destruction," "We're All in the Same Gang" was released to largely positive reviews.

"We really felt like we were making a difference, making a change," Barnes said. "We wanted to do something along the lines of 'Self Destruction' and we definitely wanted to shed light on the gang activity because it was really getting out of control.

"Everybody felt a little pride about it," added Barnes. "That was the only time that everybody on the West Coast got together. It was beautiful. I'm all about that unity, that peace and love."

"It's politics and you don't know that everywhere," said Yukmouth, half of Oakland, California, platinum rap duo the Luniz. "You're thinking L.A. is just Hollywood. You're thinking you can just go out there and chill and it's politics. Now you know when you go out there, you've got to watch where you go.

"It made me more alert on how to respect the situation," Yukmouth added, regarding the release of *Bangin on Wax*. "There's neighborhoods everywhere. Don't think you're the biggest, roughest, toughest and that you're the only dude that came from a neighborhood and you're the only dude that own a gun. Stop it. Everybody comes from some shit and it depends on how serious your disrespect is on if there will be penalties and casualties for wearing the wrong color in somebody's neighborhood or driving the wrong color car in somebody's neighborhood."

Yukmouth had learned this lesson in real life. His friend and fellow Oakland rapper Dru Down almost lost his life because he was in Los Angeles and wearing the wrong color in the wrong neighborhood.

In 1993, Dru Down was in a Rollin 60s Neighborhood Crips section of Los Angeles driving in a red car and wearing all red, the color synonymous with the Bloods. This was prior to the release of his popular "Pimp of the Year" song, meaning that Dru Down's celebrity had yet to peak and that he had yet to become a known commodity in the streets.

As he got out of his car and walked toward the door to pick up a girl, he was approached by a teenager on a bicycle. "He'd seen him getting out the car and was like, 'What's up, cuz?'" Yukmouth said, referencing the Crips' way of greeting one another with "cuz." "[Dru Down] was like, 'Ah, I don't do that shit, man' and [walked away]. That little boy rode around the corner and came back with the whole neighborhood."

The Crips surrounded the residence and Dru Down was unable to leave the house for approximately five hours. One of the elder statesmen from the Rollin 60s approached the house and asked to speak with Dru Down.

"He's like, 'Man, I'm Dru Down. I don't do this shit, man,'" Yukmouth said. "He's like, 'But you look like a motherfuckin' Blood 'cause you got the perm. You got the red shit on. You're light-skinned.' Then he said, 'Check this shit out, man. I'ma give you my shit. Take that shit off. I'ma give you my shit. Put this blue shit on. That's only how you're going to come out this house, bro. If not, good luck.'"

Dru Down obliged, changing his outfit and leaving the residence unscathed after the standoff.

"It was that serious," Yukmouth said. "So that's when we knew, 'Oh, this Blood–Crip shit is serious. We know not to go over there with this color or over there with that color.' That shit was deeper than rap. You hear the shit and you see the shit on like *Menace II Society* and shit like that, but we never *lived* it, 'cause you know we don't gangbang in Oakland. It's more about pimping and hustling."

Once Dru Down and Yukmouth took stock of the situation, they realized they'd had only a small glimpse into the gravity and intensity of gang culture in Los Angeles, despite what they'd seen in movies and heard in songs.

"We had no clue," Yukmouth said. "It was just an innocent situation. Dru was trying to pick up a girl and was in the wrong neighborhood with the wrong fuckin' clothes on. But it's something as easy as that that could get your ass knocked down if you don't know what the fuck you're doing. Thank God, the dude came in and talked to him and got the clothes or it would have been over for Dru. We wouldn't be hearing about 'Pimp of the Year' right now. So, that shit is serious, man. Those motherfuckin' gangbangers ain't playing."

> ## "'We know not to go over there with this color or over there with that color.' That shit was deeper than rap."
>
> **YUKMOUTH**

Whereas people outside of Los Angeles may not have understood the city's gang mores, the city's rappers had years of experience dealing with their region's street code. By 1993, Compton's Most Wanted had amassed a huge following, released three albums, and had their "Growin' Up in the Hood" featured as a main single on the *Boyz N the Hood* soundtrack. As a solo act, MC Eiht had his "Streiht Up Menace" featured as the lead single from the *Menace II Society* soundtrack. Like *New Jack City* and *Boyz N the Hood* before it, the 1993 film *Menace II Society* focused on urban black America in the early nineties. But unlike its predecessors, *Menace II Society* is more overtly violent and primarily focuses on the lives of the criminals and gangbangers themselves, including A-Wax, who was portrayed by MC Eiht.

As one of gangster rap's preeminent artists, MC Eiht was mindful of his gang affiliation when he would go throughout Los Angeles to promote his projects.

"If I know I'm going to do an in-store in a Blood neighborhood, I'm not finna go over there just irritating a nigga wearing all blue," MC Eiht said. "I'm finna wear green or some gray or some shit so when a muthafucka come in and get his autograph, he's still gonna be like, 'This fuckin' Crip nigga,' but he's still finna buy that motherfuckin' tape and get that motherfuckin' autograph because he's

GANGSTER TALK

SEVERAL RAP SONG and album titles reference gang affiliations. The following are some noteworthy examples.

"Get Your Walk On" (2000) by Xzibit. Mr. X to the Z delivered this popular ode to Crip Walking, the dance synonymous with the Crips.

***Crip Hop* (2001) by Jayo Felony.** The San Diego rapper's project showed that rappers beyond Los Angeles represented the Crips.

***Tha Blue Carpet Treatment* (2006) by Snoop Dogg.** Given Snoop Dogg's status as a Crip, he flipped the popular "red carpet treatment" saying to fit his gang's affinity for blue.

"Blutiful World" (2007) by Spider Loc. The one-time G-Unit affiliate rapped about a world where everything was blue—and released a striking video to match.

***The R.E.D. Album* (2011) by the Game.** The Compton rapper ushered in a new wave of attention for Bloods rappers, a point cemented by the title of his fourth major label album.

"Bicken Back Being Bool" (2014) by YG. The Compton rapper replaced the first letters in *kicken* and *cool* to reflect his status as a Bloods member.

not feeling too irritated because, let's face it, he's like, 'I like that motherfucka's song, but I'm trying to be true to where I'm from.'"

The idea of "being where you're from" was used not just to refer to where someone grew up, but to refer more specifically to the premier gang in that neighborhood. To the average listener, that distinction was often lost. In the rap world, though, the hardcore rappers in Los Angeles, who were labeled as gangster rappers, differed from their New York counterparts who adopted the same style and subject matter as gangster rappers (guns, drugs, violence, profanity) but were not viewed by many artists, journalists, and fans as gangster rappers, because they did not rap about Los Angeles gang culture. Indeed, the "gangster," "street," "reality," and/or "thug" rappers not from Los Angeles typically rapped about the blanket persona and habits of a traditional gangster and the criminal lifestyle rather than gangbanging itself.

"They're not where we're from," MC Eiht said. "L.A. is considered gangsters, Crips, Bloods. *Now* you have that in New York. But back then, when you had the Kool G Raps and the Fat Joes and the Mobb Deeps or whoever that were like, 'Yo, we're from the projects. We play craps. We're with the homies with the L [marijuana cigarette] and we're pushing that white girl [cocaine].' They were just looked at as niggas from the projects that was hustlers. They didn't symbolize with gangs. They didn't say, 'We're from 159 Bronx Crips,' so it enabled them to go, 'Yeah. There's fifteen of us on the block in front of the projects selling our shit ready to bust at you,' but they weren't looked at as gangsters because they didn't glorify, 'I'm a Blood. I'm a Crip.' That was the difference."

Another difference was that their associations with either red or blue made the Bloods and Crips easily identifiable to both people entrenched in the streets and casual observers alike. Many of the street crews from other cities were not as brazen with their attire.

Furthermore, many of the Bloods and Crips sets got their names from their specific streets or neighborhoods (i.e. Hoover [Street] Crips and Rollin' 60s Neighborhood Crips), which gave them each a geographical ground zero in addition to their color preferences.

"If we would have never incorporated red and blue into it, we would have been just like them down-south niggas, them up-north California niggas, the New York niggas," MC Eiht said. "We would have been just a group of niggas congregating. That's our crew. . . . You can go to New York and get around the same twenty niggas. Half of them got dope and guns on 'em. Half of 'em is gonna bust on a nigga that drive by their hood, but they weren't looked at as Bloods or Crips, so now you can have a Fat Joe, you can have a Mobb Deep or Kool G Rap, but they weren't looked at as, 'This nigga's wearing all red or all blue,' it took them to a different element."

That difference enabled rappers from New York, for instance, to earn a certain level of respect from the media and fans alike. New York rappers, such as Kool G Rap, for instance, were often revered for their lyrics, style, and storytelling in a way California gangster rappers weren't. The New York rappers were more respected and viewed more as artists than the Los Angeles gangster rappers.

"New York never symbolized themselves with that color shit," MC Eiht said. "That's why we always got a bad rap for it, because it made it look like it was just a gang of dumb niggas fighting over red and blue. They didn't take it for, 'This shit's been going on since the sixties and seventies, when niggas wasn't wearing colors, when niggas was wearing zoot suit hats, canes, and fuckin' shit like that. It wasn't as bad then. But when niggas going, 'I'm a Blood with my red rag. I'm a Crip with my blue rag,' that's when the shit got like, 'These dumb niggas out here killin' each other over colors.' It's not that. It's just what we symbolize with, but California is the gangbanging town, Crip, Blood, whatever. New York is crews, hustlers. That type of situation."

Although much of the discussion surrounding gangs in rap was negative at the time, Ice-T's 1993 song "Gotta Lotta Love" paid homage to the gang truce enacted by rival Watts, California, gangs just prior to the 1992 Rodney King riots. It was a remarkable act in the midst of the escalating violence that the gangs brokered their own peace accord. The gang truce did not eliminate gang

STAYING AFFILIATED

ONCE GANGSTER RAPPERS reach significant success, many remain as members of, or affiliated with, gangs. Although many people wonder why they maintain their affiliation, leaving the lifestyle and the culture isn't necessarily easy.

"Once you grow up in that environment, it actually becomes part of your psyche and your fabric of who you are," said RBX, who grew up in Long Beach, California, and who rose to prominence after appearing on Dr. Dre's *The Chronic* and his cousin Snoop Dogg's *Doggystyle* albums. "What you strive to become is kind of different, but you must always remember where you came from. So, it's a tad bit of that. Also in the hood, we were taught not to sell out and hold it together the way you was taught from your uncles and elders, and sometimes that comes off as gangbangerish."

Thus, as a rapper's star rises, he finds that bringing an overtly gangbanging persona into corporate America becomes a balancing act.

"Some people know how to turn it off or turn it down, and some people don't," RBX said. "Some people maybe use it as a badge for respect, and to some it's just a part of a thing they went through and you really can't take it [away]. It's a real slippery slope, that thing."

violence, but it did quell some of the tension between factions of the Bloods and Crips that were at war with one another.

On "Gotta Lotta Love," Ice-T explained his shock at and reverence for the treaty.

I never thought I'd live to see us chill / Crips and Bloods holdin' hands, the shit is ill / But I love it, I can't help it / Too much death on the streets, and we dealt it

Also in 1993, Ice Cube protégé Kam released the song "Peace Treaty," another cut celebrating the gang-initiated truce.

Hit the park, bailed out the car / And seen blue and red everywhere, look how strong we are / Niggas showin' up from this gang and that gang / Nobody set-trippin', 'cause it's a black thing

As Ice-T and Kam were preaching unity, Compton's Most Wanted and DJ Quik were in the early stages of their rivalry, one that would push gangster rap into new lyrical territory. When Ice Cube left N.W.A in the late eighties and Dr. Dre departed Ruthless Records in 1991, each party dissed the other on songs, but neither brought gangbanging into the discourse.

The same was initially true for DJ Quik and Compton's Most Wanted (CMW). DJ Quik had dissed his fellow Comptonites on "Real Doe," a cut from his independently released *The Red Tape*, after interpreting a line from CMW's 1991 song "Def Wish," from *Straight Checkn 'Em*, as a diss to him. DJ Quik dissed CMW again on "Tha Last Word," the closing cut from his *Way 2 Fonky* album, calling out a "no-reppin', monkey-faced, one-hit-having ass, simpleminded punk, muthafuckin'-ass nigga from CMW." CMW responded in 1992 with "Def Wish II," which featured MC Eiht dissing DJ Quik's music and his (at the time) signature perm hairstyle. In 1994, MC Eiht released his first solo album, *We Come Strapped*, and dissed DJ Quik again with "Def Wish III."

But things changed later in 1994 with DJ Quik's "Dollars & Sense." Here, DJ Quik shouted out the Tree Top Piru

Blood gang, of which he was a member, and questioned MC Eiht's affiliation with the Tragniew Park Compton Crips.

Now that the platinum-selling DJ Quik had boasted of his Blood affiliation, other prominent rappers were about to become bolder in repping their own gang ties in their songs, videos, and album art.

"People started rapping about the shit in Chicago," Yukmouth said. "We ain't knowing. Now we know. You've got to watch out for the Vice Lords, the GDs [Gangster Disciples], the Latin Kings. Boom. Okay. People start rapping about Miami shit. Okay. Now you've got to watch out for the Zoes [Zoe Pound]. You've got to watch out for the Cubans. You start getting the word from these people's raps. You know how they're moving and everybody got gang ties and everybody's from the streets. This hip-hop shit is still the streets, 'cause everybody who do it is still from the fuckin' streets."

Yet as the platform and expectation for gangster rappers to flaunt their gang affiliations increased due to authenticity demands from artists, record labels, and fans alike, the next two major milestones for gangster rap came from two dramatically different sources, one that branded a decidedly laid-back portion of the genre and another that led to the genre's expansion into another region.

G-funk Meets Mob Music

IN 1994, THE WORLD VACILLATED BETWEEN LONGSTANDING WRONGS FINALLY BEING RIGHTED AND NEW MORAL ATROCITIES.

Nelson Mandela was sworn in as South Africa's first black president, a groundbreaking step after the fall of apartheid, the country's governmental system that practiced institutionalized racial segregation and discrimination. The Rwandan genocide began after a plane with the Rwandan and Burundian presidents was shot down. The event led to the Rwandan Hutu ethnic group slaughtering approximately seven thousand members of the country's Tutsi population in a stadium in the city of Kibuye.

In the shadow of those evils, justice was served in a number of high-profile ways in the United States. Byron De La Beckwith was sentenced to life in prison thirty years after killing civil rights leader Medgar Evers. Rodney King was awarded $3.8 million in compensation from the City of Los Angeles for his

1994
Key Rap Releases

1. Warren G & Nate Dogg "Regulate" single

2. OutKast's *Southernplayalisticadillacmuzik* album

3. Nas's *Illmatic* album

US President

Bill Clinton

Something Else

Amazon.com was founded.

beating at the hands of the Los Angeles Police Department. A federal jury also convicted all four men on trial for the 1993 bombing of the World Trade Center in New York that killed six people and caused hundreds of millions of dollars in damages. The charges included using a destructive device resulting in death and the destruction of government property.

By 1994, rap was enjoying more than a decade of sustained exponential growth. The genre had grown from an almost exclusively New York–area marvel into an international phenomenon whose tentacles continued expanding into other forms of media. Gangster rappers, in particular, had also shown their keen ability to evolve and find success beyond simply making music.

Schoolly D, for instance, was working extensively on soundtracks and scores for such movies as *King of New York* and *Bad Lieutenant*, with acclaimed indie film director Abel Ferrara. After their respective breakthrough film roles in 1991, both Ice-T (*New Jack City*) and Ice Cube (*Boyz N the Hood*) were establishing themselves as bankable actors and had starred together in the heist film *Trespass*.

As rap music entered the New Year, there were two major long-simmering breakthroughs on the horizon—both able to show that gangster rap could connect with people in less menacing ways and with dramatically different sounds. The first was something that Above the Law created, Dr. Dre popularized, Snoop Dogg named, and Warren G branded.

> ## "N.W.A was on some damn-near Public Enemy shit with their beats. Above the Law came and slowed it down."
>
> **— YUKMOUTH**

The percolation began in 1990. During the height of Ruthless Records, Eazy-E signed the rap group Above the Law to his record label. Based in Pomona, California (about thirty miles east of Los Angeles), the group consisted of rapper-producer Cold 187um, rapper KMG the Illustrator, DJ Total K-Oss, and DJ Go Mack. Their first album, 1990's *Livin' Like Hustlers*, was produced by Dr. Dre, Laylaw (also the group's manager), and Above the Law, and featured the rap hits "Murder Rap" and "Untouchable," as well as the posse cut "The Last Song" with N.W.A.

Lyrically, *Livin' Like Hustlers* dealt with the common gangster rap themes of violence, drugs, and sex, but Above the Law also added a political undercurrent to much of their work, and focused on being hustlers, players, and pimps more than straight-up gangsters. They also introduced the idea of a black mafia to the rap world. Furthermore, Cold 187um (also known as Big Hutch) and KMG the Illustrator rapped differently than many other rappers of the era, choosing a more deliberate, steady delivery than that of most of their contemporaries. Additionally, Cold 187um's higher-pitched, nasal tone played well with KMG's deeper, huskier voice.

"They slowed that shit completely down to where they're talking to you," Yukmouth said. "It felt like a conversation when you're in the car. You're bumping [the music and] are like, 'Is the muthafucker talkin' to me?' It felt like that and it hit home like that. You could understand it, and it ain't too tricky to where you've got to listen to it one thousand times to figure out what this nigga said, or go look in a thesaurus or dictionary to figure it out. It was straight to the point."

It was sonically, though, that Above the Law made their most profound impact.

In the late eighties, EPMD, Eazy-E, and N.W.A had released music using funk samples in their respective works. So did conscious rap group X Clan, which rapped over Parliament's beats on their 1990 album *To the East, Blackwards*, most notably on their single "Funkin' Lesson" and album cut "Earth Bound." Similarly, Ice Cube protégé (and younger cousin) Del tha Funkee Homosapien rapped over Funkadelic's beats on his 1991 album, *I Wish My Brother George Was Here*.

But both X Clan and Del tha Funkee Homosapien rapped in esoteric rhymes, with X Clan's black nationalistic lyrics and Del tha Funkee Homosapien's equally dense songs about everyday struggles earning them cult followers among certain demographics of the expanding rap fan base. But neither of the acts (nor EPMD, Eazy-E, or N.W.A before them) made funk the foundation of their musical identity in the way that Above the Law did. They were not purely gangster rappers, either.

When Above the Law emerged in 1990, producer Cold 187um incorporated samples from, at the time, unconventional musical sources for rap, such as Quincy Jones and Isaac Hayes. The following year, Cold 187um developed the sound that would shape that of gangster rap for the next several years. He produced Above the Law's 1991 EP, *Vocally Pimpin'*. The nine-song project was anchored by the single "4 the Funk of It," which borrowed its groove and some of the lyrics of its chorus from Funkadelic's "One Nation Under a Groove," a funk music staple.

Cold 187um delved deeper into the funk vaults on Above the Law's second album, *Black Mafia Life*, which was released in 1992. He made the sound Above the Law's signature, kicking off the project with "Never Missin' a Beat," which featured a sample of Funkadelic's "(Not Just) Knee Deep." Cold 187um's cousin singer-rapper Kokane delivered vocals that mimicked the work of the Parliament and Funkadelic vocalists.

The second song on *Black Mafia Life*, "Why Must I Feel Like Dat," sampled George Clinton's "Atomic Dog" and Parliament's "I Can Move You (If You Let Me)." *Black Mafia Life* also mined Funkadelic's "Freak of the Week" for its "Call It What U Want" single featuring 2Pac and Digital Underground's Money B. Elsewhere, Cold 187um incorporated Parliament's "Mothership Connection (Star Child)" into *Black Mafia Life* cut "Pimp Clinic."

Although it didn't have a name yet, the sound Above the Law ushered in through *Vocally Pimpin'* and *Black Mafia Life* was later used by one-time collaborator and Ruthless Records labelmate Dr. Dre throughout his massively popular and influential debut album, *The Chronic*. Like Above the Law before him, Dr. Dre relied on the work of Parliament, Funkadelic, and George Clinton for what would become his album's signature material.

Dr. Dre's *The Chronic* single "__ wit Dre Day (And Everybody's Celebratin')," for instance, built its sonics on samples from Funkadelic's "(Not Just) Knee Deep" and George Clinton's "Atomic Dog." The song shares much of the sound of Above the Law's "Never Missin' a Beat," the first cut on *Black Mafia Life*.

"Let Me Ride," another *The Chronic* single, sampled Parliament's "Mothership Connection (Star Child)" and "Swing Down, Sweet Chariot" in much the same way Above the Law had on *Black Mafia Life* selection "Pimp Clinic."

But while Above the Law's *Black Mafia Life* scored rap hits with singles "V.S.O.P." and "Call It What U Want," the album sold less than five hundred thousand copies. On the other hand, Dr. Dre's *The Chronic* sold more than three million copies within a year of its release, becoming one of the bestselling and most influential albums in rap history.

Dr. Dre's next production project was Snoop Dogg's debut album, 1993's *Doggystyle*. Like *The Chronic*, it incorporated funk samples and funk elements throughout. It also featured a song called "G Funk Intro," which gave a name to the sound Above the Law had created with *Vocally Pimpin'* and *Black Mafia Life* and that Dr. Dre popularized with *The Chronic*.

"This is just a small introduction to the G-Funk era," Snoop Dogg raps on "G Funk Intro," which, like *The Chronic* single "__ wit Dre Day (And Everybody's Celebratin')," sampled Funkadelic's "(Not Just) Knee Deep." The G-Funk (gangster funk) era was officially underway, indeed, but Dr. Dre's and Snoop Dogg's popularity may have overshadowed Above the Law's innovation because, in rap, the artist who makes something commercially popular is often more revered than the person who created or inspired it.

"They were the originators of G-Funk, period," Yukmouth said of Above the Law. "N.W.A was on some damn-near Public Enemy shit with their beats. Above the Law came and slowed it down. It was groovy. Us being from the Bay, there's a lot of pimps, a lot of hustlers, so we like the slowed-down, mob, groovy shit, so we were into Above the Law. It was funky."

After Above the Law created G-Funk, Dr. Dre popularized it, and Snoop Dogg named it. The next major player in the G-Funk wave was Dr. Dre's stepbrother, Warren G, who branded the music and became synonymous with it.

SOUTH CENTRAL'S FINEST

SOUTH CENTRAL CARTEL became the first purely gangster rap act from the West Coast to release a project on one of Russell Simmons's bevy of labels. The six-member crew released their *'N Gatz We Truss* via Rush Associated Labels (RAL) in 1994 and collaborated with Ice-T, MC Eiht, 2Pac, and Spice 1 on the single "Gangsta Team." Onyx—a rap quartet from Queens, New York, whose *Bacdafucup* was released by RAL in 1993—and Bo$$—a female gangster rapper from Detroit who released her *Born Gangstaz* album in 1993 on RAL—were the first gangster rappers to release material via the hip-hop mogul.

Warren G gained notoriety in his Long Beach hometown as one-third of the group 213, which got their name from the original area code of Long Beach and also featured friend Snoop Dogg and fellow Long Beach artist and singer Nate Dogg. As 213 gained popularity in the region, Dr. Dre became familiar with Snoop Dogg's work through Warren G.

But as Dr. Dre, Snoop Dogg, and Death Row Records catapulted to superstardom, Warren G became a supporting act rather than a focal point in the Death Row Records lineup, appearing on the intro of *The Chronic* selection "Deeez Nuuuts" and rapping on *Doggystyle* selection "Aint No Fun (If The Homies Cant Have None)."

Unlike his friend and 213 partner in rhyme Snoop Dogg, Warren G didn't sign with Death Row Records, the imprint co-owned by his stepbrother, Dr. Dre. Instead, Warren G signed with Violator/Rush Associated Labels, sister labels of Def Jam Recordings, the iconic New York rap label that had released such groundbreaking acts as LL Cool J, Beastie Boys, Public Enemy, and Slick Rick.

Warren G had a reason not to sign with Death Row Records. "I didn't want to be waitin'," he said. "I wanted people to hear what I had, and I would have had to really wait for Snoop to do his thing. My brother had already did his thing when we did *The Chronic*, and I didn't feel like waiting. Dre was like, 'Warren, you need to go on and be your own man and get out there and do your thing.' So I was like, 'Shit.' It hurt, but I went out and did it."

After producing and rapping on rapper-singer Mista Grimm's 1993 song "Indo Smoke," which was featured on the soundtrack for the 2Pac and Janet

DOMINO

With a singsongy style that was often more R&B than rap, Long Beach rapper-singer Domino broke through in late 1993 with his smash "Getto Jam" single. Both "Getto Jam" and his 1993 self-titled album were certified gold in 1994. The *Domino* album was primarily produced by DJ Battlecat, a one-time KDAY mixmaster who would later produce material for Snoop Dogg, Kurupt, and Xzibit, among others. DJ Quik affiliate AMG also produced on the project.

Jackson film *Poetic Justice*, Warren G ironically got his first major exposure through a Death Row Records project. Warren G and Nate Dogg teamed up in 1994 for "Regulate," the main single from the soundtrack for the 2Pac vehicle *Above the Rim*, which Death Row Records released in March 1994.

Warren G produced "Regulate," which lifted its velvety groove from Michael McDonald's "I Keep Forgettin'." The song's smooth, laid-back sonics and airy aural atmosphere stood in stark contrast to Warren G's rhymes about getting robbed at gunpoint for his jewelry. Fortunately for Warren G, Nate Dogg was there to "regulate" the situation by shooting the assailants. After their bodies dropped, Nate Dogg sang in his stoic style about how he and Warren G were able to resume pursuing women. A car full of them agreed to accompany the crooner to the fictitious Eastside Motel.

As the song concludes, Warren G puts his stamp on G-Funk, saying it is "where rhythm is life and life is rhythm." Nate Dogg follows him by singing, "It's the G-Funk era, funked out with a gangsta twist."

Thanks in large part to the massive success of "Regulate," the *Above the Rim* soundtrack sold more than one million copies in two months and more than two million copies in less than six months, making it a double-platinum project for Death Row Records. As a single, "Regulate" sold more than one million copies in less than four months, making Warren G's first single a platinum-certified smash hit and a great launching pad for his solo career.

Released on June 7, 1994, Warren G's *Regulate... G Funk Era* branded the wave of gangster rap that Above the Law had been developing for years and that Dr. Dre had popularized through the immense success of his *The Chronic* album and Snoop Dogg's subsequent *Doggystyle* album.

But *Regulate... G Funk Era* had a much different lyrical tenor than the work of Above the Law, Dr. Dre, and Snoop Dogg. Where the lyrics by those artists were regularly rife with testosterone-filled episodes of a violent life on the streets in which they often played the victor, Warren G took a wistful approach on many of his songs. With "Do You See," for instance, Warren G rapped about the numbing effect of violence in his neighborhood and how, when Snoop Dogg was incarcerated, he made a decision to stop selling drugs and pursue music in earnest.

On Warren G's other big hit from *Regulate... G Funk Era*, "This D.J.," he rapped over smooth, high-pitched keyboards about playing basketball and heading home once the streetlights came on. He augmented his income by selling weed, but he wasn't portraying himself as a major baller or drug dealer. Instead, it was a way for him to make money and enjoy the smaller moments in his life. Warren G's world was "gangster lite," in a sense, a soft-spoken complement to the gruffer material being made by such musical partners as Nate Dogg and Snoop Dogg.

"Nate brought the gangster melodies to the game," Warren G said. "Snoop brought the smooth gangster style to the game. They've had an incredible impact. I'm the cool type."

Although Warren G's musical sensibility wasn't as harsh, aggressive, and confrontational as the rest of the gangster rap world, he is credited with showcasing a new layer of the experience with a different sound.

"That was just another side of what we brought to the table as far as gangster rap music," MC Eiht said. "It was still a part of that. You had Above the Law, you had Warren [G], you had Kokane. That was a part of Dr. Dre, Eazy[-E], that straight gangster era that we went through."

Warren G's *Regulate... G Funk Era* was a top-seller, rivaling *The Chronic*, the more acclaimed and culturally significant release from his stepbrother, Dr. Dre. The album sold more than two million copies in two months and moved an additional one million copies by August 1995.

With a combination of well-known associates, quality music, impeccable timing, and a musical movement people could gravitate toward, Warren G became the flagship G-Funk artist.

"I think Warren G exploded for it because he made it a lane, made it a movement instead of people just doing the music," Yukmouth said. "He said 'G-Funk.' They were screaming that shit in every rap. . . . They capitalized on it. They not only made the brand, made the word, made the movement, but the music. They made classic shit, 'Regulate,' one of the best G-Funk beats ever done."

KMEL

The San Francisco–based radio station was a pivotal player in breaking rap records in the region. In the late eighties, it began playing mix shows, and by the early nineties, the station had some of the most progressive programs on urban radio, including Sway (later of MTV fame) & King Tech's *The Wake Up Show*, which played a bevy of independent music and showcased freestyle raps from then-emerging acts such as JAY-Z, Eminem, and Wu-Tang Clan.

While the various practitioners of G-Funk were dominating radio, video, and the sales charts, another gangster rap movement was gaining traction in the San Francisco Bay Area: Mob Music. The divergent Northern California rap scene made its first major mark in the mideighties thanks to Oakland's Too $hort and his partner in rhyme, Freddy B, who would hawk their homemade—and later customized for consumers—rap tapes on public transit. Soon thereafter, Too $hort became a pioneering rapper from the area who was known not only for his groundbreaking music about the world of pimps, prostitutes, and sex, but who also delivered several socially aware and political songs. His often slow, stripped-down, and sonically spare music contained funk elements thanks to the use of live bass guitar and keyboards, among other things.

Much like Southern California, Northern California was rocked by violence throughout the eighties and early nineties. Even though Southern California was rife with gangs and Northern California was not, it suffered many of the same crime-related travails. In Oakland, where the population was 378,617, there were 140 homicides in 1994.

While the harsh streets of Oakland were the topic of much of Too $hort's music and helped push him to platinum success at the turn of the nineties, other rappers from the city had different stories to tell. Fellow Oakland act Digital Underground, for instance, delivered a string of popular party rap records, most notably "Doowutchyalike" and "The Humpty Dance," before introducing their protégé, roadie and dancer 2Pac, as a solo artist. Ice Cube's cousin Del tha Funkee Homosapien added another thoughtful perspective to the discussion with his

PAUL STEWART

Starting off as a DJ and record promoter, Los Angeles native Paul Stewart became instrumental in Russell Simmons's embrace of West Coast artists. With New York rap manager Chris Lighty, Stewart executive-produced Warren G's *Regulate... G Funk Era*, which was released on Simmons's Rush Associated Labels (RAL) imprint. In conjunction with his own PMP company, Stewart signed singer Montell Jordan to RAL, launching a successful career accented by platinum party hit "This Is How We Do It" (1995) and the sensuous single "Let's Ride" (1998).

stories about the struggles of the everyman trying to survive amid typical life challenges and the crime and chaos enveloping his city.

About ten miles west of Oakland, San Francisco rapper Paris had cultivated a loyal following that gravitated toward his Black Panthers–inspired messaging and political commentary. Around the same time in Hayward, fifteen miles south of Oakland, Spice 1 was emerging as the San Francisco Bay Area's preeminent straight-up gangster rapper. His overtly violent rhymes were driven by graphic murder talk on such songs as "187 Proof," "Trigga Gots No Heart," and "187 He Wrote."

Yet Too $hort, Digital Underground, Del tha Funkee Homosapien, and Paris were each capturing different segments of the rap-buying public, with Too $hort having the streets locked down, Digital Underground appealing to the college crowd, Del tha Funkee Homosapien sewing up the skater set, and Paris attracting the revolutionary minded. Even though Too $hort rapped about the world in which gangster rappers existed, he didn't present himself as a gangster. Instead, he was more focused on money and how crime was crippling his city. Spice 1 was a bona fide gangster rapper, but he was a lone wolf of sorts—albeit a hugely popular one with three gold albums. Unlike most of the gangster rappers in Southern California (Ice-T, Ice Cube) or Compton (Eazy-E, N.W.A, Compton's Most Wanted, DJ Quik), who were part of a camp of similar artists, Spice 1 was not part of a larger movement of artists that helped sustain either his success or his visibility.

Another set of artists from the area, though, was about to seize the street audience in what would later be christened as the Yay Area. Based in Vallejo

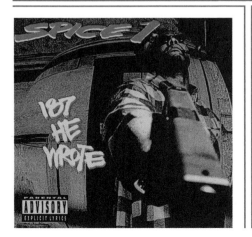

MURDER HE WROTE

Spice 1 made murder his topic of choice throughout his prolific career, as evidenced by such songs as "Money or Murder," "I'm the Fuckin' Murderer," and "The Murda Show." There was a sizable market for the one-time Jive Records artist's particular brand of grisly gun talk. Each of the Hayward rapper's first three albums (1992's *Spice 1*, 1993's *187 He Wrote*, and 1994's *AmeriKKKa's Nightmare*) went gold, selling in excess of five hundred thousand units each.

SACRAMENTO'S TREACHEROUS THREE

Southern California is often synonymous with gangster rap. Three rappers from the Golden State's capital have also been among the genre's most prolific and noteworthy because of their maniacal music and their affiliation with the Garden Blocc Crips. Two of them also have notable arrest records.

X-Raided. The release of the rapper's debut album, 1992's *Psycho Active*, was accompanied by controversy. X-Raided was arrested after authorities said some of the material on the collection described a local murder, and also claimed that the gun X-Raided was holding to his head on the album cover was the actual murder weapon. After his arrest, X-Raided recorded material over the phone while incarcerated. He was convicted of first-degree murder, which was also ruled a gang-related homicide. He was sentenced to thirty-one years to life in prison, and has released more than a dozen albums while incarcerated.

Brotha Lynch Hung. The producer of X-Raided's *Psycho Active* album for Black Market Records, Brotha Lynch Hung also signed to the Sacramento imprint, which released his *24 Deep* project in 1993. The nine-track collection's hallmark is the dark, eerie vibe on such selections as the title track, "Back Fade," and "Fundamentals of Ripgut Cannibalism (Outro)." Black Market signed a distribution deal with Priority

Records, bringing Brotha Lynch Hung's 1995 album, *Season of da Siccness*, to a national audience. In 2001, he collaborated with C-Bo for the Blocc Movement album. Nine years later, he released the first of his three LPs for Tech N9ne's Strange Music.

C-Bo. After garnering regional attention in 1994 with his *The Autopsy* and *Gas Chamber* projects, C-Bo (who appeared on 2Pac's *All Eyez on Me* album) earned national headlines four years later when he was arrested and incarcerated after the state of California determined that the content included on his 1998 *'Til My Casket Drops* album violated the terms of his parole. The terms of C-Bo's parole included provisions that restricted him from associating with gang members, as well as a stipulation that he would "not engage in any behavior which promotes the gang lifestyle, criminal behavior and/or violence against law enforcement." *'Til My Casket Drops* song "Deadly Game" includes lyrics about killing a police officer in order to avoid being arrested.

(about thirty miles north of San Francisco), E-40 and the Click (E-40's brother, D-Shot; sister, Suga-T; and cousin B-Legit) began gaining traction in the early nineties thanks to such releases as the Click's "Mr. Flamboyant" and E-40's "Captain Save a Hoe" and "Practice Lookin' Hard."

"When 'Mr. Flamboyant' came out, it just swept our whole area," Kansas City rapper Tech N9ne said. "There was nothing like it musically, and E-40 was just giving game in a way that was exciting to the fan no matter how young they were, because some of that game was over the head of the young ones, but the delivery was so new and exciting, and still is today. It sounded like nothing we'd ever heard before."

E-40's and the Click's blend of street tales—running the gamut from gangster stories and pimp tales to life lessons and business tips—made them more than just gangster rappers. Similar to the G-Funk artists, the way E-40 and the Click rapped wasn't loud, confrontational, or overtly aggressive like many other gangster rappers of the era.

> *"Anything West Coast is just West Coast.... We are these type of people that don't give a fuck. It's California. It's West Coast..."*
>
> **MC EIHT**

"E-40 was a gentler kind of gangster rap," said Leslie "Big Lez" Segar, former host of BET's *Rap City*. "I didn't really feel threatened by anything he said or depicted in his rhymes."

Furthermore, E-40's slippery delivery style and his ability to make up words, to flip phrases, and to redefine terms made him instantly identifiable.

"His vernacular and the way he rapped, he rapped like no-fuckin'-body in the Bay Area has ever rapped," said Yukmouth, who grew up in Oakland, California, about twenty-five miles south of Vallejo. "How quick he is and how sharp he is putting it together has always been the key to his success, and the words he invents from the gate. He was calling the police the 'Po-po Penelope,' the 'Federalis.' He had lingo and words that we didn't know. He put that out there and we started rocking with it."

E-40 pioneered virtually a dictionary's worth of slang, including *fasheezy*, adding *-izzle* to the end of words, and referring to marijuana as "broccoli."

"E-40 is a trendsetter," Tech N9ne said. "But his trends never die. His flow is groundbreaking. He has an ear for music."

Sonically, E-40's and the Click's music was also distinctive. It was spearheaded by producers Mike Mosley, who had met E-40 in the streets before they started making music together, and Sam Bostic, a funk and soul musician who had released *Circuitry Starring Sam Bostic* in 1985 on Atlantic Records. Mosley would play the initial take on the material and then have Bostic come in and replay it, adding another layer of musicianship to the track.

"It was a mixture of me knowing how to produce like a Quincy Jones or like a Dr. Dre, knowing to have somebody come in and give me a certain sound that I need that I couldn't necessarily play it myself all the way," Mike Mosley said. "I would play it up to a certain point, and then I would hire this guy to come in [and be like], 'Hey, play this right here.' Then he'd replay it and funk it out."

The Mob Music sound, as it would later be known, was identified by its slow, bass-heavy, groovy, and melodic qualities. "M.O.B.: musically orchestrated basslines," E-40 said. "It's a certain sound. It's gotta be sinister. It's a sound. It ain't about a shoot 'em up bang bang or whatever. As long as that bassline's heavy, or it sounds real eerie and the drums [are] kickin', [it's Mob Music]. It's a feel. That's what Mob Music is."

Although the music was coming from Northern California, Los Angeles–area rappers quickly connected with E-40's and the Click's sounds and subject matter.

"It was on a different aspect," MC Eiht said, "but it still was the same G-Funk, synthesizers, heavy basslines, so it wasn't hard for us to get into the up-north sound.

"To us, anything West Coast is just West Coast. We know that the brothas from up north get down a little differently than the Southern California dudes as far as the gang situation. But we are these type of people that don't give a fuck. It's California. It's West Coast, and it wasn't like E-40 was so far from our shit."

E-40 and the Click also had another advantage in building their fan base. E-40 and B-Legit had attended Grambling State University, a historically black college located about three hundred miles northwest of New Orleans. While there, they performed, promoted, and connected with thousands of fans outside of their hometown in ways that the average independent rappers couldn't. Thus, when E-40 and the Click began pushing their music, they had two major markets supporting them, the San Francisco Bay Area and the South.

By 1994, E-40 and the Click had released a string of successful singles, albums, and EPs, including E-40's *Mr. Flamboyant* EP, *The Mail Man* EP, and *Federal* album (which depicts a "Mob" side and a "gangsta" side in the album's cover art). The Click also released their *Let's Side* EP and *Down & Dirty* album.

Like other business-minded rappers before him, E-40 released his material on his own record label. Sick Wid' It Records was the recording home for E-40's music as well as that of the Click. E-40's entrepreneurial spirit and independent work ethic were celebrated by Northern California rap fans.

"As far as niggas in the street, they was the epitome as far as rap groups," Yukmouth said. "To have your own record label and to put on your family and to have your own Mob Music, your own production team, that was the ultimate."

The executives at Jive Records (Whodini, Steady B, Kool Moe Dee, D.J. Jazzy Jeff & The Fresh Prince, Schoolly D, Boogie Down Productions, Too $hort, Spice 1) took notice and signed E-40 and his Sick Wid' It label to a contract that took both E-40's and the Click's success from independent and regional to major label and national.

Locally, E-40's and Sick Wid' It's success helped influence and increase the profile of a legion of independent labels and artists in the San Francisco Bay Area who released their own brand of street-centered, mob- and gangster-inspired music, including In-A-Minute Records (M.C. Pooh, R.B.L. Posse), Strictly Business Records (Mac Dre, Ray Luv), Big League Records (415, Richie Rich), Young Black Brotha Records (Ray Luv, Mac Mall,), and Get Low Records (JT The Bigga Figga, San Quinn).

These acts and their imprints helped make the San Francisco Bay Area the leading locale for independent rap, specifically independent gangster rap. Many of these artists ended up signing national deals after enjoying regional success, including M.C. Pooh (then going as Pooh-Man) with Too $hort's Dangerous Music and Jive Records, Ray Luv with Atlantic Records, and Richie Rich with Def Jam.

As gangster rap continued expanding in sound, style, and regions, it was about to endure a wave of real-life violence that would cost rap music the lives of two of its most popular and most significant artists.

Death Around the Corner: The So-Called East Coast/ West Coast Beef

IN 1994, AMERICA HAD SHOWN IT WAS LARGELY INDIFFERENT TO CULTURAL TRENDS THAT FORESHADOWED SOME OF THE MAJOR EVENTS RESPONSIBLE FOR SHAPING THE COUNTRY IN THE NEXT DECADES.

OPPOSITE:
2Pac and Leslie "Big Lez" Segar.

For many people living outside of New York, the 1993 bombing of the World Trade Center was just another news story whose gravity and foreboding went unrecognized. Furthermore, the conviction of the four men charged with the crime barely resonated with a public oblivious to the anti-American sentiment growing throughout the world.

Additionally, Rodney King's settlement was seen as a far cry from a victory by a population that had witnessed and experienced decades of police brutality. The massive riots that resulted when the police were acquitted on criminal charges caught the public's attention, but only momentarily.

1996
Key Rap Releases

1. 2Pac's *All Eyez on Me* album

2. Fugees' *The Score* album

3. Nas's "If I Ruled the World (Imagine That)" single

US President

Bill Clinton

Something Else

Bill Clinton signed welfare reform into law.

While these events were taking place in courtrooms across the country, the rap world continued to evolve. Death Row Records sustained its commercial and critical dominance with hit albums from Dr. Dre and Snoop Dogg, while P. Diddy's Bad Boy Entertainment emerged as a major player thanks to the success of Craig Mack and the Notorious B.I.G. (aka Biggie or Biggie Smalls). Eazy-E also found success post-N.W.A with his own material, solo projects from MC Ren, and Cleveland rap quintet Bone Thugs-N-Harmony. Despite these successes, however, the rap world was on the brink of a civil war of sorts, one highlighted by real-world violence.

It was seldom discussed, but for years, there was real animosity simmering between rap communities from different cities. Artists who were not from New York, in particular, often felt as though they were being slighted by the New York rap elite, whether it was record labels passing them over, radio disc jockeys Kool DJ Red Alert and Mr. Magic not playing their music, or the rap media (almost all of which was located in New York) dismissing their work. Ironically, though, West Coast rap was dramatically outselling rap from New York artists. But a casual observer—and even studious rap fans who happened to be swayed more by hype than the charts—would never have known it if they lived in New York.

"I think people in general just looked down on the West Coast," MC Ren said. "Ever since we started coming out back in the day, it was like we were the little stepbrother or something. On the West Coast, it was hard getting respect from people on the East Coast. We know hip-hop started in New York, and back then, it was that feeling like, if you wasn't from New York, you're not going to get that respect. It's been hard since then and it's hard now."

As early as 1989, the Geto Boys rapper Willie D articulated this frustration on his group's "Do It Like a G.O." single. Willie D lamented the lack of support the Geto Boys' music was getting on East Coast radio, and called out the egos of New Yorkers in particular.

The explosion in the popularity of and mainstream-media attention given to Los Angeles–area gangster rappers such as Ice-T, Eazy-E, N.W.A, Compton's Most Wanted, DJ Quik, Cypress Hill, Dr. Dre, and Snoop Dogg had shifted much of the record-buying public's and the media's focus away from New York rappers. As the trend continued into 1994, several rappers—even those not from New York—began taking note of how rap had been changing and how it had moved away from its political, or so-called "conscious," direction, which had been largely spearheaded by New York acts. This was another point of contention, as New York artists were seemingly upset that they had fallen behind, especially commercially, to gangster rappers.

One song that drew the ire of several West Coast acts was Common's 1994 single "i used to love h.e.r." (The "h.e.r." is short for "hearing every rhyme.") The song traces Common's relationship with rap, which is the "girl" he's rapping about. In the second verse, the Chicago rapper (who went by Common Sense at the time) said it was cool that she went to the West Coast and that he "wasn't salty she was with the boys in the hood," a reference to either Eazy-E's 1987 landmark single or the 1991 film starring Ice Cube—or both.

In the third verse, though, Common laments how his girl is now

A gangsta rollin' with gangsta bitches / Always smokin' blunts and gettin' drunk / Tellin' me sad stories, now she only fucks with the funk

By the time "i used to love h.e.r." was released in September 1994, the robust gangster rap industry had become synonymous with the West Coast. Through such West Coast acts as Cypress Hill, among others, rap had become associated with smoking weed, blunts in particular. Then, of course, there was the West Coast's obvious affinity for funk music and funk samples, as well as its burgeoning G-Funk movement.

As much as Common's "i used to love h.e.r." rankled some West Coast acts, the animosity between artists from different regions exploded after 2Pac was shot five times on November 30, 1994, while going to meet the Notorious B.I.G. at Quad Recording Studios in New York. Prior to that, 2Pac and the Notorious B.I.G., a Brooklyn rapper signed to P. Diddy's Bad Boy Entertainment, had become friends. Even though 2Pac was born in New York and went to high school in Baltimore, he rose to national

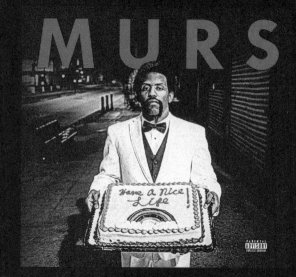

YOU AIN'T GANGSTA?!?

GROWING UP IN the Mid-City section of Los Angeles in the 1980s, Murs was affected by the same violence and gangbanging that enveloped the more famous sections of the city's metropolitan area, such as Compton, Watts, and South Central. Like many of his friends, he grew up listening to such local heroes as Eazy-E and DJ Quik, but Murs didn't want to make gangster rap. He was met with resistance when he embarked upon a nongangster rap recording career in the mid–nineteen nineties. Even the success of early nongangster rap acts the Pharcyde, Freestyle Fellowship, and Tha Alkaholiks did little to alter people's perception of what Los Angeles rap was supposed to sound like.

"LA was ready for it, but I don't think the East Coast was ready for it," Murs said. "Where I experienced the most problems was trying to get outside of LA because people would say, 'No. LA's not that.' In LA, people knew what you were. It wasn't accepted and it wasn't cool, but you had a place thanks to Unity, Rap Pages, Rap Sheet. That was the place for the Ras Kasses and the Western Hemispheres. It wasn't as big as the gangster rap scene and it wasn't as valid or respected, but it was there. Outside of LA, no hope."

prominence after relocating to the San Francisco Bay Area and becoming a member of Oakland-based rap group Digital Underground. He started off as a dancer and a roadie, touring with the outfit as their crossover songs "Doowutchyalike" and "The Humpty Dance" became major hits in 1989.

In 1991, 2Pac appeared on Digital Underground's energetic, playful "Same Song" single and released his first album, the incendiary *2Pacalypse Now*. The collection's most celebrated cut was "Brenda's Got a Baby," a somber tale about a twelve-year-old girl who gets pregnant by her cousin, throws the newborn in the trash, and gets killed after becoming a prostitute. But much of *2Pacalypse Now* focused on his disdain for police and how they often abused their authority, especially when dealing with young black men.

Also a trained actor, 2Pac became an in-demand Hollywood player thanks to his dramatic turn as the troubled Bishop in the 1992 film *Juice*. Obsessed with power, his character turns on his friends, ultimately dying during an altercation with one of them. 2Pac's star continued its ascent in 1993 with the release of his *Strictly 4 My N.I.G.G.A.Z.* album (which contained the hits "Keep Ya Head Up" and "I Get Around") and his appearance in director John Singleton's *Poetic Justice* opposite Janet Jackson.

But 2Pac's success was tempered by his increasingly serious legal issues. He was arrested six times between 1993 and when he was shot on November 30, 1994. While recuperating from his gunshot wounds, 2Pac was on trial for sexually abusing a woman. Wheelchair bound in court, on February 7, 1995, he was sentenced to one and a half to four and a half years in prison for the crime.

Later that month, the Notorious B.I.G. released a single titled "Who Shot Ya?" Although it did not directly reference 2Pac or the shooting, it was, at the least, bad timing and poor judgment to release a song called "Who Shot Ya?" while 2Pac—an alleged friend—was healing from wounds he suffered on a trip to visit Biggie. Biggie claimed the song had nothing to do with 2Pac getting shot. Regardless, the song made it appear as though something was awry between the two.

In the April 1995 issue of *Vibe* (which hit newsstands in March), 2Pac implicated former friend the Notorious B.I.G. and P. Diddy in his shooting, saying that they set him up to get robbed, beaten, and shot.

The article, according to former *Vibe* features editor Rob Kenner, "marked the first time Biggie had any idea Tupac—who was formerly a close friend—had problems with him. Our decision to change the names of two of the people in the story, both because they were not public figures but rather 'street dudes' and because we could not verify the things 2Pac was alleging about them, would come under fire in years to come."

COTTAGE BEEF INDUSTRY: THE BIGGIE & 2PAC SHOW

SEVERAL FILMS AND DOCUMENTARIES about the Notorious B.I.G. and 2Pac have been made. Here are some of the more noteworthy releases.

Biggie & Tupac (2002). This documentary film garnered media attention given director Nick Broomfield's pedigree (*Aileen: Life and Death of a Serial Killer, Kurt & Courtney*) but was derided for its lack of definitive findings regarding the murders of the rap stars despite a series of accusations that are implied but never confirmed.

Tupac: Resurrection (2003). This Academy Award–nominated film uses home movies, photographs, and 2Pac's own voice to tell the story of the late artist's life.

Notorious (2009). This biopic details the Notorious B.I.G.'s Brooklyn, New York, upbringing and his rise to rap superstardom.

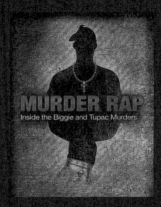

Murder Rap: Inside the Biggie and Tupac Murders (2015). This documentary is anchored by the work of retired LAPD detective Greg Kading. The film purports that the killers of both Biggie and 2Pac are not unknown. Rather, Kading says, they are simply unprosecuted because key witnesses are dead, among other factors.

All Eyez on Me (2017). Helmed by longtime video director Benny Boom, the 2Pac biopic features Demetrius Shipp Jr. starring as the late rapper and actor.

Unsolved: The Murders of Tupac & The Notorious B.I.G. (2018). This television series focuses on the travails of detectives Greg Kading and Russell Poole, among others, who worked to solve the high-profile murders of the superstar rappers.

As well intentioned as Kenner's statement may have been, it failed to address other journalistic shortcomings on *Vibe*'s part.

The publication had given 2Pac a platform to make explosive and unsubstantiated claims that were never corroborated by any research or secondary follow-up. To be fair, plenty of responsibility rests on the artists, who both ratcheted up the controversy with their actions, but *Vibe* failed in its journalistic responsibility when it neglected to notify the Notorious B.I.G. and P. Diddy about the article and its content prior to its publication. This lapse in journalistic judgment added significant fuel to the fire that eventually consumed both 2Pac and the Notorious B.I.G.

Despite rap's massive popularity in 1994, the mainstream media was still relatively reluctant to give rap much coverage. Moreover, the Internet as we know it did not yet exist, which made publications that covered rap, such as *Vibe* and the *Source*, the go-to places for information on the rap world, whether it was an album review, a story about a trend in the music, or an interview with an artist. Consequently, had the more established and respected news outlets regularly carried interviews with 2Pac and the rapidly growing rap industry, they would have likely done a more balanced job reporting on 2Pac, his allegations, and the situation regarding his shooting. If nothing else, the mainstream media typically had stricter journalistic standards.

But that didn't happen. Animosity began ramping up elsewhere, too, as Ice Cube protégé Mack 10 included the song "Westside Slaughterhouse" on his self-titled album, which was released in June 1995. The song featured Mack 10, Ice Cube, and WC blasting Common and the stance he took on "i used to love h.e.r." Ice Cube, in particular, took aim at Common and the mindset adopted by artists who felt gangster rap wasn't a valid segment of the genre.

All you suckas wanna diss the Pacific / But you busta niggas never get specific / Used to love her, mad 'cause we fucked her / Pussy-whipped bitch with no common sense / Hip-hop started in the West / Ice Cube bailin' through the East without a vest

If "Westside Slaughterhouse" served as a warning shot about the deepening animosity between acts from the East and West Coasts, entities from both sides crossed a line months later at the Source Awards, which were held at Madison Square Garden's Paramount Theatre in New York. Broadcast on August 3, 1995, the event featured a number of moments that showed the disdain that people from different rap regions held for one another.

While on stage accepting *Above the Rim*'s award for Best Motion Picture Soundtrack, Death Row Records' Suge Knight took the first shot at P. Diddy, who had become famous for appearing on the songs and in the videos of his artists and the artists he worked with. "Any artist out there [that] wanna be an artist, and wanna stay a star and won't have to worry about the executive producer trying to be all in the videos, all on the records, dancing, come to Death Row," Knight said.

"Once Suge said what he said, I knew right from there this was gonna keep going," said rapper and the *Source* executive Raymond "Benzino" Scott. "I didn't know it was going to go to the extent that it did, but at the end, you didn't see Suge and Puff hugging. Suge had over one hundred people in the audience. All from L.A. Gangbangers. I don't think New York really grasped the whole thing about gangbanging until that time. You had Bloods and Crips sitting in New York City, and I think that was the first time that was taking place."

But Suge's comment wasn't the only sore spot revealed at the event. When Snoop Dogg—far and away the bestselling and most popular rapper at the time—took the stage, he was greeted by a chorus of boos from the largely New York audience. "The East Coast don't love Dr. Dre and Snoop Dogg?" he responded with obvious disappointment, disgust, and disdain. "The East Coast ain't got no love for Dr. Dre and Snoop Dogg and Death Row? Y'all don't love us?"

While on stage, P. Diddy made a point to brush aside Knight's comments. "I'm the executive producer that comment was made about a little bit earlier," P. Diddy said. "Contrary to what other people may feel, I would like to say that I'm very proud of Dr. Dre, of Death Row and Suge Knight for their accomplishments. And all this East and West, that need to stop."

OutKast was booed after winning Best New Artist, as the New York crowd seemed unimpressed with the emerging duo from Atlanta, showing that Willie D's 1989 statements on "Do It Like a G.O." were warranted. But OutKast's André 3000 took the high road when accepting the award, saying, "The South got somethin' to say."

The fallout from the Source Awards was swift, deadly, and dramatic. On September 23, 1995, Jai Hassan-Jamal

BLACK SUPERMAN

WHEN EAZY-E DIED of complications due to AIDS in 1995, the rap world was in a state of shock. HIV/AIDS was an emerging epidemic at the time, one that had yet to take the life of a high profile heterosexual male.

The N.W.A mastermind's death ran counter to the gangster rap image. Eazy-E didn't die by the gun, but because of a medical condition.

"I think if he would have died in a gang fight or a beef somewhere, it probably would have been easier to take almost, as far as his legacy is concerned," said Cold 187um, lead rapper and producer of Above The Law, which released three albums and an EP on Eazy-E's Ruthless Records. "Being an ex-Compton gangbanger, an ex-drug dealer, if he got caught up in a fight in the streets, it'd be like, 'Oh. He went out like a G,' verses it being a health thing. At that point, we thought only gay people could get that. We weren't thinking a hip-hop artist as manly as an Eazy-E [could]."

RAP MAGAZINES

GIVEN THAT THE mainstream media largely overlooked rap until the late nineties, the rap press had a virtual monopoly on coverage. Below are several of the prominent rap magazines from the nineties and notable facts about each.

The Source. Founded by Harvard students, *The Source* grew from a newsletter to the most prominent rap publication. At one point, the New York–based publication outsold *Rolling Stone* on newsstands.

Vibe. Founded by producer Quincy Jones, the magazine positioned itself more as an urban culture magazine than a straight-up rap publication.

Rap Sheet. The Los Angeles–area publication was printed on newspaper yet packaged as a magazine.

Rap Pages. Owned by porn magnate Larry Flynt, the magazine focused on covering emerging, underground, and independent rappers, as well as rappers from the West Coast and South.

Murder Dog. The San Francisco Bay Area–based magazine featured Q&As with and album reviews of mostly independent gangster rappers from the West Coast, South, and Midwest.

XXL. Launched in 1997, the magazine made an early name for itself with its split covers, making two different covers of the same magazine for several of its first issues. It put New York's JAY-Z on one cover and New Orleans's Master P on a second cover of its first issue, for instance, in order to target two key, and distinctly different, demographics of the rap-buying public: the East Coast and the South.

Robles, a Death Row Records employee, was shot and killed in an Atlanta nightclub. Robles had been arguing with P. Diddy's employee and bodyguard Anthony "Wolf" Jones before he was shot. Neither P. Diddy nor any of his associates were questioned about the shooting by Atlanta police.

Then, in October 1995, Death Row Records duo Tha Dogg Pound (Daz and Kurupt) released *Dogg Food*, including their song "New York, New York." The song was innocuous enough, but its video was anything but. In the clip from the video, Tha Dogg Pound and Snoop Dogg (who rapped the chorus) are shown to be as tall as the city's skyscrapers. In one scene, Snoop Dogg kicks over a building. In another, a shoe is shown stepping on a car, crushing it. On top of that, while the Death Row Records crew was in New York filming the video, the trailers housing them were shot at.

Also in October 1995, 2Pac was released from prison and joined Death Row Records after the label posted $1.4 million bail to free him. At the time, he appeared optimistic about the future.

"It's been stress and drama for a long time now, man," 2Pac said. "So much has happened. I got shot five times by some dudes who were trying to rub me out. But God is great. He let me come back. But, when I look at the last few years, it's not like everybody just did me wrong. I made some mistakes. But I'm ready to move on."

Dr. Dre, though, was also moving on. In March 1996, he left Death Row Records, just three months after collaborating and producing 2Pac's "California Love," the song that catapulted 2Pac to rap's forefront. Dr. Dre gave his share of the company to Knight and founded his own company, Aftermath Entertainment, which, like Death Row, would be backed by longtime partner Jimmy Iovine's Interscope Records.

March 1996 proved to be a pivotal month for other reasons, too. 2Pac let everyone know that he hadn't totally left everything in the past when he confronted the Notorious B.I.G. and P. Diddy at the Soul Train Awards. While Biggie and his entourage were backstage waiting for their ride, 2Pac and Knight pulled up in a Hummer and started yelling at them. The situation was defused by security and others and ended when Biggie and his crew got in their vehicle and left.

Then, in June, 2Pac released the song "Hit 'Em Up," in which he claimed to have had sex with Biggie's estranged wife, R&B singer and fellow Bad Boy Entertainment recording artist Faith Evans. He also dissed East Coast rappers Junior M.A.F.I.A., Mobb Deep, and Chino XL on the song's outro, showing that his animosity now went beyond just Biggie.

Even with all the friction with some of its rappers, 2Pac had long made it clear that he had no problem with the entire East Coast, a position he reaffirmed in "Hit 'Em Up." "Now when I came out, I told you it was just about Biggie," he said in the song's outro. "Then everybody had to open their mouth with a motherfuckin' opinion."

In addition to singling out the people he had problems with on "Hit 'Em Up," 2Pac was also trying to defuse the situation by working with other East Coast artists, including Big Daddy Kane and Nice & Smooth on the unreleased album *One Nation*.

2PAC'S *ONE NATION* ALBUM

During the height of the so-called East Coast–West Coast beef, 2pac was recording *One Nation* with artists from the East Coast. He flew New York rap groups Black Moon and Smif-N-Wessun out to his Calabasas home about thirty miles northwest of Los Angeles. Big Daddy Kane and Nice & Smooth were also among the New York acts with whom 2Pac worked on the album, which he wanted to use as evidence that he had nothing against rappers from New York in general.

The media, though, didn't run with that story. In the midst of this controversy, hip-hop journals largely ignored the integration of the two coasts on rap projects. In 1995, Los Angeles's King Tee protégés Tha Alkaholiks worked with New York producer Diamond D for the group's second album, titled *Coast II Coast*. At the same time, some of the bestselling and most acclaimed albums in hip-hop history, from LL Cool J's *Bigger and Deffer* to Ice Cube's *AmeriKKKa's Most Wanted*, featured New Yorkers teaming with Los Angeles artists.

In August 1996, the rivalry between the coasts was officially branded when *Vibe* used the headline "East vs. West: Biggie & Puffy Break Their Silence" on the cover of its September 1996 issue. The following month, on September 7, after a series of back-and-forth exchanges on songs and in interviews, 2Pac was gunned down in Las Vegas by a still-unidentified assailant brandishing a .40-caliber Glock. He was hit four times, twice in the chest, once in the arm, and once in the thigh. The news traveled fast.

2Pac friend and collaborator Snoop Dogg was at Warren G's house when he started getting calls and pages urging him to turn on the news. After seeing that 2Pac had been shot, Snoop immediately sprang into action.

"I drove down there to the hospital 'cause I wanted to see my nigga, make sure he was straight," Snoop Dogg said. "I'm thinking he was gonna make it."

Snoop Dogg said he was able to speak with 2Pac in the hospital. "I had said a little prayer to him in his head and held his hand and whispered at him, said my peace with him," Snoop Dogg said. "He didn't have no consciousness, but I felt like my spirit and his spirit connected, and I felt like he got it."

2Pac held on for six days in the hospital but ultimately succumbed to his injuries and died on September 13, 1996. He was twenty-five years old.

Eminem recalled hearing about 2Pac's death while working as a cook at a sports bar. "A lot of people that worked at the job that I worked at didn't understand 2Pac or didn't understand the music, so [they] were looking at us like, 'What's wrong? What's the big deal? Get over it,'" Eminem said. "It's like, 'Nah.' This is a really fucked up day. For the longest, I think anybody who had something to do with hip-hop and loved the music, it was a sense of mourning for a long time."

Members of the *Vibe* staff say they felt partially responsible for the situation escalating and resulting in 2Pac's death, though several of them have differing takes on how "East vs. West" ended up on the cover of the publication. Features editor Rob Kenner, editor Carter Harris, and writer Larry "Blackspot" Hester say they were against it. Editor in chief Alan Light said several people were involved in the decision.

CHICAGO GANGSTER RAP

AS RAP DEVELOPED on the East and West Coasts in the eighties and early nineties, the Midwest was developing its own gangster rap style. The Legendary Traxster, who produced defining mid- and late nineties Chicago gangster rap material from Do or Die, Twista, Snypaz, and Psychodrama, among others, was influenced by the sonics coming from the West Coast, while the rappers Traxster and other beatsmiths worked with drew more inspiration from the flair and undulating flows of East Coast rappers.

Chicago gangster rappers also separated themselves by blatantly shouting out the Windy City's swath of prominent gangs, including the Gangster Disciples, Black Disciples, and Vice Lords, almost as soon as they started making music.

"A lot of those stories and a lot of that gangster rap was directly linked to the gang culture, whereas West Coast hip-hop, if you look at its origins, even though it was related to gangbanging, it wasn't as blatant as ours," Traxster said. "We were saying 'GDs,' 'BDs.' We were naming out the gangs and claiming the gangs. Early West Coast hip-hop, we didn't know if Eazy was a Crip or a Blood. Affiliations weren't really portrayed through the music. Tha Dogg Pound was

Tha Dogg Pound, but it took a while before we figured out they were Crips. Eventually they said it. From the beginning with us, it was, 'Vice Lords.' If you listen to Crucial Conflict's [1996 song] 'To the Left,' it was actual gangbanging on the record, naming the sets. I think that played a big part of what made Chicago gangster rap unique. It wasn't just about being a gangster. It was about being a member of a gang."

Although Twista enjoyed platinum success, and Do or Die and Crucial Conflict hit gold, Chicago gangster rap failed to become a bigger movement because, at least in part, there wasn't the same drive surrounding the artists as there had been with, say, rappers from Compton or acts signed to Ruthless Records or Death Row Records.

"In the nineties, it was really dominated by Twista, Do or Die, and a few other local groups, but it wasn't like now, where there was a new group coming out every week and being recognized," Traxster said. "The output of Chicago wasn't high enough. It's almost like we didn't understand that flooding the market and stimulating the market by encouraging other companies and other acts would benefit us by creating a bigger market."

CRUCIAL CONFLICT EP

CC01   1

1. Ride The Rodeo

2. To The Left

IT'S A COMPTON (RECORD-BUYING) THANG

Compton NEXT 3 EXITS

WHEN RECORD STORES were the primary way fans purchased music, rap consumers in Compton were particularly prone to support local talent. "It was the realness of what our artists spoke about and the flavor of the beat," says Arnold "Bigg A" White, who, with his brother, owned and operated Underworld Records & Tapes at 2530 E. Alondra Boulevard in Compton from 1995 to 2001. "Any artist, from DJ Quik to Eazy-E to Ice-T to King Tee to CMW, everybody was talking about what's happening on the West [Coast], the lifestyle, the lowriders, police brutality, the dress code. With the stories that they were telling, the majority of the consumer base knew somebody that knew somebody who knew somebody, so there was always that surge of energy to come in there and support. I remember when Compton was hot. Once Eazy and them broke, everybody was looking for anything from Compton. It kind of transferred to Long Beach when Death Row kicked in when Dre went over there and got Snoop and them. Everybody from Long Beach got deals, so that's what we were on."

"Other editors were involved in that," Light said. "I'm not gonna say that I know who's the one who made the decision. It was all being debated and discussed. These are collaborative enterprises. It's not a question of one person dictating what it's gonna be."

Light says that Keith Clinkscales, *Vibe*'s founding president and CEO, and Gilbert Rogin, *Vibe*'s editorial director, wanted "East vs. West" on the cover. "Was it on the cover? Yes," Clinkscales said. "Did I approve it? No. But the reality of the situation is that I didn't approve the cover in most cases. The editor approves the covers. Because of the nature of that cover, it is quite natural that I would have been involved in it except for the fact that I was going to Los Angeles. Ultimately, the mistake I made was not making sure I saw the final proof. I'm proud of the story. Proud of the job Blackspot did. Proud of the editing that was done. I'm not proud of that cover line."

As rap was reeling from the death of 2Pac, a new supergroup released their debut album. Westside Connection (Ice Cube, Mack 10, and WC) united for *Bow Down*, a scathing indictment of gangster rap's detractors, especially those in New York. The thirteen-track project featured title song "Bow Down," a warning to people who doubted gangster rap; "Gangstas Make the World Go Round," a testament to the potency of gangsters; and "All the Critics in New York," a message that each rapper was tired of being disrespected by New York rap critics.

"When *Bow Down* came out, it shut everything down in my eyes," said Dave Weiner, who worked at Priority Records, which released the album, from 1991 to 1999. "To me, Cube was one of the best shit-talkers, obviously with 'No Vaseline' being one of the hardest diss tracks in hip-hop history. He brought that same level of anger to *Bow Down*, the same level of aggressiveness. They talked shit about everybody and everything having to do with the West Coast being the Best Coast. You couldn't deny it when that record came out. If it wasn't as hard as we all thought it was, it would have just gotten laughed at and would have been removed from any part of the story, but it lived up to what we all hoped for representing the West Coast. It made us proud."

By January 1997, Westside Connection had sold one million copies of *Bow Down*, good for a platinum plaque. The LP's success illustrated that fans identified with Westside Connection's perspective that artists from the West Coast had been marginalized by rap's New York–based gatekeepers.

With tensions running high in the rap world, the echo of 2Pac's murder had not yet quieted when the Notorious B.I.G. traveled to Los Angeles to promote his forthcoming second album, *Life After Death*. After attending a *Vibe* magazine party at the Petersen Automotive Museum in Los Angeles, the rapper was leaving in his SUV. The vehicle—hired to drive him around for the night—was stopped at a traffic light when a car pulled up beside it. A man opened fire, and Biggie was hit four times. He was pronounced dead an hour later. Like 2Pac's murder, the murder of the Notorious B.I.G. remains unsolved.

After the deaths of two of rap's marquee acts, there was a definite sense of unease throughout every level of the rap business.

"You had cats on the West Coast that didn't want to go to the East Coast and you had people on the East Coast that didn't want to come to the West Coast," MC Ren said. "It was just a time where you had to be careful. You just couldn't do like you used to do. You couldn't just go anywhere. It was like a gang war, damn near, basically going on. Two coasts going at each other like how fools bang in the street. It was just a bad time."

Priority Records, which had helped make gangster rap a national phenomenon in the eighties and early nineties with Eazy-E, N.W.A, and Ice Cube, was in the midst of ramping up security in its office due to internal issues with its own artists and others by the time 2Pac and the Notorious B.I.G. were killed.

The label didn't shy away from signing gangster rappers, but it took drastic measures to attempt to ensure the safety of its employees. It installed a bulletproof entrance, which resembled the entrance to a bank vault, at its office in the CNN building on Sunset Boulevard in Los Angeles. The company also hired off-duty LAPD officers, who were housed in a secret office in the CNN building, to escort employees considered "high risk" due to either their status at the company or their relationships with artists. These employees weren't allowed to leave the office without alerting one of the officers.

"There was so much chaos and so much drama on all fronts in hip-hop that that was obviously the pinnacle, but it wasn't the only thing," said the Priority

Records employee Weiner. "There was constant drama, constant chaos with our artists within and artists trying to get at Priority Records. It shut us down when that shit happened. It wasn't like, 'Oh my God, this shit happened and now we have to take these measures.' It was more like what was expected. The reality. No one was surprised."

Similarly, the lack of journalistic integrity was not lost on those within the rap community, who realized after reading *Vibe*'s interviews with 2Pac and the Notorious B.I.G. that *Vibe* was not delivering a true journalistic service to its readers.

"They weren't speaking to each other," Brooklyn rapper Talib Kweli said. "They were reading the magazines. Then, 'Pac got shot. Big goes to an after-party at *Vibe* magazine and gets killed in front of all those people. That's not to single out *Vibe* magazine. I'm just saying the media in general is just real responsible for inflaming a lot of that shit.

"If the media would have had some responsibility," Kweli continued, "and been like, 'Listen, cut that shit out. We can't condone that activity,' instead of glorifying it, which would have made sense and been the logical, responsible thing to do especially if you say, 'I'm a media institution that represents hip-hop.' I expect that from a *Newsweek* or a *Time* or somebody that doesn't claim to represent hip-hop. But magazines and media outlets that say, 'We represent hip-hop and are all about hip-hop,' and are doing nothing but exploiting the shit when the shit was obviously a dangerous situation."

> ## "When B.I.G. took that picture, he didn't take that picture thinking 'East vs. West.' He took a picture thinking, 'I'm going to be on the cover of Vibe.'"
>
> **METHOD MAN**

Regardless of who made the decision to print 2Pac's unsubstantiated claims without fact-checking them or to put "East vs. West" on the cover, the fact that no one at *Vibe* realized putting those words in the magazine or on the cover would be inflammatory, at the least, is unfathomable and unjustifiable.

"With that East–West crap, *Vibe* has to take a lot of . . . they should've got a bullet," said Method Man, the Wu-Tang Clan member who recorded with both 2Pac and the Notorious B.I.G., appearing on 2Pac's *All Eyez on Me* album and Biggie's *Ready to Die*. "They should've got a bullet instead of 'Pac or B.I.G. When they put that cover up with B.I.G. and Puff on there, when B.I.G. took that picture, he didn't take that picture thinking 'East vs. West.' He took a picture thinking, 'I'm going to be on the cover of *Vibe*.' What came after is what solidified [the] East–West beef for all the dumb motherfuckers around that don't know how to think for themselves. Maybe they just don't like West Coast people. Maybe they just don't like East Coast people, but that fueled the fire. . . . 'Pac even said himself, 'You guys injected yourselves into a beef that was just between me and Bad Boy [Entertainment].' Had nothing to do with nobody else. He said it himself."

In the aftermath of the deaths of two of rap's biggest figures, every segment of the rap community found itself in mourning.

"People on the West Coast weren't happy when Biggie got killed, and people on the East Coast weren't happy when 'Pac got killed," Weiner said. "I never saw or heard anything like that. I never heard anyone celebrating those losses, which at the end of the day, to me, really let you know what was going on with the community. It [showed] hip-hop is based on a culture that challenges itself and everything around it, and when it came to the real shit happening, everyone stood up together and felt that loss.

"It made people realize that they went too far," Weiner added. "It made the fans, the entire community of hip-hop, realize that this shit-talking, this beef that we've all documented, been a part of, and seen develop over the years, can get out of hand."

Still, as the fallout from the deaths of 2Pac and the Notorious B.I.G. lingered, gangster rap was about to be transformed by a revolutionary artist who changed the business of rap and who brought the streets to the dance floor.

CH.
13

It Ain't My Fault: Master P and the No Limit Revolution

IN 1997, THE WORLD TOOK STEPS TO REIN ITSELF IN FROM GRIEVOUS SELF-INFLICTED WOUNDS.

Countries that had signed an agreement at the Chemical Weapons Convention of 1993 started outlawing the production, stockpiling, and use of chemical weapons. Delegates from one hundred and fifty nations met in Kyoto, Japan, and reached an agreement to control heat-trapping greenhouse gases. In Hong Kong, chickens were slaughtered in an attempt to prevent and limit the outbreak of H5N1, avian influenza, also known as the bird flu.

As pockets of the world tried to clean up these issues, rap was undergoing a similar process. The genre was reeling from the deaths of 2Pac and the Notorious B.I.G., and there was an unspoken agreement that something needed to change in the culture. The much-needed adjustment came from an unlikely force that rose to prominence and was aided by a familiar partner.

OPPOSITE:

From left: Brothers C-Murder, Master P, and Silkk the Shocker were three of No Limit Records' platinum artists. They are shown here at the Sickle Cell Celebrity Jam III at the Los Angeles Memorial Sports Arena on February 28, 1998.

1997
Key Rap Releases

1. The Notorious B.I.G.'s *Life After Death* album

2. Puff Daddy & The Family's "I'll Be Missing You" single

3. Master P's *Ghetto D* album

US President

Bill Clinton

Something Else

Steve Jobs was named Apple's interim CEO.

Back in February 1995, Dave Weiner, then a Priority Records sales rep, had taken a business trip to Oakland, California, to visit Music People's 1-Stop. At the time, Music People's was what was known as a one-stop, a business that bought albums and singles on vinyl, CD, and cassette from record companies. One-stops such as Music People's would then sell the products to the independent record stores in the region.

Weiner, who started at Priority Records in the mailroom in 1991 and had worked his way up through the sales department, had taken the trip to sell Priority projects to Music People's, namely mainstays such as N.W.A and Ice Cube. He wasn't going to find talent or to add to Priority Records' roster, but the course of rap history was dramatically transformed due to a chance encounter in the Music People's parking lot.

On the way to his car, Weiner was approached by an emerging artist. It was Percy Robert Miller, aka Master P. Since he was in the business of independent rap music, Weiner was familiar with Master P and his fledgling No Limit Records, which had been making a dent in the San Francisco Bay Area's flourishing indie rap scene.

Master P handed Weiner a copy of his *99 Ways to Die* project and told him where it would be charting on the Billboard charts the following week. Impressed by P's confidence and knowledge of the business, Weiner took the rapper-businessman's information, along with the copy of *99 Ways to Die*.

The following week, Master P's *99 Ways to Die* debuted one slot lower than P had predicted. "My mind was blown [by the fact] that he accomplished that without any real assistance," Weiner said.

Master P and No Limit Records' success with *99 Ways to Die* gave Weiner an idea. Once implemented, the idea revolutionized the music industry and made Priority Records more money than it had ever made with rap industry titans N.W.A and Ice Cube.

Weiner's idea was to have Priority Records distribute the releases of other record companies via its own distribution deal with CEMA (Capitol Records, EMI Records, Manhattan Records, and Angel Records), starting with No Limit Records. At the time, Priority Records was the only self-owned independent distributor of rap music in the United States. Prior to launching Priority Records, owners Bryan Turner and Mark Cerami both worked at compilation label K-Tel. While at K-Tel, Turner worked in A&R, putting the music portion of the albums together. Cerami, meanwhile, handled sales.

The industry standard was that the record company would send an album, single, or EP to its distributor, who would then manufacture it and ship it to retail. Upon receipt of the music, the retailer would then pay the distributor, who would then pay the label.

Through his work, though, Cerami had developed strong relationships with all the national music business accounts and wanted to sell Priority Records projects to the chain record stores, one-stops, and other businesses directly. Thus, Cerami set it up so Priority Records would manufacture and ship its material to retail, and the retailers, in turn, would pay Priority Records for the product. This was a major asset given that the labels controlled the majority of the shelf space in all the record stores, meaning that there was limited real estate on which to stock albums.

In addition to cutting out a step in the business process, Priority Records also had another distinct advantage: Its receivables were guaranteed by its manufacturer/distributor, CEMA. This meant that if Priority Records sold one hundred thousand copies of an album to retail that it would get paid full price for those one hundred thousand albums because of the massive clout that CEMA had with retailers. In return, CEMA received a small distribution fee. Without this relationship, Priority would have most likely suffered the fate of other small labels: chase retailers to get paid, get paid long after the money was due, and pay a premium on manufacturing their products.

Thus, Priority Records was, in effect, both its own national distributor and an independent record label. Unlike any other record company, Priority was set up so that it could sign an artist or label to a distribution deal itself since it could facilitate its own distribution needs.

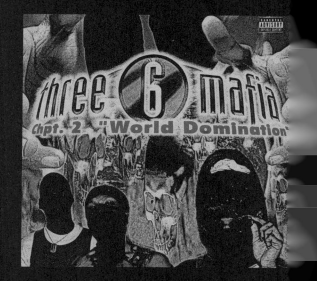

MEMPHIS GOTCHA SHAKIN'

LIKE MASTER P, Three 6 Mafia got their start in the mid-1990s releasing music independently before exploding nationally. The Memphis sextet (DJ Paul, Juicy J, Gangsta Boo, Lord Infamous, Crunchy Black, Koopsta Knicca) broke through in 1997 thanks to their hit "Tear Da Club Up '97" single and nationally released *Chpt. 2 "World Domination"* album, which went gold in nine months.

Although the group's wicked sonics (courtesy of DJ Paul and Juicy J) and gruff lyrics were inspired by N.W.A, Three 6 Mafia added a different wrinkle to gangster rap. "Our gangster was blended with some dark, wicked shit, 666 Mafia type shit," Gangsta Boo says. "Before our arrival, Memphis wasn't really nothing like that. Memphis was just all gangster. But when we brought the gangster with a bit of wickedness, it was like, 'Motherfucka, not only will we kill you, but we will kill you and burn your body. Then, when we burn your body, we'll have a fuckin' ritual with your bones. After we do that, we're going to go home and smoke a blunt.'"

This arrangement was the reason Weiner could suggest the idea for Priority Records to partner with Master P's No Limit and offer it distribution. Priority was already set up to implement that type of arrangement, one that was best-suited to its internal workings given that neither Turner nor Cerami was a devout rap fan with his finger on the pulse of the rap scene.

"Priority Records was never designed to be a hip-hop label," Weiner said. "They were doing compilations, which led to the California Raisins, which led to the financing that brought on N.W.A."

After those initial successes, Priority Records had other hits in signing and developing its own acts, most notably Ice Cube and Mack 10, but the company had yet to become a marquee destination for talent. Given Weiner's knowledge of Priority Records' structure and Master P's independent success, Weiner took his concept to his boss, Priority Records cofounder Mark Cerami.

Cerami understood Weiner's vision and agreed to sign Master P and No Limit Records to a ground-breaking deal. Master P got $250,000 and retained 100 percent ownership of his master recordings, as well as his publishing. Priority Records got the exclusive manufac-turing/distribution rights and took a distribution fee in order to guar-antee getting No Limit product into stores.

"There was no record company that was offering national distri-bution deals without taking a[n ownership] percentage of that opportunity," said Weiner, who was the freshly minted director of distributed labels at Priority Records when Priority signed Master P's No Limit Records. "It was the first deal of its kind where he got an advance and we took no publishing, no masters, and only took a distribution fee. Simple as that."

Priority Records reissued *99 Ways to Die* in June 1995. The following month, it released *True* from No Limit group TRU, whose core members were Master P and two of his younger brothers, Silkk the Shocker and C-Murder.

> *"Priority Records was never designed to be a hip-hop label. They were doing compilations, which led to the California Raisins, which led to the financing that brought on N.W.A."*
>
> **DAVE WEINER**

Now with Priority Records' national reach and more money to invest, No Limit Records began gaining new fans and getting exposure at retail, in magazines, on television, and on radio. It also had its first hit with "I'm Bout It, Bout It," a song that referenced Master P's New Orleans roots and his then–home base of Richmond, California, about twelve miles north of Oakland.

Like E-40, who was from Vallejo in the San Francisco Bay Area and went to school at Grambling State University in Louisiana, Master P had ready-made fan bases on the West Coast and in the South. Once No Limit Records' music started taking off, this geographical benefit helped bolster his ascent to stardom.

Taking advantage of this rare cross-regional opportunity, in October 1995, Master P released *Bouncin' and Swingin'*, a compilation from the Down South Hustlers. In reality, the Down South Hustlers was not a group but a name No Limit used to push the double-disc album, which featured gangster or gangster-leaning rap artists from several cities around the country, including Flint, Michigan (the Dayton Family); Memphis (8Ball & MJG); Port Arthur, Texas (UGK); Houston (E.S.G.); and, of course, its own No Limit Records acts from New Orleans (Silkk the Shocker, Mia X, C-Murder). The album proved to be a shrewd marketing move. No Limit was able to gain fans in cities throughout the country who supported any one of the more than twenty artists who were featured on the twenty-six-track project.

As would become standard practice with No Limit Records, Master P began flooding record stores with his company's material. In April 1996, he scored a significant hit with his *Ice Cream Man* album and its "Mr. Ice Cream Man" single. By September, the album had sold more than five hundred thousand units, demonstrating that Master P's acumen, Weiner's vision, and Cerami's faith were all being rewarded handsomely.

But with little—yet steadily increasing—national radio play and video support, getting No Limit albums in stores was still somewhat difficult, even with the label's early sales victories and Priority Records' decade of delivering consistently popular projects. Having longstanding relationships with the buyers at retail was one of the main reasons why Priority Records' unique positioning as both a record company and a record distributor was so critical to its sustained success.

"Accounts didn't really know how to deal with rap music, especially the chains," Weiner said. "So it was very important to have your own sales staff go out there and explain what Westside Connection was, explain what No Limit was, and explain why Silkk the Shocker needed to ship two hundred thousand units. That wouldn't have happened through a major label sales rep, who would not have

MASTER P DID IT FIRST

MASTER P ROSE to national prominence through his No Limit Records. The New Orleans native also paved the way in several key business areas.

I'm bout it. Master P's 1997 landmark direct-to-video film jumpstarted a new industry (independent rap flicks) and showed Hollywood that it could move major units even if films bypassed theaters.

Dimension Films. Master P became the first rapper to release his own movie through a major film production partner. His *I Got the Hook-Up* project was released May 27, 1998, by Dimension Films in conjunction with his own No Limit.

Converse. In 1999, Converse made Master P the first rapper to have his own shoe. Yes, other rappers had had endorsement deals with shoe companies prior to Master P's pact—most notably Run-DMC with Adidas—but those rappers didn't have their own shoes.

No Limit Sports. Master P was the first rapper to have his own sports agency. It pulled a major coup by signing running back Ricky Williams, who was drafted No. 5 by the New Orleans Saints in 1999. However, the athlete's incentive-based contract caused a black eye from which the agency never recovered.

understood what we were working on. That was a key part of the puzzle, sales guys that knew how to move hip-hop."

At this time, in the early stages of No Limit's rise to national prominence, the combination of Master P and No Limit Records' Southern slang and attitude; the imprint's often garish album covers; and the keyboard, funk, and G-Funk production of such San Francisco Bay Area producers as Al Eaton and K-Lou, among others, provided a new twist on gangster rap. As artists, Master P and the No Limit roster were combining Southern sensibilities over decidedly West Coast–sounding production. The combination proved addictive, with Master P and the growing No Limit Records lineup becoming street favorites thanks to their gruff, violent, and profanity-filled rhymes about coming up in the ghetto, hustling, and trying to make it out by any means necessary. But where other artists were revered for their lyricism, toughness, or production, Master P and his No Limit Records acts garnered respect because of their ability to hustle, to grind, and to make catchy music with memorable choruses.

Through this early work, Master P was building his brand and setting up his next major move. Industry veterans began noticing his momentum.

"You snatch the streets first," said MC Eiht, Compton's Most Wanted's front man and gold-selling solo artist. "Make the streets respect you. 'Yeah, I sold my dope.' That's why he got so much respect from that angle, because he came with the 'I started off from the bottom with y'all, too.' But when he got that [money] and he was able to start selling them records, he turned into the music dude, like, 'Everything ain't finna just be about dope and motherfuckin' hustling in the projects. Shit's finna be about making the crowd move.' That's why the shit transitioned, which was smart."

As he was laying his music empire's foundation, Master P was also transitioning in other ways. In the second half of 1996, he began shooting his debut feature film, *I'm bout it*, which he financed himself. Master P approached Priority Records to distribute the film.

"When he brought the concept of films and *I'm bout it*, none of us knew what to make of it," Weiner said.

Weiner told Master P that Priority was a record company. "Well, you're about to be a film company," Weiner recalled Master P saying to him. Master P urged Priority Records' sales staff to work with the same people at Tower Records, Warehouse, and Music Plus who bought albums from them. When P was told the people who bought movies at record stores were not the same people who bought albums, he was undeterred.

"He wouldn't take no for an answer," Weiner said. "He said, 'Well, then sell it to your music buyer.' Well, it's a video. It's a movie. We can't sell it to our music buyer. He said, 'You have to. They know who I am. They know the value of Master P.' We all looked at each other and said, 'He's got a point. Let's see if we can actually do this.'"

Thanks to Master P's insistence, Priority Records' sales staff pushed Master P's *I'm bout it* film through unorthodox channels (music people selling a movie to film people). The results were remarkable. *I'm bout it* sold more than five hundred thousand units according to Weiner. For perspective, the 2000 film *How the Grinch Stole Christmas*, starring Hollywood elite Jim Carrey and directed by the revered Ron Howard, was released on VHS in October 2001. It sold 1.4 million copies by the end of the year, meaning that Master P's *I'm bout it* sold about a third of the number of copies as a film made by major Hollywood players sold—for a fraction of the cost.

The success of *I'm bout it* was about more than money and sales, though. "I think it was solely responsible for showing independent filmmakers that you could circumvent Hollywood, put your film out, recoup your film, make some money, and move on to the next film," Weiner said. "That had never been done before through the channels that we went [through]."

Other rappers quickly understood the significance of Master P's business savvy.

"You've got to open up different avenues to people that ain't really checkin' for us or don't really know nothing about us," said Mack 10, the Inglewood,

DIRECT-TO-VIDEO RAP MOVIES

A BEVY OF rappers followed Master P's lead and released their own direct-to-video movies. Below are some of the more noteworthy projects.

Streets Is Watching. JAY-Z's 1998 film featured a number of music videos interwoven into the movie's narrative.

Thicker Than Water. Mack 10's 1999 film traces the lives of rival gang leaders who are trying to break into the music business.

Charlie Hustle: The Blueprint of a Self-Made Millionaire. E-40's 1999 film featured appearances from a number of rappers and athletes, including Gary Payton and Kurupt.

Baller Blockin'. Cash Money Records' 2000 film was a dramatized depiction of the lives of the rappers on the label, including Lil Wayne, Birdman, Juvenile, and B.G.

Choices: The Movie. Three 6 Mafia's 2001 film focused on the life of an ex-con trying to balance right and wrong as he assimilates back into society.

California, rapper and Westside Connection member who appeared in *I'm bout it*. "*I'm bout it* opened up a lot of doors for Master P, man. Somebody might see that and give one of them niggas that's in the movie a role in a major movie, or we might sell more records to people that didn't used to buy our records."

By the time Master P's *Ghetto D* album arrived in record stores in September 1997, Master P and No Limit Records had become a bona fide movement. Fans had bought into the No Limit mystique and were now buying the label's releases as soon as they came out, often without even hearing a single from the album. Buoyed by this momentum, *Ghetto D* entered the Billboard Top 200 charts at No. 1, signaling Master P's rise to the top of both the rap and music worlds.

Growing up in Hollywood, Florida, about twenty miles north of Miami, ¡Mayday! rapper Wrekonize was in seventh grade when Master P and No Limit's popularity exploded. Even though he gravitated toward the music of such New York rap acts as De La Soul, A Tribe Called Quest, and Gang Starr, and typically wasn't drawn to keyboard-driven production, he was drawn to No Limit's music, Master P's up-tempo "Make Em' Say Uhh!" single, in particular. It was, in essence, feel-good gangster rap that was also danceable.

"The whole No Limit movement swept through Broward County like heavy, heavy," Wrekonize said. "Even though Florida is such a different place than the rest of the South, we still get a lot of our influence from the South. When 'Make Em' Say Uhh!' came out, that changed everything. Our whole high school started bumping the No Limit stuff.

P brought such a creative spin on it that all the things that I thought I was stubborn about in terms of my musical taste were out the window. I was bumpin' P's shit, Mystikal's shit, Silkk the Shocker's shit. [Master P] brought such a creative spin that I didn't expect in the music. It spoke to us in that time and that area, for sure."

With a No. 1 album, a direct-to-video movie selling hundreds of thousands of units, and No Limit albums from Mia X (*Unlady Like*) and TRU (*Tru 2 da Game*) selling in excess of five hundred thousand units within months of their respective releases, Master P and No Limit Records blindsided the music industry.

> ## *"Many of Priority Records' employees and artists were actually slow to understand and hesitant to embrace the magnitude of Master P's moves."*
>
>
>
> **DAVE WEINER**

Priority Records had been enjoying significant success at the time with Westside Connection's platinum *Bow Down* album and Mack 10's eponymous debut album, which had gone gold. Yet No Limit became Priority's priority, with Master P as the label's mastermind.

"He consumed us," Weiner said. "His movement happened so fast that it went from a quiet operation to just trying to keep up."

Many of Priority Records' employees and artists were actually slow to understand and hesitant to embrace the magnitude of Master P's moves.

"There was a period when I first signed Master P where he got no love from [Ice] Cube and some of the other artists on the label," said Weiner, who ran a four-person department at the beginning of his distribution run with No Limit. "They didn't understand him or his music, and he was the little guy in the company. He got the cold shoulder. When No Limit exploded, the tables turned and all of the sudden he was the big guy in the company and everybody else was trying to do something with No Limit. He flipped the whole company on its head over the course of a couple of years and turned a staff of two hundred that didn't want to work on his records, that didn't want to help, that didn't want to be a part of it, to those two hundred people doing everything they could to get involved because they missed the boat."

NO LIMIT RECORDS' MOST GARISH ALBUM COVERS

MASTER P STANDS as one of the best marketers in rap history. After college, the New Orleans native relocated to Richmond, California, and launched his own No Limit record store and record company. He quickly realized how an eye-popping album cover would help move his independently released music.

What started off as crudely designed homages to life on the streets evolved into imaginatively garish album art that was supplied by Photoshop wizards Pen & Pixel.

Let's revisit several of the most memorable No Limit album covers in all their glory.

The Ghettos Tryin' to Kill Me! by Master P (1994). Master P's first significant foray into album art shock and awe comes from one of the last albums he released before signing with Priority Records. On this memorable cover, he has a woman on top of him seemingly participating in sex, which understandably has Master P's full attention. Unfortunately for the rapping businessman, there is an angry-looking man brandishing a firearm seemingly about to come through the bedroom window. Was it a ruse? Did the woman set him up, luring him with sex to set up a robbery? Or was Master P saying that he needed security at all times, even when he

was having sex because the ghetto was tryin' to kill him? If truly great art is in the eye of the beholder, then the cover art of *The Ghettos Tryin' to Kill Me!* is a masterpiece.

Ghetto Dope by Master P (1997). As Master P and his No Limit Records began enjoying increasing success throughout the midnineties, the execution of his entire operation improved, from his beats (now supplied from percussive production team Beats By the Pound) to his raps, as well as the caliber of his collaborators. This success also led to bigger budgets for his album art. With the album that announced his arrival as a national star, Master P wanted to hit hard. So, for his then-titled *Ghetto Dope* album art, he featured a man who appeared to be a drug addict smoking what appeared to be crack. But upon closer inspection of the smoke emanating from the purported crack vial, the "dope" the addict was smoking was actually music from the No Limit Records catalog. Perhaps not coincidentally, the cover of *The Ghettos Tryin' to Kill Me!* is one of the images included in the haze.

Ghetto D by Master P (1997). Master P was all about the dollar. So, with his stock rising exponentially in the late 1990s, he didn't want to do anything to hurt his brand— or his chance to move product. Thus, he changed the name of his *Ghetto Dope* album to *Ghetto D.* But, when Wal-Mart (which only sold clean versions of albums) and other retailers balked at carrying the original album cover featuring what appeared to be a man smoking crack, Master P revamped the cover art. Gone were the man and the purported crack consumption. In their place was an image featuring a raging flame in front of the No Limit Music Super Store. The smoke still featured the cover art of several No Limit Records albums. With Wal-Mart and others appeased, *Ghetto D* was the No. 1 album in the country its first full week in stores.

Charge It 2 Da Game by Silkk the Shocker (1998). Master P gave his family members a piece of the No Limit pie. Silkk the Shocker, one of his younger brothers, was the most commercially successful. Silkk's biggest song was "It Ain't My Fault," a collaboration with the rapid-fire, tsunami-like rapper Mystikal. The cut was included on Silkk's second studio album, *Charge It 2 Da Game.* As potent as "It Ain't My Fault" was, the album's cover became the stuff of street legends. On the image, Silkk sports stylish black shades, blinding jewelry, and a boss-like cigar. But it's what in his right hand that sets him apart. He's carrying a personalized Ghetto Express card, the epitome of ghetto fabulousness (had it been real, of course). Silkk's smirk and the ingenious double entendre of both the album title and the album art showed that Silkk and the No Limit team had panache in spades.

There's One in Every Family **by Fiend (1998).** Not to be outdone by Master P's original *Ghetto Dope* album cover, gruff-voiced No Limit Records rapper Fiend played off his stage name when crafting his debut No Limit release. *There's One in Every Family* was more than just a title. It was a motto people would use to describe the member of their family who was the black sheep. Naturally, Fiend was placed on his album cover at what appeared to be a drug market. With Fiend's focus on his flip phone as a zombielike drug addict lunged toward him, the rapper's nonchalance in the face of potential terror was either a chilling or hilarious commentary about this segment of life on the streets, depending on your perspective. Fiend rode the album cover, as well as guest appearances from Master P and Snoop Dogg, to gold album status for *There's One In Every Family.*

Rear End **by Mercedes (1999).** Master P's No Limit Records was a male-dominated operation. Mia X earned a gold album for 1997's *Unlady Like,* but beyond Mia, No Limit didn't produce a noteworthy female act. It wasn't for lack of effort, though, especially on the album cover front. Mercedes's debut album, *Rear End,* featured the rapper-singer in the background of the cover art holding a smoking cigar. But it was the foreground that stood out. This image of Mercedes featured her bent over what appeared to be a Mercedes-Benz wearing a revealing, form-fitting bikini as she looked back at the camera. Songs such as "Pu**y," "Kiss Da Cat," and "N's Ain't S**t" were balanced with her thanks yous in the liner notes, which started off with, "First and foremost I would like to thank God, for through him all things are possible."

No Limit Records had actually become bigger and more lucrative than Priority Records. An avalanche of albums from No Limit Records acts hit record stores in 1997 and the first half of 1998, with Master P and his artists Mia X, Silkk the Shocker, Mystikal, Fiend, Kane & Abel, and C-Murder all going gold or platinum and branding themselves as "No Limit Soldiers." Their signature look was to dress in military fatigues for press shots, album artwork, and in their videos.

But the military imagery was more than just motif. It extended to actual confrontation, as evidenced by the No Limit policy of boxing to solve interpersonal issues. They were literally mandated to fight through their problems. "Whoever wanna get the gloves—I don't care if you the president of the company or you clean up the office—if you feel you wanna get it in, then that's how we do," Master P said. "It take all the fear away. When you don't have no fear, you can be a better person in life."

The fearless attitude, combined with the military image and mentality, became the No Limit lifestyle. "He's always had this military-inspired approach, and that's how he built the company, with lieutenants and colonels," Weiner said. "People were appointed positions, and they followed it.

"You weren't allowed to be tired," Weiner added. "You weren't allowed to say, 'Yo, I need to catch a night's rest.' That'd be showing weakness. He led by example. He didn't sit in his hotel room and call shots. He was at every meeting, every appointment, every editing session, every recording session. I don't think he slept."

The onslaught of music and uniformity in presentation made an impression with young fans. "I could see the cohesive image and branding they had," Wrekonize said. "It was the way that they presented themselves, the way their colors matched. Just the imagery in itself was so unifying that it made you want to be a part of it. I was super drawn to it even before I knew what it was. In retrospect, I'm like, 'Man, they had such a cohesive brand image for the whole crew.' It's hard to look at it and not want to be a part of that."

The cohesive No Limit nature carried over to the imprint's production, which came to be handled by Beats by the Pound, which was made up of KLC, Mo B. Dick, Craig B, and O'Dell. The collective was churning out a massive amount of music, as Master P wanted to give his listeners their money's worth. His compilations and albums were each typically nearly eighty minutes long, the maximum amount of time that could be held on a CD. He was also a pioneer of the double-disc project, regularly releasing dual-disc compilations and albums.

"He was relentless," Weiner said. "He had a twenty-one-hour-a-day work ethic. He just wouldn't stop until he accomplished his goal. That's where I learned my lesson in the industry that as much as it's all about the talent, you need the

UNHERALDED RAP MOGULS

MASTER P IS ONE OF the preeminent rap moguls. Several other rappers who predated Master P also made impressive business moves. Here's a breakdown of several rappers who are moguls but who often don't get the credit for it.

Ice-T. Through his Rhyme Syndicate collective, which included both record company and management arms, Ice-T was one of rap's early talent scouts and executives. The company managed and released material by such respected and accomplished artists as King Tee (one of the first prominent rappers from Compton), Everlast (later part of House of Pain, famous for the anthemic single "Jump Around"), and WC (also a member of Low Profile and Westside Connection, as well as the front man of the Maad Circle, of which Coolio was also a member).

Eazy-E. The Compton rapper's Ruthless Records was home to such significant rap acts as J.J. Fad, N.W.A, the D.O.C., Above the Law, MC Ren, and Bone Thugs-N-Harmony, as well as R&B singer Michel'le. Eazy-E also struck deals with multiple labels for his acts, an unprecedented move that prevented him from being beholden to any one company as an outlet for his artists. In 1990, he started selling wares on the inside of his releases, jump-starting and planting the seeds for the rap clothing line explosion that took place in the nineties.

EPMD. The Long Island, New York, duo of Erick Sermon and Parrish Smith were among the first artists to make funk music their sonic backbone. They also were among the best talent scouts in rap history, launching the careers of K-Solo, whose signature was spelling words in his raps; Redman, a dazzlingly creative wordsmith and storyteller; Das EFX, a distinctive duo whose penchant for adding "iggity" and gibberish to some of their rhymes influenced dozens of artists, including Ice Cube; and Keith Murray, whose use of long, peculiar words made him distinctive. (Murray was released under Sermon's sole tutelage after EPMD split temporarily after their 1992 album, *Business Never Personal*.)

Ice Cube. After leaving N.W.A, Ice Cube launched his own Lench Mob Records and Street Knowledge Productions, music companies that released acclaimed albums from female rapper Yo-Yo, political rapper Kam, indie rap darling (and Ice Cube's cousin) Del tha Funkee Homosapien, rap trio Kausion, street rapper K-Dee, rap supergroup Westside Connection, and Westside Connection member WC. Ice Cube's Cube Vision film and television production company has become one of Hollywood's most bankable singles, releasing blockbuster franchises that include *Next Friday* (though not *Friday*, the first film in the series), *Barbershop*, *Are We There Yet?*, and *Ride Along*.

right guide behind the talent to help steer the ship, and those are the ones that are hard to find."

Master P's next act showed that as hardworking as he was, he was also fearless. He set his sights on acquiring an established marquee talent, namely Snoop Dogg, the preeminent gangster rapper of the nineties. Since 1996, Snoop Dogg had suffered through the departure of mentor Dr. Dre from Death Row Records, the death of friend and labelmate 2Pac, and the lukewarm response to his second album, *Tha Doggfather*. Furthermore, Death Row Records owner Suge Knight was incarcerated for being involved in a beating in Las Vegas that took place the night 2Pac was fatally shot. Knight had also developed a reputation for handling his business in gangster ways and was likely the most feared music executive.

As Snoop Dogg toured the country in 1997 in support of *Tha Doggfather*, he was letting people know that he wanted to leave Death Row Records. But given the turnover at the label and Knight being incarcerated, Snoop Dogg's future was uncertain. Master P, though, had his own pedigree on the streets and was willing to take any potential heat for bringing Snoop Dogg to No Limit. The move did not sit well with Knight and led to Death Row Records employees and artists targeting Snoop Dogg and No Limit members in public and on record, as well as confronting them at awards shows, concerts, and while traveling. Beyond the sheer audacity of taking Snoop Dogg from the most gangster record company in the country, Master P's acquisition of Snoop Dogg showed how powerful he'd become in the music world.

"It was one of the most significant moments in West Coast hip-hop in my opinion, because no one out there would challenge Suge," Weiner said. "When P decided he was going to roll out the red carpet for Snoop, Bryan Turner got on a plane and flew up and saw Suge and said something like, 'Hey, man, I got nothing to do with this,' because he was scared. In other words, Snoop was supposed to be untouchable when Suge was in jail. Bryan didn't want it to even look like he had anything to do with it, because P was making the move on Snoop and doing it with his chest out and nuts swinging and not a care in the world. He wasn't scared of [Suge]. He wasn't worried about him."

Even though it was one of No Limit's bestselling releases and it showed Snoop Dogg was still one of rap's preeminent stars, Snoop Dogg's first album for No Limit Records, August 1998's *Da Game Is to Be Sold, Not to Be Told*, was not well-received by many of his West Coast fans, who didn't appreciate Snoop Dogg rapping almost exclusively over overtly Southern soundscapes from Beats by the Pound and collaborating mostly with No Limit acts.

"It was a turning point," Weiner said. "I guess you could say that it was definitely a changing of the guards is what it felt like. It was the rise of No Limit and the fall of Death Row at that point. It was pretty clear to us that we had taken that position in the game. We were now larger than Priority. We had now eclipsed what was left of Death Row, and now we had the No. 1 living artist on Death Row at the time over on No Limit. It was surreal."

Snoop Dogg's star power coupled with juggernaut Master P helped *Da Game Is to Be Sold, Not to Be Told* move more than two million copies, rarified territory for virtually any musician. But Snoop Dogg could tell that he needed to rework his music on his next project.

"Snoop, being the man he is, explained that he needed to do something to make it right," Weiner said. "P, also being a man, said, 'All right. I understand that,' and supported that process and put that second record out, which got everything back on track with the No Limit stamp."

For his follow-up album, May 1999's *No Limit Top Dogg*, Snoop Dogg secured beats from DJ Quik and reconnected with Dr. Dre, a monumental move for Snoop Dogg, one fans had been clamoring for since Dr. Dre left Death Row Records in 1996. Dr. Dre produced three *No Limit Top Dogg* songs, including hard-hitting lead single "B Please," which also featured Xzibit and Nate Dogg. "B Please," as well as "Down 4 My N's"—a muscular, riotous single featuring No Limit labelmates C-Murder and Magic and produced by Beats by the Pound member KLC—signaled Snoop Dogg's reemergence to the elite level of respect within the rap community. Fans and critics alike loved that Snoop Dogg was delivering gritty and gruff gangster rap full of attitude, urgency, and menace.

Having creative freedom was something Snoop Dogg appreciated. "It's whoever I want to work with," Snoop Dogg said. "If I choose not to work with No Limit, [Master P] ain't got no problem with that. He just wants the best product, and that's what I'm trying to give him. I felt that working with these producers

MACK 10 AS PEACEMAKER

AFTER THE 1996 release of Westside Connection's chest-thumping *Bow Down* album—on which Ice Cube, Mack 10, and WC proclaimed the West Coast's dominance of the rap scene and their disdain for the New York–based rap critics, artists, and DJs who dismissed West Coast rap—Mack 10 wanted to help rap heal. The genre had just endured the murders of 2Pac and the Notorious B.I.G., and the rap community was feeling the effects of the so-called East Coast vs. West Coast beef. So Mack 10 reached out to artists from around the United States to appear on his 1998 album, *The Recipe*. New York rappers Fat Joe, Big Pun, Foxy Brown, and Ol' Dirty Bastard appeared on the project, which Fat Joe said was noteworthy. "We want to be known as pioneers of actually taking the step—not just talking shit about it—of bringing the East and West Coasts together," he said.

and these artists was where my heart was at, where I wanted to be on this record. Everybody in the South understands that and knows what time it is, and they're down with me regardless, because that's the best Snoop Dogg—when he's comfortable. They only want the best Snoop Dogg, regardless of who he's with. It's still No Limit."

The willingness to let Snoop Dogg cater to his audience, and not the Southern and Midwestern fan base that drove No Limit's success, showed Master P's keen understanding of rap's regionalism, even among its bestselling artists. It was also a nod to his ability to make the most of his position, something Priority Records executive Dave Weiner said other rappers didn't do.

"They didn't see the business opportunity," Weiner said. "They were artists. He probably didn't get the opportunities that Cube and Mack and some of the other artists received coming from the South and coming from the Bay. He probably was forced to put his own music out, which in turn showed him the business model, showed him where the value was, how he could retain his master, retain his publishing, and control and own.

> ## "I'm not mad when people say I'm not really a rapper. They right. I'm a hustler, a businessman. Who wanna be a rapper but ain't got no money?"
>
> **MASTER P**

"I take great pride in the fact that Master P was more of a businessman than he was an incredible artist," Weiner added. "It showed people that hard work, quality work ethic, and not taking no for an answer sometimes meant more than the music itself. So I think a lot of people looked at Master P and No Limit and said, 'Yo, if that dude made it happen to the level he made it happen, I can do that.' It felt attainable. It didn't feel like something that separated him from the average guy out there."

Master P seemed ambivalent about whether or not he was respected as an artist. "I'm not mad when people say I'm not really a rapper," he said. "They right. I'm a hustler, a businessman. Who wanna be a rapper on all these TV shows and magazines but ain't got no money? That's somebody that need to work on their fundamentals. Me? I'm more a realist than a rapper."

Master P's and No Limit's success helped open doors for several other independent Southern and gangster rap labels and crews who were enjoying their own levels of success around the same time, including Suave House Records (the Houston-based company anchored by 8Ball & MJG); Prophet Entertainment and Hypnotize Minds (the Memphis-based companies anchored by Three 6 Mafia); and Cash Money Records (the New Orleans–based company anchored by B.G., Juvenile, and later, Lil Wayne, Drake, and Nicki Minaj).

"He, in my eyes, inspired a whole movement of independents, because if Master P could do it, anybody could do it, and the ones who went out and worked hard succeeded," Weiner said. "The ones who thought it was easy and a quick hustle learned the hard way."

Gangster rap's next wave built on the momentum Master P started with the Snoop Dogg and Dr. Dre reunion. It also placed gangster rap on a platform it had yet to experience.

CH.
14

Dr. Dre and Snoop Dogg Reignite, Sending Detractors "Up in Smoke"

BY 1999, RANDOM ACTS OF VIOLENCE, WALL STREET, AND THE BUSINESS OF WAR WERE FLOURISHING.

OPPOSITE:

Snoop Dogg (left) and Dr. Dre perform in Hawaii for Los Angeles radio station Power 106's Dr. Dre and Snoop Dogg reunion concert in September 1999.

Eric Harris and Dylan Klebold shot and killed thirteen people and injured twenty-four others before committing suicide at Columbine High School in Colorado, shocking suburban America and bringing awareness to modern-day school massacres. The Dow Jones Industrial Average closed above ten thousand for the first time, signaling the United States' economic might on both domestic and global levels. The North Atlantic Treaty Organization (NATO) launched air strikes against Yugoslavia, marking the first time NATO had attacked a sovereign country.

At the same time, gangster rap had just completed its first decade of dominance, one marked by the explosion of the subgenre thanks to the massive commercial success of Ice-T, Eazy-E, N.W.A, Ice Cube, the Geto Boys, Compton's

1999
Key Rap Releases

1. Dr. Dre's *2001* album

2. Eminem's *The Slim Shady LP* album

3. Snoop Dogg's *No Limit Top Dogg* album

US President

Bill Clinton

Something Else

Bill Clinton is acquitted by the Senate in his impeachment trial.

Most Wanted, DJ Quik, Cypress Hill, Scarface, Dr. Dre, Snoop Dogg, Warren G, E-40, Mack 10, Westside Connection, and Master P, among others. The genre's success spilled over to the box office with such films as *New Jack City*, *Boyz N the Hood*, and *Menace II Society*, blockbuster movies that starred rappers and focused on the drugs, guns, violence, and socioeconomic conditions gangster rappers covered in their music.

Yet things had been largely quiet on the gangster rap front in Los Angeles, especially when compared to the artistic and commercial explosion enjoyed there in the early nineties. The specters of 2Pac's and the Notorious B.I.G.'s murders still loomed large, and the emergence of new gangster rappers from Southern California was becoming increasingly rare. Meanwhile, Master P and his No Limit Records had been dominating the rap industry for the past few years, helping spread Southern gangster rap music. Furthermore, two of the subgenre's biggest artists were rebounding from projects that weren't as well-received as much of their earlier work had been.

After leaving Death Row Records, Dr. Dre released *The Aftermath* compilation (in conjunction with Columbia Records) on November 26, 1996. It also marked the official launch of Dr. Dre's new Aftermath Entertainment company, which was distributed by Interscope Records, the label owned and operated by music executive Jimmy Iovine and Dr. Dre's home since the release of 1992's *The Chronic*.

While *The Aftermath* sold more than one million copies, it took ten months to strike platinum. It was evident that fans did not embrace the Compton rapper-producer's first project on his new imprint the same way they had his previous albums. The album was anchored by the single "Been There, Done That," which featured Dr. Dre boasting of his wealth, trumpeting his woman for being a breadwinner, and celebrating being true to oneself. Many fans, though, took Dr. Dre's musical and lyrical stance as one distancing himself from gangster rap, the genre for which he had provided the most significant, popular, and influential tracks to date.

Dr. Dre's next project was also met with commercial success by most standards, but it fell short of what most fans expected from him creatively. In October 1997, Nas, Foxy Brown, AZ, and Nature combined to create the supergroup the Firm, whose *The Album* was produced by Dr. Dre and New York production duo the Trackmasters and was released by Dr. Dre's Aftermath Entertainment.

Despite the star power of the ultrarespected Nas and Foxy Brown and the production prowess of Dr. Dre and the Trackmasters (who helmed Nas's "If I Ruled the World [Imagine That]," among other hits), the project failed to resonate with either Dr. Dre's gangster rap fan base or Nas's New York–based, adamantly lyric-hungry followers. Other than the hit "Phone Tap," the project was seemingly done in by the overtly mafioso-themed songs, which alienated many of Nas's die-hard fans, and the beats, which vacillated between ultrapopish and sinister and didn't end up appealing to either Dr. Dre's core gangster audience or the Trackmasters' more pop-friendly sound. It was an album with an identity crisis. Even though the project moved more than one million units, it was not well-received, and the Firm was no more.

As Dr. Dre was searching for his post–Death Row footing, former protégé Snoop Dogg rebounded nicely when he signed with Master P's No Limit Records and released the double-platinum *Da Game Is to Be Sold, Not to Be Told* in 1998. Like Dr. Dre, though, Snoop Dogg's first foray with No Limit was commercially successful but not embraced critically. Nonetheless, the marriage proved beneficial to both Snoop Dogg and No Limit.

"I was enjoying success because No Limit was like the hottest in the street rap and gangster rap," Snoop Dogg said. "It was the same lane, just with Southern rap. At the time, it solidified me as being a real artist that could stand the test of time and they were looked at as a real label now because they had superstars they had built from the ground [up] and they had a solidified superstar in Snoop Dogg and they handled me right. They gave me a great record, movies. They got my spirit back right, the spirit of using my pen as my sword."

Snoop Dogg's comeback came full circle with 1999's *No Limit Top Dogg*, the album that reunited him with Dr. Dre as a producer for the songs "B Please," "Just Dippin'," and "Buck 'Em." With No Limit's success and his new material with Dr. Dre, Snoop Dogg had become firmly established as one of rap's most bankable stars, regardless of who was backing him.

"When me and Dre got back together again, I was sharper than ever because I still was hot," Snoop Dogg said. "I was with the hottest label in the industry. I went from Death Row to No Limit. That was like going from the Miami Heat to the Cleveland Cavaliers when LeBron [James] did. I was still in the championship mode, still in championship spirit, and still winning."

At the same time, Dr. Dre had received a creative jolt by signing Eminem. Dr. Dre's union with Eminem came at a critical time for the producer. It followed two albums that were not well-received (1996's *The Aftermath* compilation and 1997's *The Album*) and was a major career risk for Dr. Dre. After all, he was aligning himself with a white rapper. Dr. Dre showed that, yet again, his instincts were right. His first project with Eminem was the quadruple-platinum *The Slim Shady LP*, which was released in February 1999.

Dr. Dre also welcomed the D.O.C., one of his most valuable Ruthless Records and Death Row Records collaborators, back to his creative circle. Consequently, as Dr. Dre began working on his second studio album, his collaborative energy with Snoop Dogg and the rest of his team was peaking.

"It was great for me to have my spirit right when I got back with Dre, because by that time, he had discovered Eminem and he really had a few things going for himself that he was feeling good," Snoop Dogg said. "I had Dre participating on a couple of my No Limit records, which put us back in the groove before we actually got to his groove. It was getting him back into his groove, and then keeping me on point so that once I got back with him, I knew that he would be the best for me, as far as taking me to a level that No Limit couldn't take me to musically, because he was the best producer in the world for Snoop Dogg."

As would become a hallmark later in his career, Dr. Dre used time to his advantage. With a dedicated partner in Jimmy Iovine, he was free to create on his own terms and at his own pace. The resulting project was Dr. Dre's second studio album, 1999's *2001*.

"I could have put a lot of records out just to make some money," Dr. Dre said. "But I'm trying to create a new thing, and it doesn't happen overnight. Plus, there were a lot of people out there that were real hot. I wanted to let that simmer down for a minute, and then just hit them with this new shit that I've got coming."

Snoop Dogg called friend Devin the Dude, a Houston rapper-singer who appeared on *2001* selection "Fuck You." Once Snoop Dogg started reaching out to artists, he noticed an elevated level of excitement surrounding Dr. Dre's project.

"They all wanted to work with Dre, so it was like they would never say no to Dre and they already were my friends," Snoop Dogg said, "so it was a perfect culmination of all of those periods and that music and that vibe and the attitude."

For his part, Dr. Dre felt as though he had nothing to prove with *2001*. But unlike when he left Ruthless Records and Death Row Records at their commercial heights, Dr. Dre was coming off a seven-year break between studio albums and the wake of two projects that were greeted less than enthusiastically by consumers and critics alike, a first for him. He used the criticism he'd heard regarding *The Aftermath* compilation and the Firm's album to fuel such selections as "The Watcher," "Still D.R.E.," "What's the Difference," and "Forgot About Dre."

"I think a lot of people out there on the street are like, 'Okay, well, Dre fell off,'" Dr. Dre said. "But I've been through this same situation before with the doubters when I left Ruthless. Right before I did *The Chronic*, everybody was saying the same shit. It really doesn't mean anything to me. It's just motivation."

PRODUCED BY MELMAN • RECORDED
NGINEERED BY JEAN MARIE HORVAT •
RO • MASTERED BY EVREN GOKNAR •
OMING XZIBIT ALBUM 07863-67578-1

MEL-MAN

AFTER WORKING WITH Dr. Dre on *The After-math* compilation and the Firm's album, as well as producing Xzibit's "Los Angeles Times" single, Mel-Man emerged as one of rap's most prominent beatsmiths in 1999. He produced Eminem's "Role Model" with Dr. Dre and produced (with Dr. Dre) his *2001* album. Subsequent work with Ice Cube ("Hello"), Eminem ("The Real Slim Shady," "Kill You," and "Who Knew," among others), and Xzibit ("X," "Get Your Walk On") made the Pittsburgh musician one of the most successful producers of 1999 and 2000.

Whereas *The Aftermath* compilation and the Firm album confounded Dr. Dre's supporters, they returned en masse for *2001*. Cowritten by JAY-Z, the lead single, "Still D.R.E.," featured Snoop Dogg on the chorus and Dr. Dre rhyming about his steadfast loyalty to weed, making music, and the streets, as well as his disdain for law enforcement. It was almost as if Dr. Dre had hit the reset button on his career.

The appearance of Eminem on "What's the Difference" (which also features Xzibit) and "Forgot About Dre" brought another audience to the album, fans who were smitten with the white rapper from Detroit and who may or may not have been familiar with Dr. Dre's groundbreaking work with N.W.A, Eazy-E, the D.O.C., and Snoop Dogg, among others.

Regardless, thanks to Dr. Dre's return to his gangster rap roots, Eminem's surging popularity, and the overall explosion of the sales of CDs, *2001* sold more than two million copies in less than two months. It moved another one million copies as its three-month anniversary arrived. *2001* had sold three million units in three months, while *The Aftermath* needed nearly ten months to move one million copies.

With *2001*, Dr. Dre had proven that his star was rising rather than waning. Subsequent single "The Next Episode" with Snoop Dogg, Kurupt, and Nate Dogg recaptured the Death Row magic. Dr. Dre and Snoop Dogg each handled a verse, Kurupt did ad libs, and Nate Dogg sang the outro. The skillful mixture of the various artists' talents demonstrated Dr. Dre's range as an artist and producer.

"Still D.R.E." was a menacing ode to his virtuosity, while the up-tempo, crossover "Forgot About Dre" teamed him with Eminem for an homage to Dr. Dre's ability to endure as an artist, and the sonically slinky "The Next Episode" marked a rebirth of gangster rap, one that didn't rely on funk samples in order to succeed. Instead, these three singles showed that Dr. Dre was a musical master, one whose sonic reach was ever expanding and evolving.

In fact, even songs that did not receive accompanying videos became huge underground hits, as had been the case with *The Chronic*'s "Bitches Ain't Shit" and *Doggystyle*'s "Aint No Fun (If The Homies Cant Have None)." *2001* track "Xxplosive" (featuring Hittman, Kurupt, Nate Dogg, and Six-Two) got regular burn on Los Angeles radio, while "Some L.A. Niggaz" (featuring Hittman, Defari, Xzibit, Knoc-Turn'al, Time Bomb, King T, MC Ren, and Kokane) was a street favorite that earned more radio play as time passed. Dr. Dre's "What's the Difference" with Eminem and Xzibit also became a fan favorite thanks to the three rappers' individual imaginative takes on how they were different from their detractors.

As June 2000 arrived, *2001* had sold more than four million copies, but Dr. Dre was about to spearhead something arguably more significant. Since its inception, rap had had a history of being a poor concert draw. Substandard sound, limited stage production, small crowds, and violence among the attendees made concert bookers wary of committing to large-scale rap tours.

"You're goddamn right we couldn't tour," DJ Quik said. "We were getting shot up every fuckin' night."

There were notable exceptions, of course, namely the Fresh Fest series of tours that launched with Run-DMC, Whodini, the Fat Boys, and Kurtis Blow in 1984, as well as such successful one-off outings as Public Enemy's Fear of a Black Planet Tour with Digital Underground, Kid 'n Play, Heavy D & the Boyz, and Chill Rob G in 1990. These tours played arenas of varying size, but having successful events every few years made it seem that rap was decidedly second to rock in concert appeal.

It wasn't until 1999, when JAY-Z spearheaded the Hard Knock Life Tour with DMX, Redman, and Method Man, that rappers started erasing the negative perception of rap tours. JAY-Z and DMX, in particular, were hitting the road while enjoying major success, with JAY-Z's 1998 album, *Vol. 2... Hard Knock Life*, selling more than four million copies. For his part, in 1998, DMX became the first artist in music history to have his first two albums (*It's Dark and Hell Is Hot* and *Flesh of My Flesh, Blood of My Blood*) be released in the same year and both debut as the No. 1 album in the country.

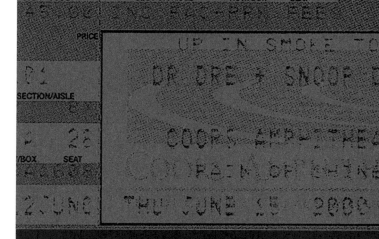

JAY-Z and DMX were two of the biggest acts in all of music in 1998 and 1999, so, in many ways, the short-term future of the rap tour hinged on what happened with JAY-Z's forty-seven-date Hard Knock Life Tour. It went off without a hitch, packing at-capacity crowds at nearly every stop and demonstrating that rap could equal rock's success, take place across the country without incident, and generate sellout crowds at arenas.

The success of the Hard Knock Life Tour was a boon to the Dr. Dre–fronted Up in Smoke Tour, which kicked off on June 15, 2000, at the Coors Amphitheatre in Chula Vista, California, just south of San Diego. With Snoop Dogg, Ice Cube, and Eminem also serving as headliners and Nate Dogg, Kurupt, Mack 10, Warren G, WC, Xzibit, Tha Eastsidaz, Jayo Felony, and others also appearing on the tour, it was the first legitimate gangster rap tour. When N.W.A and Ice-T, for instance, would tour, they would often share the bill with such non-gangster rap acts as De La Soul and Public Enemy. By contrast, the Up in Smoke Tour was an exclusively gangster rap event, other than Eminem.

The Up in Smoke Tour also arrived at a point when, thanks in large part to Snoop Dogg's resurgence, Dr. Dre's return, and Ice Cube's cultural cachet, Los Angeles–area gangster rap was again ascending and was shedding the baggage it had accumulated because of the deaths of 2Pac and the Notorious B.I.G., as well as the dissolution of Death Row Records.

"It was very significant," MC Eiht said. "We needed that tour as far as to save face for the West Coast with all the negativity we was gettin', Dre with Death Row, Snoop with Death Row. Then with all the people saying we couldn't

UP IN SMOKE
ALBUMS

THE FOUR HEADLINERS of the Up in Smoke Tour had successful albums out while the tour was in progress. Here's a snapshot of each project.

DR. DRE'S *2001*
Released November 16, 1999. Notable singles: "Still D.R.E.," "Forgot About Dre," and "The Next Episode." Certified six-times platinum November 21, 2000.

SNOOP DOGG'S *NO LIMIT TOP DOGG*
Released May 11, 1999. Notable singles: "B Please," with Xzibit, and "Down 4 My N's." Certified platinum October 13, 1999.

EMINEM'S *THE MARSHALL MATHERS LP*
Released May 23, 2000. Notable singles: "The Real Slim Shady," "The Way I Am," and "Stan," featuring Dido. Certified ten-times platinum March 9, 2011.

ICE CUBE'S *WAR & PEACE VOLUME 2 (THE PEACE DISC)*
Released March 21, 2000. Notable single: "You Can Do It." Certified gold May 31, 2000.

B PLEASE

SNOOP DOGG'S REUNION with Dr. Dre paid dividends for more than just the former Death Row Records labelmates. Xzibit's career also got a jolt thanks to his appearance on "B Please" (more commonly known as "Bitch Please"), a single from Snoop Dogg's platinum 1999 album, *No Limit Top Dogg*.

Prior to that, Xzibit had released two acclaimed albums, worked extensively with King Tee and Sir Jinx, and had become one of rap's most respected artists. Then he got a life-changing call from Snoop Dogg.

"He said he wanted to get me on the record and that Dre had the beat, and so he wanted me to meet him at the studio, at Echo Sound in the back room," Xzibit said. "It was scheduled for that day. I remember walking in. It was my first time in there with Dre. I was like, 'Yeah!' He played the beat. I wrote my verse in like 15 minutes, laid it, thanked him for the opportunity, and left. Then Snoop got on it. He called me and was like, 'Yeah. You did that, playboy.'"

Xzibit didn't know what the song would become, but he was ecstatic with the next "B Please" update.

"I get a call like, 'Yo, that's the next single off the *No Limit Top Dogg* album,'" Xzibit said. "I was like, 'Word?' I had put records out with other artists, but that was the first time it was being used as a single, especially with the big boys. It changed my life because all of a sudden, I'm here rapping alongside Snoop Dogg, one of the vanguards of our coast. It happened very quickly, and the change and reaction was immediate. I could tell, literally, that shit had changed overnight. I was on MTV rotation and I couldn't get MTV to play anything with the letter 'x' in it before that, let alone play my shit. It was just fantastic. Full rotation. Countdowns. Touring. And, that led to Dre's taking interest in me, working with me on his [*2001*] album. 'What's The Difference' came out of that. Working with Eminem on his records. Working with Snoop Dogg again. Going on the Up In Smoke Tour. All of that came from doing that record. 'Bitch Please' changed my life in a major way."

sell music anymore and that nobody wanted to listen to our type of music and that's why we were falling off and everybody was gravitating to Down South and the East Coast again. It just showed that we still had significant fans. We still were putting out good product, and it basically saved face for the West, because it brought a lot of dudes together to come and push this West Coast music."

The forty-five-date Up in Smoke Tour hit arenas in major cities such as Houston; Philadelphia; Atlanta; Dallas; Washington, DC; and Detroit, as well as two shows in the Los Angeles area. Almost all the shows sold out, and like the Hard Knock Life Tour before it, the Up in Smoke Tour took place without incident, dispelling the myth that gangster rap concerts were synonymous with violence.

Snoop Dogg, in particular, remembers the familial atmosphere he felt throughout the tour, as well as Dr. Dre's professionalism in coordinating all aspects of the tour, from the movie he showed at the onset of his and Snoop's joint set to the layout of the entire production. The tour featured a rotating cast of collaborators such as Nate Dogg, Kurupt, and Daz Dillinger, who each joined Dr. Dre and Snoop Dogg to deliver renditions of their own material.

"One thing about us, we always get classified for being violent, or making others act in a violent manner," Snoop Dogg said. "But if you really look at what we do, we're the most peaceful people in the world when it comes to making music, because we're the only ones that can get gangbangers, white people, Asian people, people from all over the world to come together and stand in a concert and rock to the rhythm of the groove and not want to fight each other

and not have issues with each other based on the music and the memories that we give them. So, I pay no attention to that, and I know that when we do what we do, we're healing the world with the music we make, even if it is gangster music. It's bringing these types of people together that would never have been in the same room together and they're singing together and rocking together. Before you know it, they became friends and realized that a gangster and a hippie's the same people. We just grew up different."

The Up in Smoke Tour concluded at the Fiddler's Green Amphitheatre outside of Denver on August 20, 2000. Four months later, the tour was immortalized with the DVD *The Up in Smoke Tour*, a two-hour concert film that captured many of the jaunt's best performances, as well as the feel-good energy of the tour.

"I think it brought [gangster rap] to mainstream America," Dave Weiner said. "I missed that tour and I regret missing that tour in person, but I can tell you I watched that DVD fifty times and with chills head to toe. It documented a magical point, and it was a successful, well-run, brilliantly executed tour, which, at that level, hadn't happened with rap music and hip-hop. The success of the DVD, the tour, the amount of people that came together on stage, from different backgrounds and different sets—and Eminem being an enormous part of launching rap into the next stratosphere of mainstream music—it was like the door was officially kicked in, man."

Like the tour, the DVD *The Up in Smoke Tour* was extremely successful, certified six-times platinum after selling six hundred thousand units.

Xzibit also reaped the benefits of the Up in Smoke Tour. The aggressive rapper, who rose to prominence as a member of lighthearted rap posse the Likwit Crew (King Tee, Tha Alkaholiks), used his work with Snoop Dogg and Dr. Dre on

MAJOR RAP TOURS PRE–UP IN SMOKE

MAJOR RAP TOURS were rare prior to the Up in Smoke Tour. Here's a look at some of the most significant ones.

Fresh Festival (1984). Also known as the Fresh Fest and the Fresh Tour, it featured the Fat Boys, Whodini, Kurtis Blow, and Run-DMC in its initial run in 1984 and the same acts, as well as Grandmaster Flash, in 1985. Both editions of the tour also featured breakdancing. The relaunched FM edition of Los Angeles radio station KDAY started throwing its own Fresh Fest in the 2010s. The lineups are made of mostly West Coast acts, often including such gangster rappers as DJ Quik, E-40, and Kurupt.

Def Jam (1987). LL Cool J headlined this early rap outing, which also featured labelmates Public Enemy. Eric B. & Rakim were also on the bill, even though they were signed to 4th & B'way/Island Records at the time, not Def Jam. The Long Island, New York, duo was managed by Rush Artist Management, though, which was Russell Simmons's management company.

No Way Out (1997). As the rap world mourned the loss of the Notorious B.I.G., mentor Puff Daddy (as P. Diddy was known at the time) launched the No Way Out Tour, which was named after the Puff Daddy & The Family album that was released less than four months after Biggie's murder. The tour featured Bad Boy Entertainment acts and collaborators, including Lil' Kim and Foxy Brown.

Hard Knock Life (1999). JAY-Z connected with his Def Jam Recordings labelmates DMX, Redman, and Method Man for a hugely successful national arena tour that reinvigorated the rap tour. While on the road, the Columbine school shooting took place. The rappers donated the proceeds from their Denver show, which took place a week after the April 20 massacre, to the families of the victims. "We've known firsthand how pointless and senseless violence always is," JAY-Z said, "and we wanted to show our support in a real way."

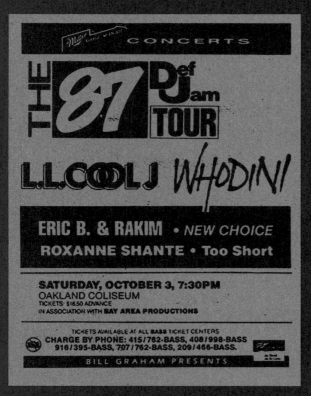

"B Please" and his time on the tour to perform in front of hundreds of thousands of new fans and to catapult himself into superstardom and into the gangster rap world. Buoyed by Dr. Dre's production and collaborations with Snoop Dogg, Eminem, and others, Xzibit's third album, *Restless*, was released on December 12, 2000. It sold more than one million copies in six weeks thanks to such muscular singles as "X" and "Front 2 Back."

"I got brought into a situation where I just stayed myself with Dr. Dre, Snoop Dogg, Eminem, and all of them," Xzibit said. "I didn't start rapping like any of them. I brought my own flavor to the table."

Established acts also built on the momentum the Up in Smoke Tour provided. With his career back in overdrive thanks to his deal with Master P at No Limit Records as well as his reunion with mentor Dr. Dre, Snoop Dogg wrapped the tour, and on December 19, 2000, he delivered his third and final No Limit album, *Tha Last Meal*. The skeletal, explosive Dr. Dre–produced single "Lay Low" featured Master P, Nate Dogg, protégés Tha Eastsidaz (whose platinum debut album Snoop Dogg released on his Dogghouse Records in February 2000), and singer Butch Cassidy, while the somber, laid-back "Wrong Idea" featured Kokane, Bad Azz, and Lil 1/2 Dead. The platinum-selling *Tha Last Meal* cemented Snoop Dogg's reign as one of rap's biggest stars and the West Coast's most prolific and consistently celebrated rapper of the era.

"I had proclaimed myself as the King of the West Coast, so I had to prove it," Snoop Dogg said. "I said it before it was actually proven. I had work to do, and that's part of my incline to get to where I am. When I looked at the great Kobe Bryant, Muhammad Ali, Magic Johnson, the people I aspire to be, I look at how they went on their runs. Their runs were consecutive and it didn't matter. They just kept running, kept doing what they did best, and that's what I was on, trying to stay on my run. So when I got a Shaquille O'Neal, a Kareem Abdul-Jabbar, or a championship-caliber player like Dre to play alongside me, it made my job easy, to where I just had to do what I do and he was going to do what he do and it came together to become something that was special and timeless."

With Dr. Dre and Snoop Dogg recording together again and having completed headlining stints on the most successful tour in gangster rap history, they helped usher in the next two gangster rap superstars, with Dr. Dre taking the lead and Snoop Dogg giving them the stamp of approval in songs, on stage, and in the media.

Your Life's on the Line

In his State of the Union address in January, President George W. Bush labeled Iraq, Iran, and North Korea an "axis of evil" and said they were guilty of state-sponsored terrorism. In March, the United States invaded Afghanistan. By November, the United Nations Security Council issued a resolution calling for Iraq's leader, Saddam Hussein, to disarm or face serious consequences.

As the world was in its latest race to global war, gangster rap was also ramping up for its own explosion. While the West Coast was enjoying a gangster rap renaissance spearheaded by Dr. Dre and Snoop Dogg, the genre was about to get a boost from a New York artist who had been left for dead, literally and figuratively.

Queens, New York, rapper 50 Cent had impressed producers Poke and Tone (aka the Trackmasters) with his song "The Hit." Poke and Tone had produced

OPPOSITE:

The Game spearheaded a new generation of West Coast gangster rap in the mid-2000s. The Compton rapper is shown here at the world premiere of *Straight Outta Compton* at the Microsoft Theatre in Los Angeles on August 10, 2015.

2003
Key Rap Releases

1. 50 Cent's *Get Rich or Die Tryin'* album

2. OutKast's *Speakerboxxx/The Love Below* album

3. JAY-Z's *The Black Album* album

US President

George W. Bush

Something Else

A United States and British-led coalition invaded Iraq.

the Firm's *The Album* with Dr. Dre and had already enjoyed success with Nas, Foxy Brown, and Will Smith. They were also executives at Columbia Records at the time.

The Trackmasters had signed 50 Cent, but as the scheduled release for his debut album approached, he failed to elicit much excitement via singles such as "Rowdy Rowdy" and "Thug Love" (the latter was a collaboration with Destiny's Child). Things changed, though, when 50 Cent recorded the controversial song "How To Rob." On the tongue-in-cheek track, which was produced by Poke and Tone, 50 Cent imagines himself robbing a bevy of entertainers, from P. Diddy and Bobby Brown to JAY-Z and Mike Tyson. Objecting to some of the lyrics, Poke and Tone had 50 Cent remove some of the rougher lines about Mariah Carey and others.

50 Cent went along with their suggestions, but truth be told, he wasn't concerned about offending anyone.

Released in August 1999 and included on the *In Too Deep* soundtrack, 50 Cent's "How To Rob" became a sensation, for better or worse. "It was an immediate shock at radio because when they played it on [influential New York radio station] Hot 97, it was over," Poke said. "Everybody was talking about this record. It immediately got him noticed, and that's what we were looking for, attention."

But with the attention came heat. Several of the rappers 50 Cent rhymed about took offense to his lyrics, including JAY-Z and Wu-Tang Clan member Ghostface Killah. Then, on May 24, 2000, 50 Cent was shot multiple times in front of his grandmother's house in South Jamaica, Queens, New York. The reported shooter, Darryl "Hommo" Baum, was killed three weeks later.

The scrutiny brought on by his being shot and by the street tension generated by his song "Ghetto Qu'ran," in which he gave detailed information about the names and operations of specific Queens, New York, drug dealers, proved unbearable for Columbia Records. 50 Cent was subsequently dropped from the label's roster. The album he recorded for Columbia, *Power of the Dollar*, was not released, even though bootleg copies surfaced once he became a superstar. (However, it was later released as an EP.)

While he was recuperating, 50 Cent recorded songs for what would become the mixtapes that gave him a second chance in the music industry. He took the innovative step of using the instrumentals from existing songs from the Geto Boys, JAY-Z, Mobb Deep, and others. 50 Cent modified the hooks of the songs and then delivered his own versions. They were instantly recognizable because of the beats and choruses of the original songs, which were already proven crowd pleasers.

As a solo artist and with his G-Unit collective (initially composed of rappers 50 Cent, Lloyd Banks, and Tony Yayo), 50 Cent released a glut of material in 2002, including the independent album *Guess Who's Back?* and mixtapes *50 Cent Is the Future* and *No Mercy, No Fear*. 50 Cent's hard-hitting, gritty, and charismatic material contained the standard gangster rap themes (guns, drugs, sex, violence) and made him one of the most buzzed-about artists in the genre, one who was booking club tours without a major record deal, an unheard-of accomplishment.

50 Cent was also relentless, releasing far more product than the typical artist. He was gaining attention and acclaim from the genre's elite. *No Mercy, No Fear* featured the song "Wanksta," which Eminem included on the soundtrack for *8 Mile*, his semi-autobiographical blockbuster film.

In about two years, 50 Cent had gone from an afterthought to signing a one-million-dollar deal with Eminem's Shady Records and Dr. Dre's Aftermath Entertainment, becoming the first artist to sign a deal with both of them. Astute businessman that he was, he had already laid the groundwork for even greater success.

"One thing about 50, he knew how to brand himself before he got with Eminem and Dre," Snoop Dogg said. "He was already popping and doing his own shit and making hot music and being controversial—doing all the shit that stars do. So, to me, 50 was already a star."

50 Cent and his handlers played up his street past in the run-up to the release of his Shady/Aftermath debut album, 2003's *Get Rich Or Die Tryin'*. His drug-dealing past and his being shot nine times gave him a hard-earned legitimacy from the perspective of rap listeners who clamored for artists who had risen up from what they considered an authentic street life.

DR. DRE AND EMINEM GANGSTER RAP

As rap evolved, getting the backing, or "cosign," from a credible, established artist became almost an unwritten rule for and requirement to the road to success. Getting two industry titans to simultaneously back an artist was virtually unheard of. Things changed when Dr. Dre and Eminem took the rare step of partnering to release 50 Cent's material, most notably 2003's *Get Rich Or Die Tryin'*. The project was executive-produced by the two rap titans and put out via Dr. Dre's Aftermath Entertainment and Eminem's Shady Records in conjunction with Interscope Records. Less than a year after its release, *Get Rich Or Die Tryin'* had sold more than six million units.

50 CENT CINEMA STAR

AFTER ESTABLISHING HIMSELF as a rap superstar, 50 Cent transitioned to Hollywood. Here are some of his more notable film and television projects.

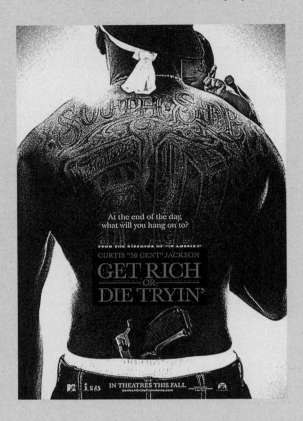

Get Rich or Die Tryin' (2005). In the film loosely based on his life story, 50 Cent portrays Marcus, an aspiring rapper who tries to leave the streets behind as he chases music stardom.

Righteous Kill (2008). 50 Cent appears in the film that reunited Robert De Niro and Al Pacino for the first time since 1995's *Heat*.

Power (2014–18). Serving as an executive producer and star, 50 Cent helped usher in STARZ's slate of original programming with this drama, which focuses on the double life of a New York nightclub owner and drug kingpin portrayed by Omari Hardwick.

"My nigga 50 was, 'I'll blast you. Nigga shot at me. We sold dope in Jamaica, Queens. The homie got one hundred years. We got the kilos, the AKs,' but he was never looked at as the gangbanger," MC Eiht said. "Never. Put him on the West Coast and tie him into one of these neighborhoods, he'd [have] been a mutha-fuckin' gangster rapper."

Although he wasn't a gangbanger from the Los Angeles area, 50 Cent catered to the demographic. On *Get Rich Or Die Tryin'* track "What Up Gangsta," for instance, the hook references the Bloods and the Crips. "What up, Blood," 50 Cent raps. "What up, cuz" comes next, using the word Crips consider a term of endearment among themselves.

Much of the rest of *Get Rich Or Die Tryin'* played like a blueprint of classic gangster rap. "Many Men (Wish Death)" featured a reflective 50 Cent detailing people who wanted to see him perish, while "Heat" featured music built around gunshots. "P.I.M.P." (and its remix featuring Snoop Dogg) played up 50 Cent's ability to sleep with a woman and then have her prostitute herself for him.

Massively popular singles "In Da Club" and "21 Questions" showed that 50 Cent was able to remain himself while parlaying gangsterism into a commercially friendly format, something mentor Dr. Dre had perfected with his own work, as well as the music he made with Eazy-E, N.W.A, Snoop Dogg, and others.

With a significant self-generated buzz, a willingness to diss the most popular rappers of the moment (Ja Rule chief among them), and the stamp of approval from Eminem and Dr. Dre, as well as the crossover smash "In Da Club," 50 Cent exploded onto the scene in 2003.

Get Rich Or Die Tryin' debuted as the No. 1 album in the country that February, showing that a new generation of gangster rappers could dominate the pop-culture consciousness.

50 Cent also came into the music industry with a distinctive focus: He was pushing his brands and was approaching his career as a multipronged business, not just as a rapper. It marked a significant evolution for both rap and gangster rap. In the eighties and nineties, for example, rappers had to walk a fine line between pursuing business opportunities and being labeled sellouts.

But by the time 50 Cent entered the conversation in 2003, Ice-T, Ice Cube, Dr. Dre, Snoop Dogg, and others had all made the transition from being looked at as exclusively hardcore rappers to being multifaceted entertainers, ones whose music, film, and endorsement work was accepted and appreciated by rap consumers, the general public, and business partners.

50 Cent used this evolution to his advantage, securing a deal with Shady/Aftermath's parent company, Interscope Records, for his own G-Unit imprint. Given his history of churning out music, his newfound fame, and his keen business sense, 50 knew that with *Get Rich Or Die Tryin'* selling more than five million copies in four months, he needed to strike again, and as quickly as possible.

In 2004, 50 Cent the executive continued his impressive run with G-Unit with the release of Lloyd Banks's *The Hunger for More* and Young Buck's *Straight Outta Ca$hville*. At this point, 50 Cent and his artists had sold more than ten million albums, and his endorsement deals with Reebok and Glacéau Vitaminwater were evidence that he was an eminently bankable persona.

"The last gangster rapper was 50 Cent," Ice-T said. "He embodied that image, that 'I don't give a fuck.' 50 Cent had you really believing you didn't want to fuck with him. I heard 50 Cent, when he was beefing with Fat Joe, was like, 'Fat Joe. I'm right down the street. It's real hard to find a nigga when you know he got a gun, ain't it?' I was like, 'Okay.' I think 50 was the last one who did it that I believed. . . . And when I say 50 Cent, I also put Game in that, because Game was part of G-Unit."

By the time 50 Cent joined Dr. Dre's Aftermath Entertainment in 2002, the Game had already been signed to the company. Unfortunately, he hadn't generated any momentum. The Game's career began to change for the better thanks to 50 Cent. After working with Dr. Dre and being around the Game, 50 Cent believed that the lyric-driven gangster rapper from Compton had enormous potential.

Part of what made the Game distinctive was his ability to adopt, incorporate, and excel at any type of rhyme style, an extraordinary skill for a rapper.

"The first thing when I listen to a beat, as soon as I hear it, I would say, 'Luda-cris would be on this,'" the Game said. "I take myself out of the equation, because I can put on any costume and become any type of MC with any style. I always figure out who can be on it first, and I attack that style. They don't necessarily have to be on it with me, but that's the way I go in to record it. The best part about that is that I get to use my city and my home and everything that I'm about to incorporate into that style."

The Game's chameleon-like rap abilities enabled him to thrive over Dr. Dre's West Coast beats, instrumentals from New York artists, and the bouncy rhythms of Southern rap acts. In seizing an opportunity to build his brand, 50 Cent found someone who would become his most commercially successful protégé, an artist who otherwise may have gotten stuck in music industry purgatory. The Game had a record deal, but no insider at Aftermath Entertainment who believed in him enough to release his material.

"When [50 Cent] got put on, he had enough gangster to pull Game off the bench, because Game was sitting on the sidelines," Snoop Dogg said. "He pulled him off the bench, put him in the game, play with him, give him a spotlight, help him shine, and create a platform that Game is still able to have to this day based off of 50 Cent looking on the sidelines and saying, 'Hey, Dre, let me put this nigga in the game. This nigga ain't getting in. He's too good to be on the sideline. As a matter of fact, let me play with him real quick and show you something.'"

Adding the Game to G-Unit brought a new dimension to the crew. With the signing, 50 Cent now had rappers from three decidedly different rap constitu-encies: New York (Lloyd Banks, Tony Yayo, 50 Cent), the South (Young Buck), and the West Coast (the Game).

The lineage of the Game signing stretched back to eighties Compton rap and had come full circle at a time when there had been a lull in new Los Angeles–area gangster rap acts.

"There was a chain being built there where 50 went in and was like, 'Okay, I need to bring someone out,'" Wrekonize said. "He created other artists to bring on his own, and it seemed like Game is that guy. It was a good time, because it seemed like it was so quiet on the West Coast in terms of artists at that time. It felt like the West was so ready for a champion, a new face. I feel like he came in almost like clockwork, at the right time for the West Coast."

On his "Westside Story" single, the Game seemed aware of how Los Angeles rap was perceived.

Since the West Coast fell off, the streets been watchin' / The West Coast never fell off, I was asleep in Compton / Aftermath been here, the beats been knockin'

The Game also rapped on "Westside Story" that he was "bringing CA back." For Big Boy, radio host on Real 92.3 in Los Angeles, the lyrics carried significant weight.

"When we got the first Game records and the energy around them, and what the city felt like and what you started to hear out the cars, and he said, 'I'm bringing CA back,' it was like, 'Hell yeah, you are,'" Big Boy said.

Furthermore, having 50 Cent perform the "Westside Story" chorus was also noteworthy given the lingering animosity between artists from the East and West Coasts. "Working with an artist like 50 from the other side of the country just helped to unify the movement," said Wrekonize.

"I would have hoped that they took a cue from us, just the trouble we got into out representing that shit," DJ Quik said of rappers promoting beef and gangsterism. "It was super, super dangerous, but at the same time, you're worse off if you play like you're not. It's going to be harder that way, to fake it. He technically put the hood on his back. He put the whole Blood card on his back. But he's such a good look, it almost made the gangbanging look secondary. You had to judge him on his talents, not how solid of a gangbanger and street brawler he is. It's really about his fuckin' music."

Fans, though, gravitated to the Game's gangster image, just as they had Ice-T, N.W.A, DJ Quik, Snoop Dogg, and others in the eighties and nineties. For the Bloods, in particular, who had not been as well represented in rap as the Crips, the Game was someone to rally around.

"He was a replica of what the millions of Bloods around the world aspired to be," Snoop Dogg said. "He was their guiding light. He was what you thought a Blood was supposed to look like, rap like, act like, because he was stamped and solidified by real Crips like myself and the Crips on the West Coast that held the throne of the rap world from day one. To be solidified by real, official rappers and Crip members, and to have your own Blood stigma and to be a youngster and to be a leader and not a follower, definitely attracted people.

"That's what it was about Game. He had leader qualities as a youngster to take the lead and not follow and do his own thing and say, 'Yeah. This is Compton Piru Blood' or whatever gang he claim, and let people know what it was that stayed down with it," Snoop Dogg continued. "He stayed true to it and that's official. One thing about us on the West, we respect when a nigga keep it one hundred. When a nigga just stay gangsta from top to bottom, that earns you more respect than anything—more respect than money and fame. I think that [was] his influence, that he was able to stand strong and tall and be him at all times and make other little homies get behind him, because everybody didn't

50 CENT: BEEF FACTORY

50 Cent had beefs with many prominent celebrities. Here's a look at several of them.

JAY-Z. 50 Cent named JAY-Z as someone he would accost on his 1999 song "How To Rob." Later that year, JAY-Z responded on "It's Hot (Some Like It Hot)," in which he rapped, "I'm about a dollar, what the fuck is 50 cents?" The two filmed a Reebok ad together in 2003 and performed together at Madison Square Garden in August 2007, though 50 Cent lobbed more disses JAY-Z's way in 2009.

Ja Rule. 50 Cent's rivalry with Ja Rule escalated into violence in 2000 when one of 50 Cent's friends robbed Ja Rule of jewelry. The rappers crossed paths in a studio, and a brawl ensued. 50 Cent was stabbed in the chest. After recovering from being shot in April 2000, 50 Cent targeted Ja Rule and his Murder Inc. crew during his ascent to stardom.

Fat Joe. In 2004, Ja Rule recorded the song "New York" and featured Fat Joe and Jadakiss on the track. To 50 Cent, Fat Joe and Jadakiss were siding with his enemy, and thus became targets. 50 Cent dissed Fat Joe throughout his "Piggy Bank" song, which also features jabs at Shyne, Lil' Kim, Kelis, and Nas. The two exchanged disses for nearly a decade.

Floyd Mayweather Jr. The former friends turned foes in April 2008. After 50 Cent put his hands in Mayweather's face at a celebrity basketball event in Michigan, the boxer threw a punch. 50 Cent claimed victory after the altercation, which allegedly started over a bet.

Rick Ross. In May 2008, the house in which one of 50 Cent's children was living with his mother burned down. Both the woman and 50 Cent's son were in the residence at the time. Rick Ross referenced the incident in "Mafia Music," a cut released in January 2009. The back-and-forth between the rappers continued for years, with 50 Cent referencing Rick Ross's past as a correctional officer, and Rick Ross claiming he's the biggest loss 50 Cent ever endured.

Jadakiss/The LOX. As was the case with Fat Joe, 50 Cent took umbrage with Jadakiss appearing on Ja Rule's "New York" single. 50 Cent included barbs aimed at Jadakiss on "Piggy Bank," saying that he was only popular in New York. The subsequent and extensive war of words included Jadakiss's "Checkmate" and 50 Cent and Tony Yayo's "I Run New York," among others. Jadakiss's partners-in-rhyme, The LOX also joined the fray, which many followers said Jadakiss won lyrically, though 50 Cent earned points by attacking Jadakiss's lack of sales.

Diddy. In 2005, 50 Cent began working with former Diddy protégé Ma$e, who, after becoming one of rap's most popular artists, had walked away from music in the late 1990s. Ever the businessman, Diddy wasn't going to let 50 Cent sign Ma$e to his G-Unit Records without being compensated handsomely. The amount, a reported $2 million, was much more than 50 Cent was willing to pay. Scathing disses soon followed. Among the most pointed was the charge that Diddy knew who killed the Notorious B.I.G. but said nothing because he was afraid he'd suffer the same fate.

Nas. One-time Columbia Records label-mates, 50 Cent and Nas's beef gained traction in 2005 when 50 Cent dissed Nas over his love for then-wife Kelis on his "Piggy Bank" track. Nas responded on 2008's "Queens Get the Money," the first track from his Untitled album, saying that 50 Cent was hiding behind the success of mentors Eminem and Dr. Dre.

Cam'ron. While doing an interview with Angie Martinez on New York radio station Hot 97 in 2007, 50 Cent fielded a call from Cam'ron, whose Diplomats company released material through KOCH Records at the time. 50 Cent had previously called KOCH a "graveyard" for recording artists, spurring an on-air argument that turned profane and hostile. 50 Cent included the blistering Cam'ron diss "Funeral Music" as a bonus track on protégé Young Buck's 2007 album, Buck the World. Cam'ron responded with the diss cut "Curtis," which is 50 Cent's given name.

Young Buck. Like the Game, Young Buck fell out of favor with his G-Unit mentor. Young Buck got off to a promising start with 50 Cent, releasing the platinum *Straight Outta Ca$hville* album in 2004 and the acclaimed *Buck The World* project in 2007. By April 2008, though, things had gotten bad enough between the pair that 50 Cent announced that Young Buck was no longer in G-Unit. Two months later, 50 Cent released a phone conversation between Young Buck and himself in which Young Buck was crying, asking 50 Cent to let him back into the crew, and explaining that he was having financial issues. The two eventually reconciled.

want to be a Crip. A lot of niggas wanted to be Bloods, and he gave them the greatest example on how to be one."

By the time the Game was gaining steam in 2004, it had been about twenty years since Los Angeles gangs had migrated to the Midwest and other regions. Ice Cube rapped about it in 1991 on his "My Summer Vacation" and DJ Quik detailed how he saw the imprint Southern California gangs had left on Oakland, St. Louis, San Antonio, and Denver on 1992's "Jus Lyke Compton."

Kansas City rapper Tech N9ne witnessed the spread of the Bloods gang firsthand. "They moved into our neighborhood in the early eighties," Tech N9ne said. "Thirty-seventh Street Fruit Town Brim moved in our neighborhood in the Fifties [as in Kansas City's Fifty-seventh Street, for instance] and brought that shit to us. So when we see people like Game repping, we realize that's a soldier over there that's been through it, so we connect that way. . . . Not only with Blood, but he was rapping his ass off. Still to this day. Lyrics, homie. That's respect."

The Game unleashed a seemingly unending quantity of material before and after he signed with 50 Cent. With 50 Cent and Dr. Dre backing him, though, the Game had a clear path to stardom.

"Nobody was in their way," DJ Quik said. "They were like the new Lakers, just to use that metaphor. Just a new, gunning team that had the legs for it and [was] going to develop into stars. That's what I saw it as. They just came in hungry and wasn't nobody standing in their way. Not even us, 'cause we had kind of moved on already. We're the old school now at this point. But they came in and looked up to us, kind of, and we gave them our music, the music we still deem to be cutting edge."

Having Eminem in 50 Cent and, by default, the Game's corner also added mainstream legitimacy to both acts and introduced them to a vast audience. After all, Eminem's 2000 and 2002 albums, *The Slim Shady LP* and *The Eminem Show*, had sold more than nine million and eight million copies, respectively, at the time.

"Eminem had become the juggernaut of hip-hop at that point," DJ Quik said. "[There] was no denying that. [This was] something we had never seen. For him to have the foresight to be able to see that 50 would be a dope artist, and then who would see that 50 would birth Game? It couldn't have landed more perfectly. That's as good a run of West Coast hip-hop mixed with East Coast hip-hop that I've ever seen. That was a whole new thing. Technically, that was the aftermath."

But 50 Cent and the Game's union was short-lived. The rappers began making comments about each other in the media, namely about 50 Cent making the

Game viable and writing the choruses for and appearing on his singles "How We Do" and "Hate It or Love It." On February 28, 2005, a few weeks after the release of the Game's debut major label album, *The Documentary*, there was an altercation and shooting outside of New York radio station Hot 97.

The Game had conducted an interview there earlier in the day and returned when 50 Cent appeared that night. The Game, though, was not allowed to enter the building, which led to an altercation and to twenty-four-year-old Compton, California, resident Kevin Reed being shot. 50 Cent announced on the radio station that night that he was kicking the Game out of G-Unit because he was disloyal. 50 Cent had taken issue with the Game because he would not side with him on his laundry list of beefs, including Nas, with whom the Game wanted to record.

> *"You had to judge him on his talents, not how solid of a gangbanger and street brawler he is. It's really about his fuckin' music."*
>
> **DJ QUIK ON THE GAME**

Even though 50 Cent and the Game stopped working together and continued dissing each other, the Game pulled off a remarkable feat over the next several years: Despite being 50 Cent's protégé and being disparaged by his mentor, he launched and sustained a significant career, one that continues today and has expanded to film (*Waist Deep*, *Street Kings*) and television (*Marrying the Game*). Like 50 Cent, the Game kept his name in the headlines by taking shots at other artists. More importantly, though, he continued releasing quality material.

"I think he was all right after leaving G-Unit because he still delivered records," Big Boy said. "He stayed extremely relevant. Usually when you're in that kind of crew, the big dog can silence a mothafucker. . . . But Game, I think he took off and ran."

With 50 Cent and the Game established as gangster rap's latest superstars, the genre moved into its third decade.

Money Turned Boys into Men

IN 2005, THE WORLD SUFFERED BOTH NATURAL DISASTERS AND MAN-MADE TERROR.

urricane Katrina devastated large swaths of the US Gulf Coast, killing more than 1,800 people and causing a reported $115 billion in damages. London's public transport system was rocked by coordinated bomb blasts, which killed fifty-two people and injured another seven hundred.

Nonetheless, progress was being made. The G8, a forum featuring representatives from the world's major highly industrialized economies (Canada, France, Germany, Italy, Japan, Russia, United Kingdom, United States), pledged to provide $50 billion (USD) in aid to Africa by 2010. The Provisional Irish Republican Army also ended its thirty-year armed campaign in Northern Ireland.

OPPOSITE:
Snoop Dogg (left) and Archbishop Don "Da Magic" Juan attend a Player's Ball in Chicago, November 30, 2002.

2005
Key Rap Releases

1. The Game's *The Documentary* album

2. 50 Cent's *The Massacre* album

3. Kanye West's *Late Registration* album

US President

George W. Bush

Something Else

WikiLeaks is launched.

As these events were unfolding and the aughts passed their middle point, many of rap's detractors still saw the genre as a disruptive force. Nonetheless, rap had enjoyed sustained commercial success for more than twenty-five years, even as independent record stores had mostly gone out of business and major record retailers, such as Tower Records, were on their last legs as a result of music becoming digital. The music business and artists were taking serious blows, and most didn't know how to reinvent themselves.

Mainstream rappers Will Smith, LL Cool J, and Queen Latifah were among the rare few who had graduated from being consistent hit makers in the music world to mainstream stars with award nominations and their own television shows and/or film franchises to their credits.

It is also worth noting that gangster rappers had arguably enjoyed more success than the rappers from all other subgenres of the music combined. Ice-T landed a role on *Law & Order: Special Victims Unit*, which is on its twentieth season, making him the longest-running black actor currently on television, having joined the show in the second season. If Ice-T and *Law & Order: SVU* return for a twenty-first season, the rapper will hold the all-time record for the longest-running black actor on a program in television history.

Additionally, Ice Cube, Dr. Dre, Snoop Dogg, and 50 Cent were among the preeminent gangster rap acts who had parlayed their success into multi-million-dollar deals (and even one multibillion-dollar pact) that stretched beyond the creation of music.

> "...*In the hood or the ghetto communities, people admire strength over wealth.*"
>
> **ICE-T**

Just like their mainstream rap counterparts, gangster rappers excelled at selling records, topping the Billboard charts, delivering box-office success, becoming mainstays on television, and connecting with audiences around the globe. Gangster rap had the rare ability to appeal to listeners of all racial and socioeconomic backgrounds on personal, visceral, and intellectual levels.

Their reality isn't always positive, but that doesn't matter to listeners. It's the authentic perspective that they crave.

"Why these particular artists tend to have good careers goes back to what it was originally called: reality rap," Ice-T said. "These artists tend to be more honest. They're telling the truth. They're saying unabashedly how they feel about things and people gravitate toward that. Now, especially in the hood or the ghetto communities, people admire strength over wealth. If you're strong, willing to break the rules, say, 'Fuck 'em,' then people dig that. So, of course, the gangster is the epitome of that. That's the person who says, 'Hey, I'm going to do it my way regardless.' So, there's a lot of admiration that goes along with that, whether it be a negative image you're portraying or a positive image."

"We have a business mentality," Snoop Dogg said. "We all looked at the gangsters we watched as kids, whether it was movie stars or gangsters in our neighborhood, drug dealers, kingpins, they all had a mentality about themselves. Some of the best *Fortune* 500 company runners are in the penitentiary right now as drug dealers. Those are guys who ran business from a street perspective, who gave us inspiration to do it, so when we was able to get into the game of doing it the right way, we definitely were going to maximize and learn and figure it out and not just be mean and tough and gangster. We were going to be gangster with this business, too."

Ice-T, for one, presented himself as gangster, but like many of his musical successors, he also portrayed himself as a player, a pimp, a mack, and a hustler. The gangster rap forefather broke into acting playing a rapper in *Breakin'* (1984) and *Breakin' 2: Electric Boogaloo* (1984). He took the ultimate career risk by going against type—and against the foundational gangster rap ethos of "Fuck tha

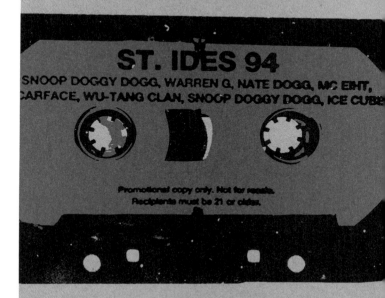

ST. IDES: FROM BILLY DEE TO KING TEE

MALT LIQUOR BRAND St. Ides was among the first companies to embrace gangster rap stars and hire them as pitchmen. The Geto Boys, MC Eiht, and Snoop Dogg were among the hardcore acts that made commercials about their love of the beverage, whose alcohol by volume concentration of 8.2 percent was significantly higher than most other drinks. Ice Cube was perhaps St. Ides's biggest endorser, appearing in several commercials and boasting his own poster for the malt liquor company. King Tee (the first rapper with a pact to endorse the brand) and Ice Cube's song for the company, "King Tee's Beer Stand," was included as a track on King Tee's 1993 album, *Tha Triflin' Album*. Thanks to the heavy push from rappers, St. Ides supplanted Colt 45 (famously pushed by actor Billy Dee Williams) as the malt liquor du jour of the urban community.

Police"—by taking on the role of police officer Scotty Appleton in *New Jack City* (1991), his first starring role.

"For him to say, 'You know what, man, I'm Ice-T, and I'm going to play a cop in this movie.' The shit that you've been rapping about, and now you're playing this motherfucka. 'But it's a role, and I'm an actor now,' and then can still come back and jump on that music, I think that he navigated his career extremely well," Los Angeles radio personality Big Boy said.

After earning acclaim for his turn in *New Jack City*, Ice-T landed a string of high-profile roles in films with Denzel Washington (1991's *Ricochet*), Rutger Hauer (1994's *Surviving the Game*), and Keanu Reeves (1995's *Johnny Mnemonic*). In 2000, he was cast in a role that made television history. The gangster rap pioneer has starred in more than four hundred *Law & Order: Special Victims Unit* episodes.

Ice-T credits his willingness to play diverse, even surprising roles for his success as an actor. "If you're going to act and you're going to limit yourself to roles, you're very stupid," Ice-T said. "Playing a cop and a gangster is the exact same acting. You both have an attitude. You both have a gun. You both want answers, and there'll be a consequence. So when I'm sitting on *Law & Order* and I'm doing an interrogation, in my brain, I might not even be thinking I'm a cop. I'm thinking like, 'This fool better tell me what I want to know,' in the same way I might be dealing on some street shit."

RAPPERS SPORT THE SHIELD

ICE-T WENT AGAINST type by portraying police officer Scotty Appleton in 1991's *New Jack City*. Soon thereafter, rappers became regularly featured as police officers in film and on television. The Fresh Prince, aka Will Smith, portrayed a cop in the successful *Bad Boys* film franchise that launched in 1995, while Dr. Dre played a corrupt officer in *Training Day* in 2001. LL Cool J has also played a police officer in film (2003's *S.W.A.T.*) and on television (2009's *N.C.I.S.: Los Angeles*). Ice Cube, who came up with the song idea for N.W.A's "Fuck tha Police," played cops in two blockbuster film franchises: the *21 Jump Street* reboot that launched in 2012 and *Ride Along*, which launched a popular series two years later. Ice-T, of course, came full circle in his acting career by portraying Odafin Tutuola on *Law & Order: Special Victims Unit*.

While Ice-T has become a television fixture, Ice Cube has become one of Hollywood's most bankable stars and producers. In addition to his films, which have combined to gross more than $1 billion at the box office, the Los Angeles artist's Cube Vision production company released several of Hollywood's most successful franchises, including films such as *Next Friday*, *Barbershop*, *Are We There Yet?*, and *Ride Along*.

Showing his versatility as a director (*The Players Club* [1998]) and writer (*Friday* [1995], *The Players Club* [1998], and *All About the Benjamins* [2002], among others), Ice Cube made himself more valuable, and he didn't have to chase roles. He created his own opportunities.

"You've got a lot of hip-hop artists that go from hip-hop and that make the transition into movies," MC Ren said. "Cube took it to a whole 'nother level, producing, writing, directing, and still going strong. He's always sitting down putting a movie out, writing a movie. He's always got that going on, so it's like one movie drops, he's already got another one ready to go. He's shooting out movies like singles."

Underpinning his myriad talents, Ice Cube has made his mark by having a supreme belief in himself, a confidence that nearly no one else did. After all, he left N.W.A when it was rap's most exciting and influential group.

"Cube left an organization in N.W.A at its hottest time and stepped out on faith, even if he couldn't see the whole staircase," Big Boy said. "That was a person that was determined. It takes a formula of the talent, determination, timing,

GUARD YOUR *GANGSTA GRILLZ*

As mixtapes gained popularity in the early 2000s, DJ Drama delivered the benchmark for the genre with his heralded Gangsta Grillz series. Revered for having album quality, lyric-driven content, the projects from such Southern rap stars as Lil Wayne, T.I., Killer Mike, Jeezy, Bun B, and Yo Gotti put a spotlight on street-centered artists with a gangster edge who heretofore were not typically thought of as top-tier artists.

"I felt like artists that were more lyrical and, in a sense, what I called 'Quality Street Music,' weren't getting the attention that they deserved," said DJ Drama, who has released more than 150 Gangsta Grillz projects. "Gangsta Grillz, it was almost that was like the movie of the South at the time, the gangster film. You knew you were going to get the most quality essence of it."

work ethic. Everything's gotta be aligned right, because everybody doesn't have it. I think there's some cats that need to superserve their fan base, but you do have to know how to maneuver.

"Then when we're not buying records, it's like, 'Well fuck it. I'm going to put some concentration into movies,'" Big Boy continued. "So these cats became brands, and we supported the brand. As long as you didn't give us the bullshit, yeah, we'll support the brand. Do we do that for everybody? Nah."

Perhaps the strongest brand of all gangster rappers belongs to Dr. Dre. After being the sonic architect of Ruthless Records in the eighties and early nineties, as well as Death Row Records in the early and midnineties, he struck out on his own with Aftermath Entertainment. With a roster that included Eminem, 50 Cent, the Game, and Kendrick Lamar, as well as his own material, Dr. Dre's vanity label was one of the most dominant imprints in all of music in terms of sales, with more than sixty million albums sold.

Launched in 2006, Beats Electronics made Dr. Dre one of the richest members of the rap world. The company, founded by Dr. Dre with longtime business partner and record executive Jimmy Iovine, was purchased by Apple in 2014 for a reported $3 billion. Dr. Dre earned a paycheck in the neighborhood of a reported $600 million for the transaction.

By remaining focused on making high-quality music and music-related products, Dr. Dre has stayed true to the foundation of his work.

"We've been through so many styles of rap and so many different phases of 'This is what's hot,' and trends and fads, but there's some cats that never swerved," Big Boy said. "You can swerve a little bit and say, 'Oh, I'm getting into this and I'm getting into headphones,' but you still say Dr. Dre. We know him as Andre Young, but that dude didn't do a 360 on us and say, 'Don't call me Dr. Dre.'"

Despite their success in film, television, and electronics, Ice-T, Ice Cube, Dr. Dre, and Snoop Dogg haven't abandoned music. In fact, they remain in-demand musicians. Both Snoop Dogg and Ice Cube tour regularly and still release music, while Dr. Dre's *Compton: A Soundtrack* was released in 2015 and sold more than five hundred thousand units, robust numbers for an artist whose music career started in the mideighties. Ice-T's band Body Count tours to major festivals in the United States and abroad, and their latest LP, *Bloodlust*, was released twenty-five years to the day after their first album and was nominated by *Loudwire* for Best LP, with the band earning a Best Group nomination.

These artists have remained musically significant for several decades. "Cube is still a beast on the mic," MC Ren said. "He still makes good records. He still puts on a good stage show. Dre's still a beast on the beats. Nothing changed.

XZIBIT DETAILS WHAT HE LEARNED FROM DR. DRE

"Dre is a mentor to me, and he is also someone I respect very highly as a businessman, as a family man, and just as someone who's been to the fuckin' mountaintop. I've seen him go through the best of times and the worst of times. One thing remains true, which is that you've got to keep going. You never settle. Great is not good enough. It has to be undeniable. I think that seeing him build these dynasties that somehow came back to bite him, and how he's able to rise back up and do it even bigger, better, and brighter has inspired me. Underestimation is a beautiful thing, if you know how to accept it.

"I've learned to persevere because of what I've seen from him, and he's given me super direction as far as some of the decision-making that I had problems with. I'd go and talk with Dre and he could simplify it and make clear what the right thing is.

"I never had a Plan B. I was always driven, and people may have drive, but they sometimes drive themselves in the wrong direction. I think what I learned from Dre was to make better choices and don't be just blindly driven. Be focused, and driven.

He also told me that this is the record business. Yeah, we make music, but you have to be just as good at business, and that's something that I definitely raised the eyebrow to and found very interesting.

"He's never told me what to do. He's either given me an example of something that he went through at the time, or he'll say something that makes you feel like, 'Damn. I'm stupid. I should have thought of that shit. Damn. What the fuck was I thinking?'

"Sometimes the best lessons are learned by observation. I've seen the process from the first step of when they press the first button to make the beat, to a lyric, to a mix, to a master, to a video, to big as fuck. So, I saw that process, and then the business around it, and how it was promoted, and how it how it was received. When you see it like that, that's like watching a plant grow right in front of you. That is more valuable than him sitting down and writing a book, or putting it on paper and handing it to me. That was valuable because now I see, 'Oh. This is how it's done.'

"The relationship I have with Dr. Dre, I think it's a mutual respect. He values the relationship we have, and he values my opinion. From being a kid who was a fan of his before I actually got to meet him, and to be considered family at this point, is amazing. I'll never turn my back on Dr. Dre. Ever."

A lot of people, they kind of decline over the years, but they just . . . And they don't even have to if they don't want to. They done made boatloads and boatloads of money, but it's like that drive keeps 'em going. That drive that they have keeps them successful."

The consumer base that supports gangster rappers doesn't seem to be fading, either. Masta Ace, whose *SlaughtaHouse* album with Masta Ace Incorporated provided a stark commentary on gangster rap and some of its less positive aspects, believes that America's voyeuristic affinity for the bona fide bad guy keeps them intrigued by the persona gangster rappers present.

"If they believe the lyrics that are being said on the song, they're a little bit more interested in them and excited about these acts and what they're talking about, because it's like an escape," Masta Ace said. "You're going to your nine-to-five, dealing with your asshole boss, sitting in your cubicle doing your job. You can put your headphones on and escape into another world where it's like putting on a movie. There's shootings, car chases, police, police chases, rape, and who the hell knows what else. Gangster music kind of goes down that wormhole, and it takes these listeners living these boring lives, I guess, it takes them with them, and they can escape for a few hours to be violent in their minds and be in this other world, and then come back to their reality."

> *"These cats became brands, and we supported the brand. As long as you didn't give us the bullshit, yeah, we'll support the brand. Do we do that for everybody? Nah."*
>
> **BIG BOY**

MC Ren thinks that once the door was opened to the explicit world of gangster rap, there was no turning back.

"What makes [Eazy-E] bigger, Dre bigger, Master P, 50 Cent, it's because of the content, what they're talking about," MC Ren said. "Before they called it gangster rap, people wasn't rapping about—you know a few was, like KRS[-One], Schoolly D, and Ice-T—but the majority of people wasn't rhyming like that. Now you've got a lot of people doing it, and that's just what people want to hear. The door's been kicked open and people want to hear that. Back in the day, that was a Richard Pryor record. Once Richard Pryor came out doing his thing, cussing, all the jokes and all of that, all the comedians after Richard Pryor did it like Richard Pryor. You go somewhere now, if you go see a comedian and they're not cussing and they're not talking that shit, you're like, I don't want to see this. Same way."

The N.W.A brand demonstrated its staying power when *Straight Outta Compton* arrived in theaters on August 14, 2015. Ice Cube, Dr. Dre, and Tomica Woods-Wright (Eazy-E's widow) produced the film, which stars O'Shea Jackson Jr. portraying his father, Ice Cube. Made for a reported $28 million, *Straight Outta Compton* was, at the time it finished its run in theaters, the highest-grossing film of all time by a black filmmaker (F. Gary Gray), with a worldwide box office of $201 million.

"That movie wasn't successful just because forty-five-year-old black men went to see the motherfucka," Big Boy said. "I saw this one little Caucasian kid. He was probably like nine years old. He had a Compton hat on. To this day, I'm still like, 'That shit is fuckin' crazy.' I know he probably hasn't walked the streets of Compton. Maybe he has. I don't know. He got a tire rotation in Compton? I don't know, but he's rockin' the hat."

Straight Outta Compton won twenty-five awards, including Movie of the Year at the AFI (American Film Institute) Awards. It was also nominated for an Academy Award for Best Original Screenplay, a testament to the power of the film and its story, which traces how N.W.A's members met, their rise from unknowns to stardom, their eventual breakup, the death of Eazy-E, and Ice Cube's and Dr. Dre's subsequent successes.

Although the movie focused on the lives and careers of the group members, the story also includes poignant examinations of social ills, racism, and betrayal. *Straight Outta Compton*'s universal themes made it more than just a movie about rap.

"When I saw *La Bamba* and when I saw *The Buddy Holly Story*, I didn't really know the music," Big Boy said. "I wasn't alive to know Buddy Holly or Ritchie Valens. I didn't know 'La Bamba' or 'Donna.' But I enjoyed the story. Then that got me into, 'Oh, who's this guy?' I think that people that didn't know [N.W.A], they got intrigued, and then they enjoyed the movie once they sat down."

In the film, Snoop Dogg, portrayed by Lakeith Stanfield, is introduced as Dr. Dre's protégé once he leaves Eazy-E's Ruthless Records and starts Death Row Records with Suge Knight. The movie doesn't delve much into Snoop Dogg and his career, but after becoming the first artist in music history to have a debut album enter the Billboard Top 200 charts at No. 1 (*Doggystyle*),

Snoop Dogg has become one of the most lauded and embraced figures in rap history.

Since he arrived on the scene in 1992, the Long Beach, California, native has recorded with virtually every rap artist of note (Eminem, 2Pac, JAY-Z, and so on), pop icons (Mariah Carey, Katy Perry, Justin Timberlake), and even country icons (Willie Nelson). His music has been used more than one hundred and seventy times in movies or on television programs.

Beyond music, though, Snoop Dogg has arguably the most diverse and successful presence in rap history. In 2005, he founded the Snoop Youth Football League (SYFL), which he also owns and operates. The 501(c)(3) nonprofit organization provides inner-city children between the ages of five and thirteen the opportunity to play football without the worry of having to pay for equipment. Several of its players have made it to the NFL, including Super Bowl champion running back Ronnie Hillman, kick returner and wide receiver De'Anthony Thomas, and John Ross, who was selected as the ninth overall pick in the 2017 NFL draft by the Cincinnati Bengals.

As an actor, Snoop Dogg's roles have ranged from comedic (1998's *Half Baked*, 2004's *Soul Plane*) to gangster (2001's *Baby Boy* and *Training Day*) and have expanded to include voice-over work (2003's *Malibu's Most Wanted*, 2013's *Turbo*).

In addition, he has hosted *Saturday Night Live* with Avril Lavigne (2004), anchored *Snoop Dogg's Father Hood* reality show about his life and family (2007–09), appeared on *WWE Raw* several times (2007–15), and showed his culinary knowledge and ability to charm on the hit celebrity cooking show *Martha & Snoop's Potluck Dinner Party* (2016), and he is the host of the rebooted game show *The Joker's Wild* (2017). He also handled a four-episode run on the soap opera *One Life to Live* (2013).

Snoop Dogg's reach as a pitchman is also global. He has hawked everything from Hot Pockets and Air New Zealand to Chrysler and Adidas. The latter also has a partnership with the SYFL.

Even though he made his initial mark as a gangster rapper, Snoop Dogg said his ability to show people the other sides of his personality and character have allowed him to thrive in the business world.

While Snoop Dogg has become one of entertainment's most popular people, 50 Cent earned one of the largest one-time checks outside of Dr. Dre's Beats Electronics payout. An early investor in Glacéau Vitaminwater, 50 Cent earned a reported $60–100 million in 2007 when Coca-Cola bought parent company Glacéau for a reported $1.2 billion.

50 Cent has also made significant inroads in film and television. As of this writing, he has an overall deal with cable network STARZ, which airs *Power*, the program in which he appears and which he executive-produces, through at least September 2018. The deal also includes *Tomorrow, Today*, a superhero-themed series about a falsely imprisoned veteran who is set free after being used in an experiment by an insane prison doctor.

Even those who are not gangsters can appreciate the way gangsters work, also leading to their appeal.

"The gangster by nature is an entrepreneurial, enterprising character," Wrekonize said.

THE WORD:

AT THE MOVIES WITH DJ QUIK: THE ICE CUBE EDITION

DJ Quik provides succinct reviews for several Ice Cube films.

Boyz N the Hood (1991). Accurate.

Trespass (1992). Seriocomic.

Friday (1995). Hilarious.

Anaconda (1997). Funny.

The Players Club (1998). Groundbreaking comedy.

Next Friday (2000). Ambitious.

All About the Benjamins (2002). Dope.

Barbershop (2002). Fresh.

Friday After Next (2002). Cool.

Barbershop 2: Back in Business (2004). Hard.

Are We There Yet? (2005). Endearing.

xXx: State of the Union (2005). Spectacular.

Are We Done Yet? (2007). Likable.

First Sunday (2008). Funny.

The Longshots (2008). Oscar-worthy.

The Janky Promoters (2009). Favorite.

Lottery Ticket (2010). Empathetic.

21 Jump Street (2012). Fleetingly brilliant.

Ride Along (2014). Sidesplitting.

Barbershop: The Next Cut (2016). Necessary.

"If you're about that life and you're about hustling and you're about getting your shit, then that goes hand in hand with success and entrepreneurialism. So I feel to be a successful artist or businessman and you consider yourself to be a gangster or whatever by nature, you kind of have to make shit happen. You have to be hungrier than the next guy. It's a very competitive way to be. I feel like most gangster rappers, eight out of ten, are gangsters in general. . . . They're out there to get it."

In the early stages of rap, the genre was not embraced by corporate America. This exclusion made a portion of the rap world vocal about distancing itself from any ties to corporate commercialization. But as the genre grew and its artists became multifaceted stars, the way rappers were received and perceived by the corporate world, as well as their fans, also shifted.

"People can call them whatever they want at the end of the day. They can say, 'Ah, sellout. He was never real,'" Big Boy said. "But you know what, man, they turned their business into a business. It wasn't like, 'Ah, man, there's no more royalties. Streaming is stealing music. I can't get on a record label.' These motherfuckas just went and turned themselves into an enterprise. Cube can do *Jimmy Kimmel* on Thursday and get on stage somewhere and do 'Fuck tha Police' and then do his premiere the next Tuesday. We accept all that from these cats."

More than thirty years after its inception, gangster rap is firmly entrenched in American pop culture. If there was a short list of the pillars of gangster rap, Schoolly-D, Ice-T, N.W.A (Eazy-E, Dr. Dre, Ice Cube, MC Ren, DJ Yella), and

POWER VS. EMPIRE

After becoming one of rap's most popular artists, 50 Cent expanded his brand to television, executive-producing and appearing in the hit STARZ network program *Power*. The Queens, New York, rapper brought his confrontational ways to promoting his show, engaging in social-media wars with Taraji P. Henson and other principals from the record-breaking music-based show *Empire*. *Empire* featured Xzibit in a recurring role as gangster Shyne Johnson, while Snoop Dogg, Ludacris, and other A-list rappers also appeared on the program.

Snoop Dogg would be on it. They pioneered an art form, repeatedly reinvented themselves like no artists before them, and became cultural icons. Where the genre is headed and what its legacy will be have yet to be determined, but MC Ren, DJ Quik, Dee Barnes, and Vince Staples provide perspective on what gangster rap means historically and how it continues evolving.

Epilogue

Gangster Rap at Thirty

THE WORLD HAS UNDERGONE SIGNIFICANT CHANGES SINCE 1985.

Technology has exploded, as has the access to information. Mobile phones are virtually omnipresent throughout the world. DNA testing and scanning social media have become routine and critical parts of police work. An increasing number of surgeries are handled laparoscopically, while GPS systems have essentially replaced paper maps. Music, which was once packaged on vinyl and cassette, graduated to CDs, which were then made obsolete by the various forms of digital distribution (ringtones, downloads, and streaming).

Thanks in part to rap's omnipresence and cultural penetration, gangster rap, which turned thirty in 2015, has thrived during each of these shifts. Since its inception, the forefathers of the rap subgenre have become grandfathers, with

OPPOSITE:
Kendrick Lamar is an artist who represents the evolution of gangster rap, according to industry insiders.

2015
Key Rap Releases

1. Kendrick Lamar's
To Pimp a Butterfly
album

2. Drake's *If Youre
Reading This Its Too
Late* album

3. Future's *DS2* album

US President

Barack Obama

Something Else

Donald Trump
launched his presi-
dential campaign.

offspring who live far removed from the world their elders rapped about and the environments in which they were raised. They went from the bottom of America's societal structure to being some of the most accomplished and acclaimed figures in American culture.

As artists such as Schoolly-D, Ice-T, Ice Cube, Dr. Dre, MC Eiht, DJ Quik, Snoop Dogg, 50 Cent, the Game, and others thrived during the past thirty years, they sold tens of millions of albums, performed in front of millions of fans around the world, starred in dozens of Hollywood blockbusters, and influenced society through their overall look, attitude, and perspective.

"Gangster rap is an image of society," Tech N9ne says. "If society wasn't like this, it wouldn't be no gangster rap. We're just the street poets that's telling you what the fuck's going on in society. So if it's going on in society, of course it's going to be a movie. Of course they're going to do documentaries, have *Gangland* on TV, because we tell you the reality. The people that didn't know, thanks to the gangster rappers, people like Ice Cube, Ice-T, N.W.A, told you what was going on in case you were blind to it, you live in the suburbs and it ain't happening in your hood. It's a camera on the neighborhood and what's going on in society."

For the artists themselves, the anger was counterbalanced with a sense of pride in making music, paying homage to the positive and negative aspects of their lives, and making a name for themselves in the highly competitive rap game and the legit business world. The members of N.W.A, for instance, aspired to be like their New York predecessors.

"The reason we wanted to put Compton on the map so much was that back then in hip-hop, everybody in New York would be hollering out their borough or their city or whatever," MC Ren said. "It was either Brooklyn, the Bronx, Queens, [or] Long Island in hip-hop. I can't remember nothing else. So it was like, 'Shit. We've got to talk about Compton.' We wanted Compton to be in the same sentence with the Bronx, Brooklyn, Queens, Long Island. People thought we was crazy. They thought we wasn't gonna do it. I had one fool come up to me. This was before we blew up. He was like, 'Y'all know you ain't never gonna be big like them New York cats.' My homeboy when I was growing up, he told me that. We were sitting on the curb. Then we blew up, and he started trying to rhyme."

Naming Compton specifically ended up being particularly significant. Once N.W.A rose to national superstardom and became one of the most important groups in rap history, the group's championing of Compton made it stand out in the competitive rap world.

N.W.A, which was inducted into the Rock and Roll Hall of Fame in 2016, also stands among the rare group of musicians whose work graduated from the music world into the broader pop-culture universe.

Straight Outta Compton, the album on which "Fuck tha Police" appeared, was among the twenty-five recordings named to the Library of Congress's National Recording Registry in March 2017. Other honorees include Judy Garland, for her 1939 rendition of "Over the Rainbow," and the Eagles, for *Their Greatest Hits (1971–1975)*, the second-bestselling album of all time, behind only Michael Jackson's *Thriller*.

"It's still moving," Snoop Dogg said. "I don't think it's done. Ice Cube is the hardest gangster rapper to ever come out. He's one of the kings of Hollywood right now, as far as movies, production, behind the scenes. So you tell me how far gangster rap can go. Dr. Dre was the hardest gangster rap producer ever. Beats by Dre sold for a couple billion dollars. You tell me how far gangster rap can go. Snoop Dogg is one of the realest gangsters to ever come up out of the rap game, catching cases, doing real shit, being around the best of the best, and look at where he is now as far as in the TV world, the movie world, the business world, just the public acceptance world."

> *"Gangster rap is an image of society.... you live in the suburbs and it ain't happening in your hood. It's a camera on the neighborhood and what's going on in society."*
>
> **TECH N9NE**

Like Snoop Dogg, gangster rap's status in pop culture has undergone a dramatic shift. When Schoolly D, Ice-T, Boogie Down Productions, and Just-Ice started making gangster rap in the mideighties, the genre was an emerging segment of rap that was still finding its footing. Within a few years, Ice-T, Eazy-E, N.W.A, Ice Cube, and Dr. Dre had become some of rap's bestselling and most controversial artists.

And they remained among the genre's bestselling artists for years, outlasting the second and third generations of gangster rappers. This initial wave of gangster rap artists, ones who emerged before the term "gangster rap" even existed, all possessed an uncanny hustle. They had to overcome boycotts, protests, censorship, and government pressure, all of which seemed to instill a type of

THE NEW STYLE

HERE'S A LOOK at some of the most promising Los Angeles–area gangster rappers of the 2010s, highlighting their hometowns, main songs, and albums.

YG
Hometown: Compton
Noteworthy song: "My Nigga" (2013)
Project of note: *My Krazy Life* (2014)

NIPSEY HUSSLE
Hometown: Los Angeles
Noteworthy song: "I Don't Give a Fucc" (2011)
Project of note: *Crenshaw* (2013)

VINCE STAPLES
Hometown: Long Beach
Noteworthy song: "65 Hunnid" (2014)
Project of note: *Hell Can Wait* (2014)

G PERICO
Hometown: Los Angeles
Noteworthy song: "Bout It" (2016)
Project of note: *Shit Don't Stop* (2016)

AD
Hometown: Compton
Noteworthy song: "Juice" (2015)
Project of note: *Blue:89* (2015)

KENDRICK LAMAR
Hometown: Compton
Noteworthy song: "Ronald Reagan Era (His Evils)" (2011)
Project of note: *Section.80* (2011)

artistic resolve and personal fortitude that served them well in the studios and in the boardrooms.

By the time N.W.A alumnus Dr. Dre was working with Eminem, the best-selling rap artist of all time, gangster rap had grown, evolved, and become an established part of rap and of pop culture in general. The road formed by gangster rap had long been paved. Eminem's lyrics were similarly shocking, but at that point, mainstream America had been exposed to rap's violent, profane, and hypersexual side for more than a decade.

"I think we scared the world so quickly, but then once Eminem did it, they were like, 'Okay,'" Ice-T said. "Now people are kinda conditioned to it. It's not like when Cube came out and said, 'Crazy muthafucka named . . .' and you were like, 'What the fuck? Who are these mother-fuckas?' Now everybody's like, 'Okay. Cool. Y'all gonna Crip Walk and dance,' but it's not as threatening now."

The image of N.W.A wearing all black and dark sunglasses, of gangster rappers toting semiautomatic firearms to interviews and in their videos, of Crips wearing exclusively blue and Bloods exclusively red, and of generally being viewed as ominous has waned signifi-cantly as time has gone on.

"Back in the days, a gangster looked a cer-tain way," said Los Angeles 92.3 KRRL radio personality Big Boy. "Now these motherfuckas are gangster and you're like, 'Oh shit.' There's no more uniform. Some cats can tuck a red rag or a blue rag, but back in the days, you knew what a muthafucka was this or that. There was no in between where, 'Oh, I'm just wearing this.'"

"I think now the new trap rappers [Southern rappers who tend to rap about street topics, doing drugs in particular], they've convinced me they can get high," Ice-T said. "They've convinced me that maybe they can sell a little drugs. They don't scare me. I think a gangster rapper has to scare you a little bit."

The perceived lack of shock current gangster rappers deliver can be partly explained by the novelty of the genre wearing off. It can also be attributed to the changing criteria of fans, who may seek different things from their artists than fans of previous generations.

"It used to be that you had to have your stripes in the nineties," Dave Weiner said. "You couldn't step up to a mic without a real, legitimate story. The story had to be real. The fights had to be real. The gunshots had to be real. It was a pedigree. It was who you are and where you came from. If you were a fraud, your music never even got the time of day, and that changed with rap taking on the mainstream appeal that it did through the end of the nineties and the 2000s, being ushered along by Eminem. But it evolved."

In the 2010s, the current manifestation of gangster rap has numerous forms. Kendrick Lamar, who many believe to be among the best of the current crop of gangster rappers, has a decidedly different approach than the cornerstones of the culture, yet he shows the ways in which gangster rap has changed and remains dominant.

"It's still reigning," Tech N9ne said. "It's a gangster that's blowing up that's multitalented though, so you don't really put him in that category because he's artistic. That's Kendrick Lamar."

After releasing his own mixtapes and collaborating with fellow Top Dawg Entertainment (TDE) rapper Jay Rock, Kendrick Lamar garnered widespread acclaim in the rap world in 2010 for his *Overly Dedicated* mixtape. The project's lyricism, social commentary, and the myriad of ways in which he could deliver his high-caliber rhymes endeared the rapper to a wide range of fans.

The *Overly Dedicated* song "Barbed Wire," for instance, features Kendrick Lamar rapping about evading crooked cops, succeeding by not having to kill other black men, and living his dreams. Toward the end of the song, though, he raps that there's always barbed wire preventing true progress. A gunshot ends the selection.

In 2011, Kendrick Lamar released *Section.80*, his first studio album. The project included "Ronald Reagan Era (His Evils)," a commentary about, among other things, how the children growing up in Compton fell victim to the policies of President Reagan, which included expanding the "War on Drugs" and an explosion of the incarceration of nonviolent drug offenders, many of whom were lower-class black males.

"Ronald Reagan Era (His Evils)" and other Kendrick Lamar songs, such as the lyrical showcase "A.D.H.D.," helped land Lamar a recording contract with Dr. Dre's Aftermath Entertainment. Although not overtly gangster, Kendrick Lamar's subject matter, his willingness to discuss Compton, and his regular references to the gangs that inhabit the city and that helped define his life give his music gangster rap elements.

"I think Kendrick keeps a nice little hood edge on his shit, so you know he's from Compton," Ice-T said. "You know he's from the hood."

Like Ice Cube before him, Kendrick Lamar grew up in a gang-infested environment but doesn't present himself as an active gang member in his music or in his interviews, even though they both rap about the gang lifestyle and its ripple effects throughout their respective communities specifically and society in general.

"If you're in that neighborhood, you're affiliated by association, basically," said Dee Barnes, one half of rap group Body & Soul and former host of the rap video show *Pump It Up!* "I think Ice Cube is a good comparison because Ice Cube to me, as far as N.W.A, he was their conscious. I feel like that's how Kendrick is. Kendrick is the conscious of Compton, of gangster rap. He's more to me on that tip than anything because he's telling stories of what's happening in his neighborhood, what has happened from his perspective, and from a worldview. He's taken it to just a whole other level.

"He gets the real hardcore gangsters to stop and think about some things for a minute," Barnes continued. "And, I think that's good, to get them to listen, to get their attention."

Yet Kendrick Lamar's list of accolades shows how differently gangster rap is received in the 2010s compared to the eighties or nineties. The Compton rapper has won twelve Grammy Awards and has been nominated twenty-nine times as of the 59th Grammy Awards presented in 2018. Snoop Dogg, by comparison, has never won a Grammy, despite being nominated fifteen times. Kendrick Lamar also made history in 2018 when he became the first rapper to win the Pulitzer Prize for Music for *DAMN.*, his 2017 album.

This type of critical disparity could be attributed to any number of factors, from perceived authenticity to the legal drama surrounding an artist to the overall climate in the music business at the time of an artist's popularity. Regardless, this variance speaks to how different artists may have been received differently in subsequent eras.

"What would Kendrick have meant in the midnineties?" Weiner asked. "He's an undeniable talent, but he wasn't coming from that gangster mentality. He wasn't hard enough. I see him as the best example of the evolution of gangster rap, because that's where he grew up and that's what he was surrounded by, and he lived that life without living that life, so to speak."

The majority of the other prominent gangster rappers emerging, from the Los Angeles area in particular, boasts of living the gangster lifestyle and of coming from that environment. Kendrick Lamar's TDE labelmate ScHoolboy Q, for instance, uses an uppercase *H* in his name, song titles, and writings in order to pay homage to his affiliation with the 52 Hoover Gangster Crips.

ScHoolboy Q's 2014 album, *Oxymoron*, featured the song "Hoover Street," which detailed his growing up around robberies, guns, drugs, and gangs. The album title itself refers to the paradoxical life he was living.

"The oxymoron in this album is that I'm doing all this bad to do good for my daughter," ScHoolboy Q said. "That's why I'm robbin'. That's why I'm stealing. That's why I done shot you, and got on, and took your car. Whatever it is that I'm talking about in my album negative, it's always for a good cause, for my daughter."

G Perico, another Los Angeles gangster rapper who rose to prominence in the 2010s and who is among the first wave of artists signed as part of the relaunching of Priority Records, raps about the gangster rap bedrocks of gangs, crime, guns, drugs, and women. Like ScHoolboy Q, though, he looks at what life is, what it was, and what he wants it to be.

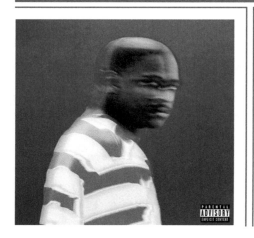

GANGSTER RAP'S BIGGEST SELLERS

Album: *All Eyez On Me* (1996) by 2Pac. Ten million albums sold. Released by Death Row/Interscope Records.

Top Artist (in Terms of Album Sales): 2Pac, 36.5 million albums sold

Top Artist (in Terms of Digital Single Sales): YG, 5 million digital singles sold

FIVE THINGS BIG TRAY DEEE LEARNED FROM GANGSTER RAP

One half of the platinum gangster rap group Tha Eastsidaz, Big Tray Deee reflects on five things he learned from gangster rap.

1. It was amazing that I could tell the truth and be myself and the whole world would be interested in my perspective, and be willing to support me for over two decades just being me.

2. Gangster rap, when it's real, you feel it. When it comes on, you feel it. You get that with certain WC, Jayo Felony, Ice Cube, Scarface songs. As soon as the beat drops, it's like, "Ah. Yeah. This is one of them right here."

3. Everybody that's a gangster rapper isn't a gangster. At least people in Cali, we're going to want to know if what you're saying is certified and if you're really who you say you are, and if the people you say you represent really respect you. We're going to break down your whole resume.

4. You can't be too serious in gangster rap. You still got to have fun. You still got to be able to make the women enjoy a song or two. You've still got to be able to show that you're more aware of life than, "I don't give a fuck and I'll kill you." You have to maintain some lyricism that hip-hop demands to be a real truly respected gangster rapper.

5. Gangster rap will have your muthafuckin' ass in prison, just on the fact of keeping it real. There's no off days of being a gangster. If you're a gangster rapper that gets pushed up on, you might have to go all the way with it. If you're not really with it like that, you might be put into a situation that you're really not equipped to handle, and it could cause you and the people around you their lives.

OPPOSITE:
Gangsters and rappers respect Big Tray Deee.

LEFT:
G Perico is a rising rapper whose esthetic harkens back to the look of Los Angeles area gangster rappers of the 1980s.

"My risk-taking is pretty much done," G Perico said. "The biggest risk I take is just still being around, because motherfuckers will try to kill me. I don't gamble money, but you could say I'm gambling my life a little bit. I'm prepared, though."

More so than maybe any other gangster rapper to emerge in the 2010s, G Perico has components of the uniform of a gangster rapper from the eighties and early nineties. The Los Angeles artist sports a Jheri curl, favors white T-shirts, and almost always wears blue apparel in order to identify himself as a Crip.

"When I first saw that muthafucka with a Jheri curl, he was cut from that cloth," Big Boy said of G Perico. "I was like, 'Oh shit.' Then when you explore [his music], he reminds me of what that West Coast fire was. I don't want to say 'rebirth' or 'the new,' but you hear that mothafucka and he go. Does radio have him? Not like radio should. Is that mothafucka gonna sell out at his next show? You mothafuckin' right he is. It's crazy because he's another one that stays in his path and we're walking over to him. He's like, 'Nah. Nah. You've got to cross the street over here because I'm not crossing the street and coming over there. If you want me, come over here.'"

Compton rapper YG is the most prominent gangster rapper to emerge in the 2010s and enjoy massive commercial success and critical acclaim. After his ode to one-night stands "Toot It and Boot It" became a West Coast hit in 2010, YG signed with Def Jam Recordings. His breakthrough single with the company was 2013's "My Nigga" (the radio version was "My Hitta"), a nod to his loyalty to the people with whom he grew up and to the friends he can rely on in the streets and in life. The song, which featured Atlanta rappers Jeezy and Rich Homie Quan, sold more than one million copies in less than five months. By October 2016, "My Hitta" had sold more than three million copies.

Def Jam Recordings formally paired YG with Jeezy, who helped YG shape the direction of his major label debut album, 2014's *My Krazy Life*. Song titles such as "BPT," "Bicken Back Being Bool," and "Bompton," as well as the album title, paid homage to his affiliation with the Bloods, as the words replace the letter *C* with either a *B* or a *K* in order to show solidarity to the Bloods.

Thanks in part to the success of "My Hitta," as well as the "Who Do You Love?" single with rap superstar Drake, YG's *My Krazy Life* was certified gold in March 2016 and platinum in April 2017, even as record sales industry wide continued to wane. In order to address the shifting ways people consume music, the "album equivalent unit" was enacted in December 2014. In this new way of counting music for sales purposes, one album sale equals ten song downloads. One album sale is also equal to 1,500 song streams.

In 2016, YG's *Still Brazy* album built upon YG's momentum and showed his willingness to make incendiary political statements. In addition to the gold single "Why You Always Hatin?," the project also featured "FDT," short for "Fuck Donald Trump." A collaboration with Los Angeles gangster rapper Nipsey Hussle, "FDT" featured both artists bashing the then–presidential candidate for his anti-Mexican rhetoric and in response to black students being kicked out of a Trump rally during his presidential campaign.

Another *Still Brazy* cut, "Blacks & Browns," features YG and mentee Sad Boy examining some of the issues plaguing their respective communities. YG laments black on black crime, high levels of incarceration, and lackluster educational opportunities. For his part, Sad Boy Loko (as he's also known) examines the traps of the green card system, the preponderance of dead-end jobs, and police brutality.

The ability to make songs that trumpet his gang affiliation as well as political statements makes YG a credible artist.

"YG don't go into a phone booth and come out and say, 'Okay, I'm YG now,'" Big

Boy said. "YG, any time you sneak up on him, you're gonna find YG. When I turn the microphone on, YG. When I turn the microphone off, that's YG. I think that YG is another one that musically is gangbanging around the world. Now I think we're also seeing that he knows how to make records, too. That's one thing that you couldn't deny when you're fucking with anything as far as the Xzibits, the Cubes, Death Row. Those were records. YG is making records and building up his catalog. He's also another one that's from the street and telling the world where he's from. He's not running away from that shit. Is he glorifying shit? Call it what you want, but that's him. He's not stealing a lifestyle from anyone."

Like YG, Long Beach rapper Vince Staples dedicates some of his music to political topics. He follows the mold of Ice-T and Ice Cube with his blend of incendiary social commentary and scintillating street reporting on such songs as "Versace Rap" and "65 Hunnid." He is an insightful storyteller with a keen grasp of history, social injustice, and the streets as he weaves the evolution of America's institutionalized racism into "C.N.B." "The sheets and crosses turned to suits and ties," he raps.

> ## "I don't want to make that kind of music. I'm not on that. [Violence] ruined my life. It killed my homies."
>
> **VINCE STAPLES**

Similar to the first generation of gangster rappers, Vince Staples infuses his music with the reality of life on the streets. He raps about his paranoia, his doubts, and his anger about the circumstances in which he was raised. Vince Staples's music may discuss mayhem, but he does not advocate mindless violence.

"I don't want to make that kind of music," Vince Staples said. "I'm not on that. That ruined my life. It killed my homies."

The business-oriented Los Angeles rapper Nipsey Hussle made headlines in October 2013 by selling his *Crenshaw* mixtape for one hundred dollars apiece. He said he sold one thousand copies, good for one hundred thousand dollars in revenue for a project that would typically be given away for free on the Internet.

A self-proclaimed avid reader, the rapper read the book *Contagious*, by Wharton professor Jonah Berger, which details unusual and counterintuitive business successes. In the book, Berger tells the story of a restaurateur who charged one hundred dollars for his Philly cheesesteak and was both applauded and derided for the move. That tactic is where Nipsey Hussle drew inspiration for his mixtape.

Nipsey Hussle said his idea was hatched on music's value in the marketplace. "It's time we acknowledge what we all know: The music is free," Nipsey Hussle said. "We shouldn't force people to buy it. What we should do is create different methods to monetize the connection."

Signed to Epic Records in 2009, Nipsey Hussle left the label the following year and resumed building his brand independently. In 2017, he announced he'd signed with Atlantic Records and, in 2018, released his major label debut album, the acclaimed *Victory Lap*.

Priority Records, which relaunched in 2017, returned to its gangster rap roots and tapped into the current generation of artists, including G Perico and AD. The latter is a Compton Crip rapper who embraces the evolution of gang relations in his city, as evidenced by his 2016 song "Thug," which featured YG, a Blood.

"Compton is a different place now," AD said. "As far as the gangbanging culture, Crips and [Bloods gang faction] Pirus don't necessarily beef anymore. More Pirus beef with Pirus and more Crips beef with Crips. I and YG come from two different areas who originally wouldn't get along with each other, but we don't have problems with each other. I got a relationship with a lot of his homies from way back. For 'Thug,' once we came up with that, I told him to bring his whole hood to the video shoot. It was dope, man."

More than thirty years after its inception, gangster rap shows that it continues to evolve and remains relevant to a wider range of people, ones who grew up listening to the music and forming their worldviews based in part on the gangster rap music they consumed. Gangster rap fans are now teaching school in suburban Maryland, working at post offices in Florida, and selling derivatives at Smith Barney in New York.

These are the people who were fascinated by gangster rap, the generation who looked at black kids from the ghetto with a more informed view and who voted for Barack Obama. It is a group of people who didn't base their opinions solely on what they saw on the nightly news and how it depicted young black men in particular.

For today's generation of listeners, the appeal remains, in essence, the same. In a brutal and ironic similarity, the current generation of gangster rappers has no shortage of material from which to draw, as racism, police brutality, drugs, guns, and gangs remain as relevant today as they were in the mideighties.

"It made a whole new reality in business, music, film," DJ Quik said. "These dudes just became the trendiest dudes, bigger than the sum of their parts."

Much of the success I have experienced in writing comes from the love, support, and inspiration provided by my parents, Alberta and Stanley Baker. They allowed me to embrace rap and dedicate virtually all of my free time (beginning at age ten) to consuming it, even though the music was foreign to them and had a largely negative rep.

My father, in particular, has been my rock and my foundation throughout my personal and professional life. Among dozens of other things, he drove my friends and me (and waited in a lounge for us) to see my first concert: Public Enemy, Digital Underground, Heavy D & the Boyz, Kid 'n Play, and Chill Rob G at the Capital Centre in Landover, Maryland, in 1990. My dad also recorded go-go mixes from Washington, D.C., radio stations and mailed the cassettes to me while I was in college so that I could stay connected to the other form of music I loved.

While attending Xavier University in Cincinnati, I began writing professionally. With my father's encouragement, I began to keep a database of all the articles I have written. At present, the total exceeds 3,500 articles published. I've also written more than a thousand other things and millions of words, including the ninety-thousand or so in this book. Thank you, Mom and Dad, for loving me and for supporting me in every step of my life.

Thank you, Grant Baker, for being a great brother, for all of your help with my writing, and for sharing my love of Ol' Dirty Bastard and Ludacris.

I've been blessed to have two phenomenal women in my day-to-day life in my adopted home of Southern California. My daughter, Loren, brings me immeasurable joy every day. Her intelligence and exuberance are two of the major motivating factors that push me. As you know, Loren, I love you infinity times infinity plus infinity infinities. DaVida Smith, thank you for blessing me with your love. You are the best partner anyone could hope for. I love you.

Jorge Hinojosa, after you heard me on KDAY hosting *Open Bar Radio* with Xzibit, you gave me a call to reconnect and to ask me why I wasn't writing any of the major rap books hitting the market. Thanks to your belief in me, I am now. Thank you for managing me through this process, pushing me to make the book better, and connecting me to a world I'd been trying to break into. I look forward to our next steps together.

Jorge's instincts proved correct when he suggested we submit *The History Of Gangster Rap* proposal to Samantha Weiner, a keen and talented editor at Abrams. Thank you, Samantha, for making this dream of mine come true—to be able to write a book that shows how and why this rap subgenre has been so important and influential. It has been a pleasure working with you and learning from you. I am grateful for this opportunity and am excited about our future collaborations. And a big thank you to the extended Abrams team, Jennifer Bastien, Kimberly Lew, Mary O'Mara, and Devin Grosz.

I am amazed that I now know and am friends with several of the artists I grew up admiring. To have been able to interview so many of them for this book has been a humbling experience. Thank you to all of the artists, executives, businessmen, and personalities who gave me exclusive interviews for this book: Jorge Hinojosa, Hi-Tek, Chris LaSalle, Faisal Ahmed, Yukmouth, MC Eiht, MC Ren, Dave Weiner, Wrekonize, DJ Quik, Snoop Dogg, Dana Dane, Tech N9ne, Masta Ace, Ice-T, Big Boy, the D.O.C., Hen Gee, Paris, Schoolly D, Cormega, Leslie "Big Lez" Segar, Kokane, CJ Mac, Arnold "Bigg A" White, Yo-Yo, the Legendary Traxster, DJ Drama, Murs, Cold 187um, Glasses Malone, Tony Draper, Scarface, Big Tray Deee, Gangsta Boo, RBX, Dee Barnes, Amir Rahimi, and Xzibit. Each one of you has inspired me in a myriad of ways.

To Jay R Jay, Brian Coleman, Richie Abbott, Lisa Barton, Brian Shafton, Chad Kaiser, Giovanna Melchiorre, and Jarrold Taylor, thank you for facilitating some of the interviews featured herein. Your work helped make this book better.

Thank you, Andres Tardio, for the great author photo. Also, Ural Garrett, Leslie "Big Lez" Segar, Dave Weiner, Alisa Childs, Paris, Hen Gee, Evil E, Hi-Tek, Gangsta Boo, and Amir Rahimi, thank you for submitting photos for consideration.

Thank you to my friends who helped make this possible, especially Steven Reissner, Daylan Williams, and Ahmed Sabir-Calloway for helping me get some of these interviews on camera. Victoria Hernandez, thank you for holding me down when I had to make things happen. Thank you, Monika A. Tashman, for your legal guidance.

Billy Johnson Jr., Shawndi Johnson, William "B-Luv" Taylor, Tracii McGregor, Tom Ruge, Aren Rostamian, Vidal Marsh, Slink Johnson, J. Wells, James Kreisberg, Omar Burgess, Maurice Thomas, Valerie Sakmary, and Andre Grant, thank you for your friendship and support.

Thank you to my family for championing me. In particular, Uncle Michael Johnson, thank you for recommending me for my first book deal, and for helping me launch my line of self-published books in 2011. Uncle Dion Baker, thank you for your steady love and support.

Thank you, Jacob Covey, for the brilliant design and everyone at Abrams for making this book an incredible experience. Toshitaka Kondo, thank you for your notes and suggestions on ways to improve the book, which they did.

Finally, thank you to the readers of this book. I appreciate your support.

Acknowledgments

RHYME PAYS

9   25602-4

SIRE

CA 1-4787

CRIMINAL MINDED
BOOGIE DOWN PRODUCT

STRAIGHT OUTTA COMPTON

RCA

JIVE

SUPPORT THE
STOP THE
VIOLENCE
MOVEMENT

SCHOOLLY-D
AM I BLACK ENOUGH FOR YOU?

1237-4-J

AmeriKKKa's
MOST WANTED

ICE CUBE

THE GETO BOYS

9 2430

PCT-1402

DJ QUIK
QUIK IS THE NAME

PROFIL

DOLBY B NR

SCARFACE of the GETO BOYS

4XL 57167

RAP-A-LOT
RECORDS

INTRODUCTION

Big Tray Deee, in discussion with author, February 15, 2018.

Dana Dane, in discussion with author, February 13, 2018.

CHAPTER 1

Big Boy, in discussion with author, May 18, 2017, Burbank, California.

DJ Quik, in discussion with author, April 5, 2017, Los Angeles, California.

Ice-T, in discussion with author, May 10, 2017, Beverly Hills, California.

Jayo Felony, in discussion with author, April 26, 2005, Glendale, California.

Questlove. "Questlove's Top 50 Hip-Hop Songs of All Time." *Rolling Stone*, December 17, 2012.

Schoolly D, in discussion with author, August 1, 2017.

Schoolly D, in discussion with author, March 2003.

Tech N9ne, in discussion with author, May 2, 2017.

CHAPTER 2

2nd II None, in discussion with author, November 25, 2014, Los Angeles, California.

Brackett, Nathan, and Christian Hoard, eds. *The New Rolling Stone Album Guide*. New York: Fireside, 2004.

Christgau, Robert. "Christgau's Consumer Guide." *The Village Voice*, February 23, 1988.

CJ Mac, in discussion with author, December 5, 2017, Culver City, California.

DJ Quik, in discussion with author, April 5, 2017, Los Angeles, California.

Hen Gee, in discussion with author, July 31, 2017.

Ice-T (@FINALLEVEL), "I even say that. PSK inspired 6 n the morning. Schoolly was hinting at it.. I just said it.," Twitter, August 15, 2015, 10:52 a.m., https://twitter.com/FINALLEVEL/status/632610910343954433.

Ice-T, in discussion with author, August 2000.

Ice-T, in discussion with author, May 10, 2017, Beverly Hills, California.

Jorge Hinojosa, in discussion with author, May 3, 2016.

Schoolly D, in discussion with author, August 1, 2017.

CHAPTER 3

CJ Mac, in discussion with author, December 5, 2017, Culver City, California.

Cormega, in discussion with author, August 14, 2017, Sherman Oaks, California.

DJ Quik, in discussion with author, April 5, 2017, Los Angeles, California.

DJ Yella, in discussion with author, August 2007.

Heller, Jerry, with Gil Reavill. *Ruthless: A Memoir*. New York: Simon Spotlight Entertainment, 2006.

Ice Cube, in discussion with author, August 2007.

Kendrick Lamar, in discussion with author, May 23, 2011.

Kool Rock Ski, *Unsung*. Season 3, Episode 11, "The Fat Boys." Narrated by Gary Anthony Williams. Aired October 18, 2010, on TV One.

MC Ren, in discussion with author, March 17, 2017, Indio, California.

Paris, in discussion with author, July 31, 2017.

Steve Hochman. "Compton Rappers Versus the Letter of the Law: F.B.I. Claims Song by N.W.A Advocates Violence on Police." *Los Angeles Times*, October 5, 1989.

The D.O.C., in discussion with author, June 1, 2017.

Westhoff, Ben. "Who Invented the Term 'Gangsta Rap'? It's Complicated." *LA Weekly*, May 5, 2015.

CHAPTER 4

"29 Black Music Milestones: BET, Yo! MTV Raps' Launch." *Billboard*, February 16, 2011.

"Ice Cube AmeriKKKa's Most Wanted Retrospective [20 Years Later]." *XXL*, May 16, 2010.

Billboard's Hot R&B/Hip-Hop Songs - 1988 Archive, https://www.billboard.com/archive/charts/1988/r-b-hip-hop-songs.

Boyer, Peter J. "THE MEDIA BUSINESS; After Rebellious Youth, MTV Tries the System." *New York Times*, May 19, 1988.

Causo, Jorge and Wes Smith. "Racial Strife Grips Miami for 2nd Night." *Chicago Tribune*, January 18, 1989.

CHAPTER 5

Chris LaSalle, in discussion with author, December 5, 2016.

Coleman, Brian. *Check the Technique: Volume 2: More Liner Notes for Hip-Hop Junkies*. Massachusetts: Wax Facts Press, 2014.

DJ Quik, in discussion with author, April 5, 2017, Los Angeles, California.

DJ Quik, in discussion with author, April 5, 2017.

Financial Audit: Resolution Trust Corporation's 1995 and 1994 Financial Statements. United States General Accounting Office, 1996. www.gao.gov/archive/1996/ai96123.pdf.

George, Nelson, and Steven Dupler. "BET Boycotts Profile Product." *Billboard*, August 23, 1986.

Greene, Andy. "Flashback. David Bowie Rips Into MTV for Not Spotlighting Black Artists." *Rolling Stone*, January 13, 2016.

Heller, Jerry, with Gil Reavill. *Ruthless: A Memoir*. New York: Simon Spotlight Entertainment, 2006.

Ice Cube, in discussion with author, Encino, California, April 4, 2006.

Ice Cube, in discussion with author, March 2008.

Kokane, in discussion with author, August 24, 2017.

Leland, John. "Armageddon In Effect." *SPIN*, September 1988.

Leslie "Big Lez" Segar, in discussion with author, August 22, 2017.

Markman, Rob. "Documentary of a Gangsta." *XXL*, June 2010.

MC Eiht, in discussion with author, November 30, 2016, Culver City, California.

Mitchy Slick, *Myths Exposed*, "Mitchy Slick & Choosing To Join A Gang | MYTHS EXPOSED | Episode 19," November 29, 2016. https://www.youtube.com/watch?v=vjg-xxZh2cc&index=1&list=UUCG196St-2rjRK77RWI58sA.

Rangel, Jesus. "Student Takes Gun to School; Another Is Caught With Fake." *New York Times*, January 13, 1989.

Report of The Sentencing Project to the United Nations Human Rights Committee Regarding Racial Disparities in the United States Criminal Justice System. The Sentencing Project, August 2013. http://sentencingproject.org/wp-content/uploads/2015/12/Race-and-Justice-Shadow-Report-ICCPR.pdf.

The D.O.C., in discussion with author, June 1 and August 25, 2017.

Vh1 Rock Docs. "Yo! The Story of Yo! MTV Raps." Directed by Mimi Adams. Aired June 7, 2012 on Vh1.

Westhoff, Ben. "Straight Outta Compton: Fact-checking the film . . . with Ice Cube." *The Guardian*, August 13, 2015.

woops, "MTV Top 100 Music Videos of 1998," inthe00s.com, January 4, 2009. http://www.inthe00s.com/archive/inthe80s/smf/1231060820.shtml.

Yo-Yo, in discussion with author, December 7, 2017.

Yo! MTV Raps interview with NWA, 1988. https://www.youtube.com/watch?v=fUDFWWcEFiY, accessed November 2016.

Yo! MTV Raps interview with N.W.A, April 8, 1989. https://www.youtube.com/watch?v=x3Avlv6g0rU&t=59s, accessed November 2016.

CHAPTER 6

Andy Kellman, review of *Grip It! On That Other Level*, by the Geto Boys, AllMusic.com.

AP. "Violent Crimes Increase by 5.5% For 1988, Establishing a Record." *New York Times*, August 13, 1989.

DJ Quik, in discussion with author, April 5, 2017, Los Angeles, California.

Hochman, Steve. "Maybe They Should Issue Stickers For Everyone's Ears." *Los Angeles Times*, July 22, 1990.

Jordan, Brad Scarface, with Benjamin Meadows-Ingram. *Diary of a Madman: The Geto Boys,*

Life, Death, and the Roots of Southern Rap. New York: Dey St., 2015.

Koshkin, Brett. "How Tipper Gore Helped the Geto Boys Popularize Southern Rap." *Village Voice*, June 28, 2013.

Pareles, Jon. "Distributor Withdraws Rap Album Over Lyrics." *New York Times*, August 28, 1990.

Tewksbury, Drew. "Six Most Idiotic Attempt to Blame Musicians for Violent Events (or, the Tuscon Tragedy Was Caused by a Crazy Person, Not by Drowning Pool's 'Bodies Hit the Floor')." *LA Weekly*, January 13, 2011.

Wetrogan, Signe I. *Projections of the Population of States, by Age, Sex, and Race: 1988 to 2010*. U.S. Department of Commerce Bureau of the Census, October 1988. https://www.census.gov/prod/1/pop/p25-1017.pdf.

CHAPTER 7

Amir Rahimi, in discussion with author, March 30, 2018.

Box office release information: boxofficemojo.com, imdb.com, rottentomatoes.com

DJ Quik, in discussion with author, April 5, 2017.

Heller, Jerry, with Gil Reavill. *Ruthless: A Memoir*. New York: Simon Spotlight Entertainment, 2006.

Hiatt, Brian. "N.W.A: American Gangstas." *Rolling Stone*, August 27, 2015.

Philips, Chuck. "Rap's Bad Boy to Get Lunch With the Prez." *Los Angeles Times*, March 18, 1991.

Rap sales information: https://www.riaa.com/

"Rapper Bushwick Bill Gives Details of Being Left 4 Dead In Houston Morgue." whenrapwasreal.com, November 7, 2015. http://whenrapwasreal.com/bushwick-bill-gives-details-of-coroner-leaving-him-dead-in-houston-morgue/2/.

Roger Ebert, review of *New Jack City*, rogerebert.com. May 1, 1991.

Sherrill, Martha. "Guess Who's Coming to Lunch?" *Washington Post*, March 19, 1991.

Thompson, Derek. "1991: The Most Important Year in Pop-Music History." *Atlantic*, May 8, 2015.

Yo! MTV Raps interview with N.W.A. https://www.youtube.com/watch?v=fUDFWWcEFiY, accessed November 2016.

CHAPTER 8

Bill Duke, in discussion with author, June 4, 2016, Culver City, California.

Chuck D. "The 50 Greatest Hip-Hop Songs of All Time: 1. Grandmaster Flash and the Furious Five, 'The Message.'" *Rolling Stone*, December 5, 2012.

Eazy-E, *The Arsenio Hall Show*. https://www.youtube.com/watch?v=TpNtFBAI0V8, accessed February 2017.

"Eazy E sues Sony Music, others." *Variety*, October 16, 1992.

Hi-Tek, in discussion with author, December 12, 2016, Culver City, California.

Light, Alan. "The Rolling Stone Interview: Ice-T." *Rolling Stone*, August 20, 1992.

"Los Angeles Riots Fast Facts." cnn.com, March 27, 2018. https://www.cnn.com/2013/09/18/us/los-angeles-riots-fast-facts/.

Reckard, E. Scott. "Charlton Heston Shocks Shareholders With Reading of Controversial Lyrics." Associated Press, July 17, 1992.

Rosenthal, Andrew. "THE 1992 CAMPAIGN: White House; Bush Denounces Rap Recording and Gives D'Amato a Hand." *New York Times*, June 30, 1992.

Rule, Sheila. "Ice-T and Warner Are Parting Company." *New York Times*, January 29, 1993.

The D.O.C., in discussion with author, June 1, 2017.

West, Kanye. "100 Greatest Artists: 56. Dr. Dre." *Rolling Stone*, December 2, 2010.

Yamayo, Jen, "'Straight Outta Compton' Fact-Check: How True Is the Explosive N.W.A. Biopic?" dailybeast.com, August 4, 2015.

CHAPTER 9

Baker, Soren. "Joe Cool Details Drawing Snoop Dogg's 'Doggystyle' Album Cover," HipHopDX.com, November 29, 2013, https://www.hiphopdx.com/news/id.26416/title.joe-cool-details-drawing-snoop-doggs-doggystyle-album-cover#.

Billboard's Hot Rap Songs, week of January 1, 1994, https://www.billboard.com/charts/rap-song/1994-01-01.

Chazanov, Mathis, and Chuck Philips. "Rap Singer Faces Charge of Murder." *Los Angeles Times*, September 4, 1993.

DJ Quik, in discussion with author, April 5, 2017, Los Angeles, California.

Masta Ace, in discussion with author, May 2, 2017.

Snoop Dogg, in discussion with author, April 18, 2017.

Snoop Dogg, in discussion with author, April 2007, Los Angeles, California.

Snoop Dogg, performance of "Murder Was the Case," *1994 MTV Video Music Awards*, September 8, 1994.

"Snoop Dogg parties with the players in Chicago." *Chicago Tribune*, December 4, 2002.

The D.O.C., in discussion with author, June 1, 2017.

The Game, in discussion with author, June 28, 2011, Los Angeles, California.

Warren G, in discussion with author, May 2004, Los Angeles, California.

Weinstein, Henry. "Lawyer for Rap Mogul Known for Aggressive Work." *Los Angeles Times*, October 29, 1996.

CHAPTER 10

Billboard's Top 200, week of May 22, 1993, https://www.billboard.com/charts/billboard-200/1993-05-22.

Cohn, D'Vera. "Gun Homicide Rate Down 49% Since 1993 Peak; Public Unaware." pewsocialtrends.org, May 7, 2013.

Dee Barnes, in discussion with author, March 16, 2018.

Drake, David. "DJ Quik Tells All: The Stories Behind his Classic Records." *Complex*, April 24, 2012, http://www.complex.com/music/2012/04/dj-quik-tells-all-the-stories-behind-his-classic-records/.

"History of Bandanas – The Iconic Piece of Square Clot," http://www.customonit.com/history-of-bandanas, accessed May 3, 2018.

"History of the Bandana," http://www.bandanashop.com/bandanahistory.html, accessed May 3, 2018.

Hubler, Shawn. "Homicides in 1992 Set Record for L.A. County: Violence: 2,589 killings in 1992 represent an 8% rise over previous year. Cultural changes and accessibility of guns cited as factors." *Los Angeles Times*, January 5, 1993.

MC Eiht, in discussion with author, November 30, 2016, Culver City, California.

RBX, in discussion with author, March 15, 2018.

Yukmouth, in discussion with author, February 20, 2017, Culver City, California.

CHAPTER 11

Arnold, Paul. "Producer Mike Mosley Recalls His Historic Work With 2Pac, E-40." HipHopDX.com, December 3, 2010, http://hiphopdx.com/news/id.13212/title.producer-mike-mosley-recalls-his-historic-work-with-2pac-e-40.

Baker, Soren. "Paroled Rapper's Fighting Words Land Him Back In Jail." *Los Angeles Times*, March 6, 1998.

Big Lez, in discussion with author, June 22, 2017.

Devi Dev in conversation with Warren G, "Warren G on Death Row, his Brother Dr. Dre and why they havent done a song together," hardknocktv, January 19, 2010. https://www.youtube.com/watch?v=kJMTSS1K--4.

"E-40, Too Short & B-Legit Definition of Mob Music," E40TV, YouTube.com, November 2, 2012. https://www.youtube.com/watch?v=mbq-3I1hmrU.

Harris, Harry. "Gradually, Oakland a less deadly place." *East Bay Times*, August 15, 2016.

MC Eiht, in discussion with author, November 30, 2106, Culver City, California.

Tech N9ne, in discussion with author, May 2, 2017.

Warren G, in discussion with author, May 2004, Los Angeles, California.

Yukmouth, in discussion with author, February 20, 2017, Culver City, California.

CHAPTER 12

"(August 3, 1995) – Suge Knight Disses Puff Daddy [The Source Awards]," Felix Montana, YouTube.com, August 3, 2014. https://www.youtube.com/watch?v=mv2OMXngkEs.

Arnold "Bigg A" White, in discussion with author, December 7, 2017.

Branch, Chris. "Method Man Goes Off On Hip-Hop Media, 'Once Upon A Time In Shaolin' And Cilvaringz." *The Huffington Post*, March 11, 2015.

Cantor, Paul. "How the 1995 Source Awards Changed Rap Forever." *Complex*, August 3, 2015, http://www.complex.com/music/2015/08/how-the-1995-source-awards-changed-rap-forever.

Dave Weiner, in discussion with author, March 27, 2017.

"Death Row Diss," LokoSomoan, YouTube.com, April 11, 2006. https://www.youtube.com/watch?v=JpgpS3ogvMM.

James, George. "Rapper Faces Prison Term for Sex Abuse." *New York Times*, February 8, 1995.

Kenner, Rob. "Back Issues: The Real Story Behind 'Vibe''s East vs. West Cover." *Complex*, February 22, 2016, http://www.complex.com/music/2016/02/vibe-1996-east-coast-vs-west-coast-cover.

MC Ren, in discussion with author, March 17, 2017, Indio, California.

Meara, Paul. "Mafia Dons Recall Notorious B.I.G./Tupac Altercation At The Soul Train Awards." HipHopDX.com, October 19, 2014.

"Outkast winning Best New Rap Group at the Source Awards 1995," TheMaxTrailers, YouTube.com, October 12, 2014. https://www.youtube.com/watch?v=vwLG7aSYM3w.

Philips, Chuck. "Possible Link of 'Puffy' Combs to Fatal Shooting Being Probed." *Los Angeles Times*, January 17, 2001.

Philips, Chuck. "Rapper Dr. Dre to part ways with Death Row, start new record label." *Los Angeles Times*, March 22, 1996.

Philips, Chuck. "Tupac Shakur: 'I am not a gangster.'" *Los Angeles Times*, October 25, 1995.

Talib Kweli, in discussion with author, September 2003.

The Legendary Traxster, in discussion with author, December 7, 2017.

"Where Were You When Tupac Died?" kawa2007, YouTube.com, October 24, 2007. https://www.youtube.com/watch?v=NoBGJA9ESYA.

CHAPTER 13

Billboard's Top 200, week of September 27, 1997. https://www.billboard.com/charts/billboard-200/1997-09-20.

Dave Weiner, in discussion with author, March 27, 2017.

Fat Joe, in discussion with author, July 1998, Los Angeles, California.

Mack 10, in discussion with author, July 1998, Los Angeles, California.

Marriott, Rob. "American Gothic." *Vibe*, May 1988.

MC Eiht, in discussion with author, November 30, 2016, Culver City, California.

Snoop Dogg, in discussion with author, May 1998, Claremont, California.

"VHS Sales Chart: 2000 Full Year," LeesMovieInfo.net. http://www.leesmovieinfo.net/Video-Sales.php?y=2000&type=4, accessed May 3, 2018.

Wrekonize, in discussion with author, April 3, 2017.

CHAPTER 14

Baker, Soren. "He's Unleashing an Experiment." . *Los Angeles Times*, December 10, 2000.

Baker, Soren. "Roots' Material Runs Deep." *Los Angeles Times*, February 14, 1999.

Dave Weiner, in discussion with author, March 27, 2017.

DJ Quik, in discussion with author, Los Angeles, California, April 5, 2017.

"Jay-Z, DMX To Help Families Of Columbine Victims." MTV.com, April 26, 1999, http://www.mtv.com/news/1428204/jay-z-dmx-to-help-families-of-columbine-victims/.

MC Eiht, in discussion with author, November 30, 2016, Culver City, California.

Snoop Dogg, in discussion with author, April 18, 2017.

CHAPTER 15

Ahmed, Insanul. "Trackmasters Tell All: The Stories Behind Their Classic Records (Part 2)." *Complex*, http://www.complex.com/music/2012/09/trackmasters-tell-all-the-stories-behind-their-classic-records-part-2/.

Baker, Soren. "He's Unleashing an Experiment." *Los Angeles Times*, December 10, 2000.

Big Boy, in discussion with author, May 18, 2017, Burbank, California.

Callahan-Bever, Noah. "Anger Management." *Vibe*, February 2004.

DJ Quik, in discussion with author, April 5, 2017, Los Angeles, California.

Ice-T, in discussion with author, May 10, 2017, Beverly Hills, California.

MC Eiht, in discussion with author, November 30, 2016, Culver City, California.

Snoop Dogg, in discussion with author, April 18, 2017.

Tech N9ne, in discussion with author, May 2, 2017.

The Game, in discussion with author, August 11, 2011, Inglewood, California.

Warner, Ralph with Christ Yuscavage and Kyle Neubeck. "Things You Didn't Know About Mike Tyson." *Complex*, September 22, 2017.

Wrekonize, in discussion with author, April 3, 2017.

CHAPTER 16

Big Boy, in discussion with author, May 18, 2017, Burbank, California.

DJ Quik, in discussion with author, April 5, 2017, Los Angeles, California.

Ice-T, in discussion with author, May 10, 2017, Beverly Hills, California.

Masta Ace, in discussion with author, May 2, 2017.

MC Ren, in discussion with author, March 17, 2017, Indio, California.

Snoop Dogg, in discussion with author, April 18, 2017.

Tech N9ne, in discussion with author, May 2, 2017.

Wrekonize, in discussion with author, April 3, 2017.

Yukmouth, in discussion with author, February 20, 2017, Culver City, California.

EPILOGUE

Big Boy, in discussion with author, May 18, 2017, Burbank, California.

Dave Weiner, in discussion with author, March 27, 2017.

Dee Barnes, in discussion with author, March 16, 2018.

DJ Quik, in discussion with author, April 5, 2017, Los Angeles, California.

Garrett, Ural. "AD Breaks Silence On Shooting At 'Thug' Video Shoot With YG." Hiphopdx.com, June 30, 2016, http://hiphopdx.com/news/id.39446/title.ad-breaks-silence-on-shooting-at-thug-video-shoot-with-yg.

Ice-T, in discussion with author, May 10, 2017, Beverly Hills, California.

MC Ren, in discussion with author, March 17, 2017, Indio, California.

Robehmed, Natalie. "Rapper Nipsey Hussle And The $100 Mixtape." *Forbes*, November 6, 2013.

"Schoolboy Q talks Gang Past, Groupies, Lean + His conversations with Kendrick Lamar!," HOT 97, YouTube.com, January 22, 2014. https://www.youtube.com/watch?v=5Q2jMXu7qk4.

Snoop Dogg, in discussion with author, April 18, 2017.

Tech N9ne, in discussion with author, May 2, 2017.

Vince Staples, in discussion with author, August 16, 2016.

Weiss, Jeff. "Rapper G Perico Took a Bullet and Still Played a Show That Night." *LA Weekly*, October 5, 2016.

KEY: Page Number, Subject (Photographer & credit)

Back Flap, Soren Baker Author Photo (Photo by Andres Tardio)

Back Cover, Dr. Dre; v, MC Eiht and Mack 10; 44, Fab 5 Freddy and Ice-T; 99, 2nd II None; 106, Snoop Dogg and Dr. Dre; 120, Kurupt; 122, Snoop Dogg; 126, Dr. Dre and Snoop Dogg; 136, CJ Mac and WC; 150, Warren G and Sir Jinx; 195, Ice Cube; 200 Snoop Dogg and Dr. Dre; 207, Up In Smoke Ticket; 209, Xzibit and Lord Finesse; 224, Snoop Dogg and The Arch Bishop Don Magic Juan; 252, Snoop Dogg and Soren Baker; 262, concert tickets (Photos by Soren Baker for Orange Line, Inc.)

Front Cover top, Snoop Dogg; 88, DJ Quik; 163, E-40; 182, C-Murder, Master P, and Silkk The Shocker; 212, The Game (Photos by Alisa Childs)

IV, collection of cassettes; 100, Ice Cube Death Certificates; 254, cassette tapes (Photos by Amir Rahimi)

Front Cover bottom, Ice Cube and Ice-T (Photo by Jay Blakesberg)

8, Schoolly D art (Original artwork courtesy of Schoolly D)

12, Ice-T and King Tee; 24, DJ Evil E and Ice-T (Photos courtesy of Evil E)

50, Warren G, Biz Lez, and Kurupt; 166, 2Pac and Big Lez (Photos courtesy of Leslie "Big Lez" Segar)

58, Ice-T, Hen Gee, Chuck D, and Ice Cube (Photo courtesy of Hen Gee Garcia)

71, Gangsta Boo (Photo courtesy of Lola "Gangsta Boo" Mitchell)

231, Dr. Dre and Xzibit studio recording session photo (Photo courtesy of Xzibit)

238, Kendrick Lamar; 247, G Perico (Photos by Ural Garrett)

246, Big Tray Deee (Photo courtesy of Big Tray Deee)

Above the Law, 103, 152–155

Above the Rim (soundtrack), 157

AD, 242, 250

The Aftermath (Dr. Dre), 202

Aftermath Entertainment, 175, 202, 215, 217–218, 230, 244

The Album (Firm), 202–203

All Eyez on Me (2Pac), 245

All Eyez on Me (film), 171

AmeriKKKa's Most Wanted (Ice Cube), 66–73

André 3000, 173

Arabian Prince, 39–40, 116

Archbishop Don "Da Magic" Juan, 224–225

Bad Boy Entertainment, 168, 181, 210

Bangin on Wax (Bloods & Crips), 141, 144

Barnes, Dee, 142–143, 244

"Batterram" (Toddy Tee), 9, 21

Baum, Darryl "Hommo," 214

Beastie Boys, 7, 14, 64

Beats by the Pound, 192, 194, 196–197

Beats Electronics, 113, 230, 235, 241

Berger, Jonah, 249–250

Big Boy, 9, 219, 223, 228–230, 233, 236, 242, 247–249

Big Daddy Kane, 64, 125, 175

Biggie & Tupac (film), 171

Big Hutch, 152–154, 173

Big Mike, 84

Big Tray Deee, vi, 246–247

Black Mafia Life (Above the Law), 103, 154–155

"Blacks & Browns" (YG & Sad Boy), 248

Bloodlust (Body Count), 230

Bloods & Crips, 141, 144

Bo$$, 71–72

Body & Soul, 142–143

Body Count, 109, 111, 139, 230

Bomb Squad, 30, 65–66

Boogie Down Productions, 16–19, 30, 62–63

Bouncin' and Swingin' (Down South Hustlers), 187

Bow Down (Westside Connection), 178–179, 191, 197

Bowie, David, 48

Boyz N the Hood (film), 83, 97–98, 109, 141, 235

"The Boyz-N-The Hood" (N.W.A), 33–36

"B Please" (Snoop Dogg), 208, 211

Breakin' (film), 93, 227

"Brenda's Got a Baby," 170

Brotha Lynch Hung, 161

Bushwick Bill, 76–77, 79–86, 97

By All Means Necessary (Boogie Down Productions), 19

Cam'ron, 221

C-Bo, 161

CEMA, 184–185

Cerami, Mark, 184–186

Charge It 2 Da Game (Silkk the Shocker), 193

The Chronic (Dr. Dre), 113–121, 124–126, 129, 154–156

Chuck D, 30, 57, 58–59, 65–66, 69, 115

"Chuckie" (Ghetto Boys), 81

CJ Mac, 22, 33, 84, 136–137, 141

Click, 162–164

Clinkscales, Keith, 178

C-Murder, 182–183, 186

Cold 187um, 152–154, 173

Colors (film), 25, 54, 138, 141

"Colors" (Ice-T), 25–27, 51–52, 138

Combs, Sean. *See* P. Diddy

Common (formerly Common Sense), 7, 50, 169, 172

Compton: A Soundtrack (Dr. Dre), 230

Compton's Most Wanted, 57, 97–98, 104–105, 145, 148–149

Concepcion, Michael, 142–143

conscious rap, 19, 62–63, 69–70, 117, 153–154, 168–169

Contagious (Berger), 249–250

Convicts, 84

"Cop Killer" (Body Count), 109, 111

Cormega, 33

Crenshaw (Nipsey Hussle), 242, 249–250

Criminal Minded (Boogie Down Productions), 18–19

Crucial Conflict, 177

Cube Vision, 195, 229

Cypress Hill, 98, 105, 114

Da Game Is to Be Sold, Not to Be Told (Snoop Dogg), 196–197, 203

DAMN. (Lamar), 244

Daniel, Darryl "Joe Cool," 128

"The Day the Niggaz Took Over" (Dr. Dre), 118

Daz, 118, 121, 131, 134–135. *See also* Tha Dogg Pound

Death Certificate (Ice Cube), 99–102, 108–109, 140

Death Row Records, 112–113, 116, 119, 127, 134–135, 156, 168, 172–175, 196–197

"Deep Cover" (Dr. Dre), 110–112, 125

Def Jam, 85, 210, 248

Delicious Vinyl, 64

Del tha Funkee Homosapien, 153–154, 159–160

Devin the Dude, 84, 204

Digital Underground, 159–160, 170, 206

DJ Code Money, 1, 7

DJ Drama, 229

DJ Evil E, 24

DJ Quik, 5, 18, 32–33, 36, 40, 47, 53, 62, 73, 81, 86, 88–91, 96, 104–105, 114, 125, 130–131, 135, 140–141, 148–149, 197, 206, 219, 222, 235, 250

DJ Ready Red, 76–77, 79, 83–84

DJ Scott La Rock, 18–19

DJ Yella, 29, 31–32, 38, 40, 95, 99, 116, 124

DMX, 206–207, 210

the D.O.C., 34–35, 38–39, 43, 46, 53, 62, 73, 108, 112, 119, 124, 130, 132, 204

Dr. Dre, 29, 31–32, 35, 37–40, 54, 57, 62, 89–90, 95, 99, 104, 106–107, 109–121, 124–126, 129, 131–132, 134–135, 138–139, 152, 154–156, 173–175, 197, 200–209, 211, 215–218, 226, 228, 230–233, 241–242

Dog, Tim, 104

Dogg Food (Tha Dogg Pound), 174

"Doggy Dogg World" (Snoop Dogg), 131–132

Doggystyle (Snoop Dogg), 125, 127–134, 155, 156

"Do It Like a G.O." (Ghetto Boys), 78–81, 84, 168

"Dollars & Sense" (DJ Quik), 135, 148–149

Domino, 156

Do or Die, 84, 177

"Dope Man" (N.W.A), 36–37

Down South Hustlers, 187

"Do You See" (Warren G), 157

Dru Down, 144–145

Duke, Bill, 110–112

Dylan, Bob, 15–16

E-40, 162–164

Eazy-Duz-It (Eazy-E), 41, 62, 63, 116, 124

Eazy-E, 28–29, 32–41, 43, 54, 60–63, 72–73, 91, 96, 99–101, 109–113, 116–117, 124, 138–139, 153–154, 168, 173, 195, 233

Efil4Zaggin (N.W.A), 95–96, 108–109, 116

Eminem, 17, 176, 203, 205–207, 209, 211, 215, 222, 242

Empire (television program), 236

"Endangered Species (Tales from the Darkside)" (Ice Cube), 69–70, 73

EPMD, 64, 153–154, 195

Fab 5 Freddy, 44–45, 51, 53–54, 56

Fat Joe, 197, 220

"FDT" (YG), 248

Fear of a Black Planet Tour, 206

Fiend, 193

50 Cent, 213–223, 226, 235–236

Firm, 202–203

"Forgot About Dre" (Dr. Dre), 205–206

Foxy Brown, 202–203

Freddy B, 35, 159

"Freedom of Speech" (Ice-T), 17

"Free Style Cutting" (Schoolly D), 7

Fresh Festival, 206, 210

"Fuck Compton" (Snoop Doggy Dogg), 117

"Fuck tha Police" (N.W.A), 37–39, 42–43, 53

Funkadelic, 154–155

Furious Five, 2, 51

the Game, 91, 132, 146, 212–213, 217–219, 222–223

Gangsta Boo, 70–71, 185

Gangsta Grillz projects, 229

"A Gangsta's Fairytale" (Ice Cube), 69, 73

"Gangster Boogie" (Schoolly D), 2–3

"Gangster of Love" (Ghetto Boys), 81–82

Ganksta N-i-P, 81

Gardner, Brian "Big Bass," 32

Geffen Records, 85–87

The Geto Boys (Geto Boys), 85–87. *See also* Ghetto (Geto) Boys

Get Rich Or Die Tryin' (50 Cent), 215–217

"Getto Jam" (Domino), 156

G-Funk, 154–158, 163

"G Funk Intro" (Snoop Dogg), 155

Ghetto (Geto) Boys, 60, 74–87, 97, 168, 227

Ghetto D (Master P), 190, 192–193

Ghetto Dope (Master P), 192

"Ghetto Qu'ran" (50 Cent), 214

The Ghettos Tryin' to Kill Me (Master P), 192

"Gin and Juice" (Snoop Dogg), 130

Goines, Donald, 4

"Gotta Lotta Love" (Ice-T), 147–148

G Perico, 242, 245, 247–248, 250

Grandmaster Flash, 1–2, 51, 210

Grip It! On That Other Level (Ghetto Boys), 78–85

"Growin' Up in the Hood" (Compton's Most Wanted), 97–98

"Gucci Time" (Schoolly D), 6–7

Guess Who's Back (50 Cent), 215

G-Unit, 215, 217–218, 221

Hard Knock Life Tour, 206–208, 210

Heller, Jerry, 33–35, 41–42, 61–62, 101

Hen Gee, 22–23, 58–59

Hinojosa, Jorge, 14, 23–24

Hi-Tek, 118, 120–121

"Hit 'Em Up" (2Pac), 175

"Hoover Street" (ScHoolboy Q), 245

"How To Rob" (50 Cent), 214, 220

Iceberg Slim, 4, 15, 22

Ice Cream Man (Master P), 187

Ice Cube, 29, 33–40, 43, 54–55, 58–59, 61–62, 65–73, 89–90, 95, 97–102, 104–105, 108–109, 115–117, 125, 132, 135, 139–140, 152, 172, 178–179, 195, 205, 207, 222, 226–230, 232–233, 235, 241–242, 244

Ice-T, 4, 6, 12–17, 20–27, 44–45, 51–52, 58–59, 60, 92–93, 109, 111, 138, 139, 147–148, 152, 195, 217, 226–228, 230, 242–244

"I Don't Like Rock 'N' Roll" (Schoolly D), 7–8

I'm bout it (film), 188–190

"I'm Bout It, Bout It" (Master P), 187, 188

Interscope Records, 113, 175, 202, 215, 217

Iovine, Jimmy, 113, 202, 204, 230

"It Ain't My Fault" (Silkk the Shocker), 193

"It's a Man's World" (Ice Cube), 72, 73

"It's Funky Enough" (the D.O.C.), 119

"It's Hot (Some Like it Hot)" (JAY-Z), 220

It Takes a Nation of Millions to Hold Us Back (Public Enemy), 30

"i used to love h.e.r." (Common), 169, 172

Jackson, O'Shea, 95. *See also* Ice Cube

Jackson, O'Shea, Jr., 233

Jadakiss, 220

Ja Rule, 220

Jayo Felony, 2, 146, 207

JAY-Z, 7, 174, 190, 205–207, 210, 220

Joe Cool, 128

J. Prince. *See* Prince, James "J."

Juice (film), 104–105, 170

"Jus Lyke Compton" (DJ Quik), 140–141, 222

"Just Say No" (Toddy Tee & Mix Master Spade), 9

K9 (Sir Rap-A-Lot), 76–77

Kam, 148

Kenner, Rob, 170, 172, 176

Kill at Will (Ice Cube), 90

King Tee, 12–13, 31, 34, 125, 138, 195, 227, 230–231

KK, 14, 98, 99

KMG the Illustrator, 152–153

Knight, Marion "Suge," 110, 112, 116, 127, 135, 172–173, 175, 196

Kokane, 72–73, 103, 154
KRS-One, 18–19
Kurupt, 51, 118, 120–121, 131, 134–135, 205, 207. *See also* Tha Dogg Pound

La Chat, 71
Lady of Rage, 71, 118, 120–121
Lamar, Kendrick, 30, 238–239, 242–245
Last Poets, 54–55
Law & Order: Special Victims Unit (television series), 226, 228
"Lay Low" (Snoop Dogg), 211
Legendary Traxster, 177
"Let a Ho Be a Ho" (Ghetto Boys), 82
"Let Me Ride" (Dr. Dre), 115–117, 126
Life Is... Too $hort (Too $hort), 31, 125
Light, Alan, 176, 178
Lil' J. *See* Prince, James "J."
Livin' Like Hustlers (Above the Law), 152–153
LL Cool J, 76, 228
"Lodi Dodi" (Snoop Dogg), 132
Lord Finesse, 209
Luke Skyywalker, 117

Mack 10, 172, 178–179, 189–191, 197, 207
Macola Records, 34, 41–42
Making Trouble (Ghetto Boys), 76, 78, 83
Marley Marl, 124, 133
Marrow, Tracy, 15. *See also* Ice-T
Masta Ace, 124, 133, 232
Masta Ace Incorporated, 133
Master P, 174, 182–184, 186–199, 211
Mayweather, Floyd, Jr., 220
MC Eiht, 52, 55–57, 98, 135, 138–139, 145–147, 149, 158, 163–164, 188–189, 207, 216, 227
MC Ren, 29, 32–33, 38, 95, 99, 109, 116, 124, 168, 179, 229–230, 232–233, 240
Melle Mel, 2, 51
Mel-Man, 205
Menace II Society (film), 145
Mercedes, 193
"The Message" (Furious Five), 2
Method Man, 10, 180–181, 210
Mia X, 71, 193
Michel'le, 32, 99, 104, 112, 140, 195
Miller, Percy Robert. *See* Master P
"Mind of a Lunatic" (Ghetto Boys), 82, 84–86, 97
"Mind Playing Tricks on Me" (Geto Boys), 97
Mix Master Spade, 3, 9
Mob Music, 159–165
"Mr. Flamboyant" (Click), 162
Mr. Scarface Is Back (Scarface), 98–99
MTV, 48–57. *See also* Yo! MTV Raps
Murder Dog (magazine), 174
Murder Rap: Inside the Biggie and Tupac Murders (film), 171

Murder Was the Case (film and soundtrack), 134–135
"Murder Was the Case" (Snoop Dogg), 134
Murs, 169
"My Hitta" (YG), 248
My Krazy Life (YG), 248
"My Nigga" (YG), 248
"My Summer Vacation" (Ice Cube), 140, 222

Nas, 202–203, 221
Nate Dogg, 125, 134, 156–158, 205, 207, 211
"Natural Born Killaz" (Snoop Dogg), 135
Natural Born Killers (film), 135
New Jack City (film), 91–93, 95, 228
"New Jack Hustler (Nino's Theme)" (Ice-T), 92–93
"New York" (Ja Rule), 220
"New York, New York" (Tha Dogg Pound), 174
"The Next Episode" (Dr. Dre), 205–206
Nice & Smooth, 175
"The Nigga Ya Love to Hate" (Ice Cube), 67–68, 73
Niggaz Wit Attitude. *See* N.W.A
99 Ways to Die (Master P), 184, 186
Nipsey Hussle, 242, 248–250
No Limit Records, 184, 186–199, 203, 211
No Limit Top Dogg (Snoop Dogg), 197–198, 203
No Mercy, No Fear (50 Cent), 215
Notorious B.I.G., 169–172, 175–176, 179–181
"No Vaseline" (Ice Cube), 99–101
No Way Out Tour, 210
"Nuthin' But a 'G' Thang" (Dr. Dre), 115, 119
N.W.A, 28–43, 51–54, 60–63, 72–73, 89–90, 95–96, 99–101, 104–105, 108–109, 116, 124, 153–154, 233, 240–242
N.W.A and the Posse (compilation), 34

"O.G. Original Gangster" (Ice-T), 93
"Once Upon a Time in the Projects" (Ice Cube), 70
100 Miles And Runnin' (N.W.A), 89–90
One Nation (2Pac), 175–176
Overly Dedicated (Lamar), 243
Oxymoron (ScHoolboy Q), 245

"Pain" (Ice-T), 22
Parents Music Resource Center (PMRC), 17, 25, 87
Paris, 17, 33, 139, 160
Parker, Lawrence "Kris," 18–19
Park Side Killers, 6. *See also* "P.S.K. What Does It Mean?" (Schoolly D)
P. Diddy, 168, 170, 172–176, 181, 210, 221
"Peace Treaty" (Kam), 148
Penicillin on Wax (Tim Dog), 104

"Piggy Bank" (50 Cent), 220–221
Pimp: The Story of My Life (Iceberg Slim), 15
PMRC (Parents Music Resource Center), 17, 25, 87
Poke. *See* Trackmasters
Power (television series), 216, 235–236
Power of the Dollar (50 Cent), 214
Prince, James "J.," 75–81, 85, 97
Prince Johnny C, 76–77, 79, 83–84
Priority Records, 41–42, 63, 96–97, 113, 139, 178–180, 184–187, 189, 191, 193, 250
Pryor, Richard, 3, 5, 233
"P.S.K. What Does It Mean?" (Schoolly D), 4–6, 14, 114
Psycho Active (X-Raided), 161
Public Enemy, 30, 47, 62–63, 65–66, 125, 206
Puff Daddy. *See* P. Diddy
Pump It Up (television program), 50
"Put Your Filas On" (Schoolly D), 7–8

Queen Latifah, 64
Quik Is the Name (DJ Quik), 90–91, 96, 125

Raheem, 76
Rap-A-Lot Records, 75–84, 87, 97
Rap City (television program), 50
Rap Pages (magazine), 174
"Rapper's Delight" (Sugarhill Gang), 1
Rap Sheet (magazine), 174
RBX, 118, 120–121, 126
reality rap, 22, 33, 40, 86, 227
Rear End (Mercedes), 193
"Rebel Without a Pause" (Public Enemy), 47
The Recipe (Mack 10), 197
Redman, 210
Reed, Kevin, 223
"Regulate" (2Pac), 157–158
Regulate... G Funk Era (Warren G), 157–159
Rhyme Pays (Ice-T), 20, 23–25
Rhyme Syndicate collective, 195
Righteous Kill (film), 216
Roadium Open Air Market, 36
Robles, Jai Hassan-Jamal, 173
Rock, Jay, 243
Rogin, Gilbert, 176
"Ronald Reagan Era (His Evils)" (Lamar), 243–244
Rose, 142–143
Ross, Rick, 220
Rubin, Rick, 85–87, 97
Run-DMC, 76
Rush Associated Label, 156, 159
Ruthless Records, 32, 34–35, 41–42, 61–62, 72–73, 96, 109–113, 116, 119, 139, 195

Sad Boy (Loko), 248
St. Ides, 227

"Saturday Night" (Schoolly D), 10
Saturday Night! –The Album (Schoolly D), 10–11
Scarface, 60, 76–80, 82–87, 97, 98–99
ScHoolboy Q, 245
Schoolly D, vi, 1–11, 14, 18–19, 114
Schoolly D (Schoolly D), 7–9
Schoolly-D Records, 4, 9
Scott, Raymond "Benzino," 173
Scott-Heron, Gil, 54–55, 56
Season of da Siccness (Brotha Lynch Hung), 161
2nd II None, 99
Section.80 (Lamar), 243–244
Segar, Leslie "Big Lez," 50–51, 162, 166–167
"Self Destruction" (Stop the Violence Movement), 143
Sermon, Erick, 195
Sever, Sam, 65–66
Silkk the Shocker, 182–183, 186, 193
Simmons, Russell, 85, 159
Sire Juke Box, 76, 79, 83
Sire Records, 20, 24, 109, 139
Sir Jinx, 66, 68, 150–151
Sir Rap-A-Lot, 76–77
"6 'N the Mornin'" (Ice-T), 14–16
SlaughtaHouse (Masta Ace Incorporated), 133, 232
The Slim Shady LP (Eminem), 203, 222
Smith, Parrish, 195
Snoop (Doggy) Dogg, 106–107, 110–112, 115–123, 125–135, 146, 152, 155–158, 173–174, 176, 196–198, 200–201, 203–205, 207–209, 211, 215, 218–219, 222, 224–227, 230, 233–235, 241, 244
Snoop Youth Football League (SYFL), 234
"Some L.A. Niggaz" (Dr. Dre), 206
The Source (magazine), 174
Spice 1, 160
"Squeeze the Trigger" (Ice-T), 20–21
Staples, Vince, 242, 249
Stein, Seymour, 20, 23–24
Stewart, Paul, 159
Still Brazy (YG), 248
"Still D.R.E." (Dr. Dre), 205–206
Stop the Violence Movement, 143
Straight Checkn 'Em (Compton's Most Wanted), 98
Straight Outta Compton (film), 233–234
"Straight Outta Compton" (N.W.A), 51–53, 62
Straight Outta Compton (N.W.A), 31–32, 38–40, 63, 116, 124, 241
"Stranded on Death Row" (Dr. Dre), 118
Street Knowledge Productions, 195
Strictly 4 My N.I.G.G.A.Z. (2Pac), 170
Suave House Records, 80, 199
Sugarhill Gang, 1–2
"The Symphony" (Marley Marl), 124, 133

Take a Look Around (Masta Ace), 133
Tech N9ne, 162, 222, 240, 243
Tha Chill, 98
Tha Doggfather (Snoop Dogg), 196–197
Tha Dogg Pound, 131, 134–135, 174, 177
Tha Eastsidaz, 207, 211
Tha Last Meal (Snoop Dogg), 211
Tha Triflin' Album (King Tee), 227
There's One in Every Family (Fiend), 193
3rd Bass, 64
"This D.J." (Warren G), 157–158
Three 6 Mafia, 71, 185, 190
"Thug" (AD), 250
Tila. *See* King Tee
'Til My Casket Drops (C-Bo), 161
Tim Dog, 104–105, 117
Toddy Tee, 9, 21
Tomorrow, Today (series), 235
Tone. *See* Trackmasters
Tone Loc, 64–65, 114
Too $hort, 31, 35, 81, 125, 159–160
To the East, Blackwards (X Clan), 153
"To the Left" (Crucial Conflict), 177
Trackmasters, 202–203, 213–214
Tupac. *See* 2Pac
Tupac: Resurrection (film), 171
Turner, Bryan, 184, 186, 196
24 Deep (Brotha Lynch Hung), 161
Twista, 177
2Pac, 102–103, 156–159, 166–167, 169–172, 174–176, 180–181, 245
2Pacalypse Now (2Pac), 102–103, 170
2001 (Dr. Dre), 204–206

Underworld Records & Tapes, 178
Universal Zulu Nation, 79
Unsolved: The Murders of Tupac & The Notorious B.I.G (film), 171
Up in Smoke Tour, 207–209, 211
The Up in Smoke Tour (film), 209
"Us" (Ice Cube), 102

Vibe (magazine), 170, 172, 174, 176, 178, 180–181
Violator Label, 156
Vocally Pimpin' (Above the Law), 103, 154–155
Vol. 2… Hard Knock Life (JAY-Z), 206

Warren G, 50–51, 110, 128–129, 134, 150–152, 155–159, 207
Way 2 Fonky (DJ Quik), 141
WC, 103, 136–137, 141, 172, 178–179, 195, 207
We Can't Be Stopped (Geto Boys), 81, 83, 97
Weiner, Dave, 178–181, 184, 186–189, 191, 194–196–199, 208–209, 243, 245
"We're All in the Same Gang" (The West Coast Rap All-Stars), 139–140, 142–143

The West Coast Rap All-Stars, 139–140, 142–143
Westside Connection, 178–179, 191, 197
"Westside Slaughterhouse" (Mack 10), 172
"Westside Story" (the Game), 218–219
"What's the Difference" (Dr. Dre), 205–206
"What Up Gangsta" (50 Cent), 216
"What Would U Do?" (Tha Dogg Pound), 135
White, Arnold "Bigg A," 178
"White America" (Eminem), 17
"Who Am I (What's My Name)?" (Snoop Dogg), 128–130
Who Am I?, 103. *See also* Kokane
"Who Shot Ya?" (Notorious B.I.G.), 170
Williams, Alonzo, 32–33
Willie D, 77–85, 97, 168, 173
"__ wit Dre Day (And Everybody's Celebratin')" (Dr. Dre), 117–118, 154
Woldemariam, Philip, 127
Woods-Wright, Tomica, 233
Wrekonize, 190–191, 194, 218–219, 235–236
Wright, Eric, 91. *See also* Eazy-E

X Clan, 153–154
X-Raided, 161
XXL (magazine), 174
"Xxplosive" (Dr. Dre), 206
Xzibit, 146, 205–209, 211, 232, 236

YG, 146, 242, 245, 248–249, 250
Yo! MTV Raps, 41, 48–57, 79, 96
Young, Andre. *See* Dr. Dre
Young Buck, 221
Young MC, 64–65
Yo-Yo, 66–67, 72–73, 103
Yukmouth, 144–145, 149, 153, 155, 158, 162, 164

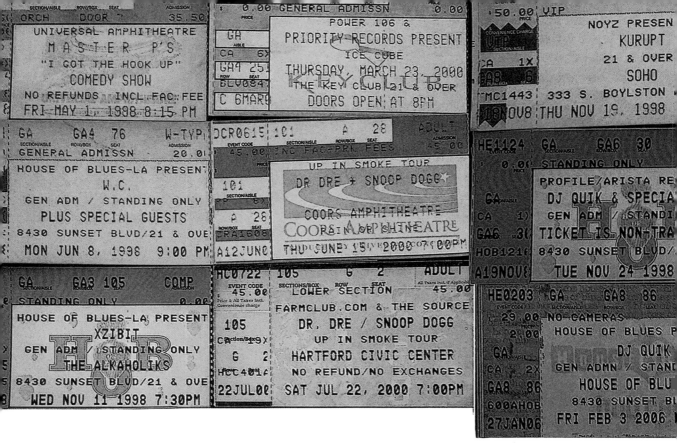

EDITOR: Samantha Weiner

DESIGNER: Jacob Covey

PRODUCTION MANAGER: Rebecca Westall

Library of Congress Control Number: 2017956854

ISBN: 978-1-4197-2915-7

eISBN: 978-1-68335-235-8

Printed and bound in the USA

10 9 8 7 6 5 4 3 2 1

ABRAMS The Art of Books
195 Broadway, New York, NY 10007
abramsbooks.com